Rhyme's Rooms

Alfred A. Knopf

New York   *2022*

Rhyme's Rooms

THE ARCHITECTURE

OF POETRY

Brad Leithauser

THIS IS A BORZOI BOOK
PUBLISHED BY ALFRED A. KNOPF

Copyright © 2022 by Brad Leithauser

All rights reserved. Published in the United States by Alfred A. Knopf,
a division of Penguin Random House LLC, New York, and distributed in
Canada by Penguin Random House Canada Limited, Toronto.

www.aaknopf.com

Knopf, Borzoi Books, and the colophon are registered trademarks
of Penguin Random House LLC.

Pages 347 and 348 constitute an extension of the copyright page.

Library of Congress Cataloging-in-Publication Data
Names: Leithauser, Brad, author.
Title: Rhyme's rooms : the architecture of poetry / Brad Leithauser.
Description: First edition. | New York : Alfred A. Knopf, 2022. |
"This is a Borzoi book"
Identifiers: LCCN 2021025741 (print) | LCCN 2021025742 (ebook) |
ISBN 9780525655053 (hardcover) | ISBN 9780525655060 (ebook)
Subjects: LCSH: Poetics—History. | Poetry—History and criticism. |
LCGFT: Literary criticism.
Classification: LCC PN1042 .L36 2022 (print) | LCC PN1042 (ebook) |
DDC 808.1—dc23
LC record available at https://lccn.loc.gov/2021025741
LC ebook record available at https://lccn.loc.gov/2021025742

Jacket painting: *Architectural Fantasy* by Antonio Joli © Leeds Museums
and Galleries/Bridgeman Images
Jacket design by Jennifer Carrow

Manufactured in the United States of America

First Edition

CONTENTS

Author's Note   ix

Foreword: A First Step, A First Stop   xi

Chapter One: Meeting the Funesians   3

Chapter Two: The Prosodic Contract   16

Chapter Three: Poetic Architecture   29

Chapter Four: Stanzas   42

Chapter Five: Enjambment   54

Chapter Six: Defining and Refining   67

Chapter Seven: The Marriage of Meter and Rhyme (I)   81

Chapter Eight: Iambic Pentameter   95

Chapter Nine: Iambic Tetrameter   110

Chapter Ten: Rhyme and Rhyme Decay   125

Chapter Eleven: Spelling and the Unexpected Rhyme   139

Chapter Twelve: Rhyme Poverty, Rhyme Richness   154

Chapter Thirteen: Rhymes, and How We Really Talk   166

Chapter Fourteen: Off Rhyme: When Good Rhymes

    Go Bad   178

Chapter Fifteen: Rim Rhyme   192

Chapter Sixteen: The Marriage of Meter and Rhyme (II)   203

Chapter Seventeen: Wordplay and Concision   217

Chapter Eighteen: The Look of Poetry   229

Chapter Nineteen: Song Lyrics   244

Chapter Twenty: Poetry and Folly   261

Chapter Twenty-One: Dining with the Funesians   277

Chapter Twenty-Two: Drinking with the Funesians   294

Chapter Twenty-Three: The Essential Conservatism

    of Poetry   308

Chapter Twenty-Four: The Essential Radicalism

    of Poetry   324

Glossary   343

Permissions Credits   347

Acknowledgments   349

Gratefully

to

William Pritchard

and

Ryan Wilson—

Two of the most inspiring readers I know

I'm hoping to attract the specialist: the practicing poet, the high-minded critic, the esteemed professor. But none of these is the primary target of this book. I want to lure here, more than anyone else, the reader who loves words and literature but maybe feels some trepidation, and a little nervous resentment, as well as various unvoiced cravings, on confronting a poem on a page.

Over the years, a passion for twentieth-century American popular song has led me to publish essays on Irving Berlin, Cole Porter, Ira Gershwin, Lorenz Hart, Johnny Mercer, Stephen Sondheim et al. In the following pages I often look to them for illumination and example. For many readers of advancing years, these have been the modern poets most closely lived beside, and loved beside. We all owe them, and I'm happily seeking to repay a long-standing debt.

Biologists employ a term for creatures like frogs or salamanders: They are indicator species. Their well-being, or lack of it, is a reflection of the broader conditions governing the environment. You want to know if your marshland is thriving or dying? Look to the frogs.

And you want to know if a literary marshland is thriving? Look to the poets, and the poetry readers, who together compose a froglike indicator species. Their croaking alerts us to the overall vigor of our ecosystem. If while croaking they're *croaking,* so are a host of other creatures, including both writers and fans of short stories, novels, literary essays, even personal memoirs. Where poetry languishes, every book lover should feel pangs of foreboding.

I mean this book as a modest dose of medicine—supplied to a literary culture not always fully appreciative of those solitary figures, besieged and fumbling, who spend their days with poetic structures, pondering how some small handful of words might be grouped, or regrouped, or grouped once more, to engineer a satisfying line.

All poems begin by saying the same thing. It doesn't matter if the poem is written in your native language, or in a language acquired later in life, or even in one in which you're wordless. It doesn't matter if the writing goes from left to right, or right to left, or descends vertically down the page. The first message it sends you is *Slow down*. It asks to be read less hurriedly than you typically read.

If the poem is in English, it's likely to be justified (aligned vertically) along its left margin. Its right margin, though, will be rutted and raggedy—like a rumble strip on a highway. That ragged edge is a series of little speed bumps telling you, the driver/reader, to take your foot off the accelerator. And to wake up fully if you've begun to drowse.

Rhyme's Rooms

◻

CHAPTER ONE

Meeting the Funesians

Let us begin with a tribe of people residing high in the Andes Mountains, where the brisk air is thin and vistas are arrestingly clear. We'll call them the Funesians. They are a small and in many ways unexceptional community, subsisting mostly on boiled potatoes and pickled turnips and a mild rhubarb brandy. Days roll by, decades pass, marked chiefly by a gratified uneventfulness. The Funesians are remarkable in only one aspect, really: They are, far and away, the finest readers of poetry in the world. They hear things the rest of us don't hear. The question this book poses is what can you—whether you live in New York or London, in Johannesburg or Jakarta, in a tidal shack or a yurt or a submarine or a castle—learn from the Funesians?

Plenty, I think. In their modest but dizzying excellence, the Funesians instruct and enlighten us about our limitations as readers and thinkers. Perhaps all art is an expression of human restlessness against our bodily confines and of our adaptations within them; perhaps every art form is an arena for measuring the mettle of our physiological and mental capabilities. Even so, poetry—like its sister arts music and architecture—is a medium that constantly brings this testing into sharp relief, with pointed and poignant models.

Let's open with a valedictory poem by Dylan Thomas, "Prologue," completed in 1952, shortly before his death. Thomas himself did not suspect it, but at his close he was writing for the Funesians. "Prologue" initially appears to lack a rhyme scheme. You have to reach the poem's exact mid-point, lines 51 and 52, to meet your first rhyme, a couplet:

> Sheep white hollow farms
> To Wales in my arms

From here on out, the rhymes unfold punctually, systematically. The next line, line 53, turns out to rhyme with line 50, and line 54 with 49, and so forth, each later line finding its earlier, coordinated partner, until finally the second-to-last line rhymes with the poem's second line, and its final line with its first. Everything's neatly paired.

"Prologue" is a wildly eccentric construction. Thomas built it mostly for himself, I suppose; poets are forever erecting self-imposed obstacles that the general reader is unlikely to appreciate, or perhaps even notice. For an ordinary reader, "Prologue" offers a peculiar experience. If it comes across as an unrhymed poem for most of its length, there's a fleeting middle interlude, beginning with line 52, when something else occurs: You hear the rhymes chiming away, creating an ever-dwindling music. Depending on your ear, you may hear the rhymes for four or six lines, eight, ten, maybe twelve, but no one is going to hear all fifty-one of them.

No one except a Funesian. To hold inside their brains, in order, fifty-one rhymes—why, it's a piece of cake for the

Funesians. Let's assume that, as a little joke, Thomas had created a random and minuscule disorder: The rhyme that was supposed to fall at line 89 (linked to line 14) actually fell at line 88. You and I would never notice. But the Funesian reader's eyebrows would lift, followed by a slight but unmistakably quizzical shaking of the head. *What is he doing?* our Funesian wonders. *The rhymes are out of whack.*

When a poem is placed before a Funesian, he or she, though human in all other tastes and talents, becomes a kind of extraterrestrial. The Funesians notice *everything.* Every variant of rhyme, every sonic repetition (not merely of word but of syllable and phoneme), every tiny buried euphony and dissonance, every metrical variation, every little tension and release in the rhythms, every pun, every punctuational inconsistency—there is no end to all the things they notice.

For the rest of us (mere human readers), rhymes fade and are meant to fade. Evanescence is the essence of rhyme. Our ears move on. Rhymes live, in Shakespeare's phrase, within a "dying fall." For a few instants, a rhyme chimes inside the ear, recalling an earlier sound. An echo is celebrated, then discarded as another echo surfaces.

In poems written for ordinary human beings, the rhymes are therefore proximate, especially with the most popular forms, like the ballad or Shakespearean sonnet or limerick. But as any handbook of poetic forms will show, this propinquity of rhymes is true of rarefied forms as well (the villanelle, the ballade, terza rima, ottava rima, rhyme royal). Most rhyme schemes require partnered sounds to fall no more than thirty syllables apart—and usually much closer. Sounds come and go within a poem, as each line, with its unique freight of resonances, in effect replaces and supplants a previous line, with its own unique freight. A poem is a compact sonic parade, marching clamorously through the tunnel of the ear canal, an ever-shifting zone of commotion in which the most recent sounds serially dominate.

It turns out that thirty syllables (three lines of **iambic pentameter**—see the glossary for words in boldface type) represent a chasm both sizable yet bridgeable. A rhyme spaced at an interval of thirty syllables speaks of resuscitation, of a spirited and robust call-and-response across that black and echoless abyss that threatens every poem. Having composed poetry for more than a millennium, experimenting all the while with echoes and durations, English-language poets have learned that readers can be trusted to hear rhymes across this distance.

Among popular poetic structures, the Miltonic son- net maintains the longest interval between rhymes. It's an inflexible form in its octave, or first eight lines (they rhyme ABBAABBA), though highly flexible in its sestet, or final six lines, which allow rhymes to fall where they may, provided no lines remain unrhymed. These rhymes can therefore achieve a gap as long as fifty syllables, the distance between the end words to lines 9 and 14.

Beyond fifty syllables, the distance evidently becomes too great. The web strand linking any two words grows increasingly attenuated, then breaks. Of course, poets live to challenge accepted limitations, and they will often (in their spidery ingenuity) contrive to stretch a rhyme as far as it will go.

This is what's happening at the conclusion of Robert Frost's "After Apple-Picking." (Speaking of spiders, Frost created one of the most memorable web weavers in world literature with his sonnet "Design," to which we'll turn in the next chapter.) "After Apple-Picking" is a poem of forty-two rhymed lines that follow no established scheme. At the start, the rhymes are unavoidably clangorous:

> My long two-pointed ladder's sticking through a tree
> Toward heaven still,
> And there's a barrel that I didn't fill
> Beside it, and there may be two or three
> Apples I didn't pick upon some bough.
> But I am done with apple-picking now.

But the rhymes grow quieter at the close, as the exhausted speaker/farmer, his harvesting duties accomplished, begins to drift off. And it's surely no accident that the longest wait for a rhyme consummates with the poem's last word, a full seven lines removed from its mate. The poet, like the farmer he's depicting, can now say, *All done at last*, as the concluding rhyme drops with an almost subliminal echo into the drowsing mind:

> For all
> That struck the earth,
> No matter if not bruised or spiked with stubble,
> Went surely to the cider-apple heap
> As of no worth.
> One can see what will trouble
> This sleep of mine, whatever sleep it is.
> Were he not gone,
> The woodchuck could say whether it's like his
> Long sleep, as I describe its coming on,
> Or just some human sleep.

Frost has kept the final rhyme alive partly through internal rhyme, thrice slipping *sleep* into these eleven lines before it materializes as the final rhyme word. Even so, the last rhyme is, appropriately, the softest and sleepiest in the poem. And—perhaps no coincidence—it arrives fifty syllables after its partner (fifty-one, actually); in roundabout fashion we've arrived at a familiar threshold.

Fifty syllables. It's a sizable distance—the extent of three haikus, and longer than some immortal whole English-language poems (Frost's "Hannibal," A. E. Housman's "Here Dead Lie We," Robert Herrick's "The Coming of Good Luck"). Much can be uttered in fifty syllables—asserted, questioned, contradicted, resolved. But while the reader is following these assertions, questions, contradictions, resolutions, she is also holding aloft a sound in her head, waiting for it to encounter its soul mate, and waiting for the two united sounds, now bound in wedlock, to be put to bed. Any good reader of poetry is a born multitasker.

One of my favorite sonneteers, John Crowe Ransom (1888–1974), concluded virtually every sonnet with a fifty-syllable rhyme gap. In each case, it's the longest such unanswered stretch in the poem. The result, as in "After Apple-Picking," is a muted tolling at the close—a musical effect in keeping with that air of wise resignation that suffuses so many of Ransom's lovely verses. Here's the finale of "Parting at Dawn," where we contemplate two lovers, a Romeo (the "Sir" of the poem) and a Juliet (the "Madam"), whom society has grievously separated:

> And then? O dear Sir, stumbling down the street,
> Continue, till you come to wars and wounds;
> Beat the air, Madam, till your house-clock sounds;

And if no Lethe flows beneath your casement,
And when ten years have not brought full effacement,
Philosophy was wrong, and you may meet.

Brain and heart are once more at odds. But it appears that the intellect (philosophy) was never a trustworthy guide. Nor was common sense. Or social mores. All along, the steadfast heart knew what it knew, in the face of all rational objections. Well, after a barren decade, after much loneliness and pain and seclusion, the heart triumphs, the solitary lovers at last "may meet," just as, after a stretch of fifty barren syllables, the unpartnered rhyme words "may meet." The last line announces a kind of quiet double wedding.

Rhymes fade partly because sounds naturally fade into the air, and partly because in any good poem other compelling activities are happening, often leaving the rhymes unremarked in the general welter. Rhymes are merely one contribution to the poem's music, and its music is itself often contending with its meaning. Typically, the poem will be singing about some actual subject or event (singing its heart out, let's hope!), and we readers are trying to catch all the attitudinal nuances in the lyrics even as we appreciate the melody.

Sometimes one comes upon a critic or poet confidently asserting that a poem's form and content, or its music and meaning, are the same thing. Not closely intertwined, but the same thing.

This strikes me as soft thinking: a dangerous and distortional half-truth. Yes, form and content are the same thing—in heaven. Or, less fancifully perhaps, the same thing among the Funesians.

But not with us. Among mere human writers and readers, they're not at all the same thing. A poem's music naturally

attempts to harmonize with its meaning, and in a successful poem the relationship draws intimately close. Yet there's
always a rift—a mortal falling short of that ideal where music
and meaning are indivisible.

As a piece of music, a poem suffers the unshakable burden of having to carry meaning. Though this meaning may
well be conventional and predictable (*Gather ye rosebuds while
ye may,* or *All is vanity,* or *Love is chancy*), it is hardly expend-
able. Poets of various ears and eras have sought to jettison this
ancient burden of needing to *say something.* They've sought
at times to create a poetry of "pure music," liberated from
meaning. In the hands of composers of nonsense verse, the
projected audience may be children; in the hands of some
militantly avant-garde poets, the audience may be a mili-
tant avant-garde. But the poetic result typically lacks staying
power. Who can fail to love the meaningless cavalcade of
Lewis Carroll's "Jabberwocky," which opens in a universe
whose nouns and verbs and adjectives are untethered to any
recognizable reality:

> 'Twas brillig, and the slithy toves
>   Did gyre and gimble in the wabe:
> All mimsy were the borogoves,
>   And the mome raths outgrabe.

But a century and a half after Carroll assembled these
words, how many such poems exist, universally loved and
embraced for their nonsensicality? Typically, the poem that
doesn't attempt to say anything—winds up saying nothing.

And it turns out we readers of poetry, insecure in our
acoustical shortcomings, imperfect in our focus, usually ask
a poem to reward us by saying something. Our betters—the

Funesians—may be fully content with a poetry of pure music, sound divorced from meaning. But *our* ears are frail and faulty, and simple sounds, divorced from meaning, won't sustain us.

So, ordinary human readers read simultaneously for meaning and for sound. It's a bifurcated experience: one half of your brain trying to catch the poem's music, the other half going after its meaning. The two halves are likely imbalanced, operating at different levels of efficiency. Over time I've learned about myself that I tend to read first for sound and second for sense. On an initial reading, I may well pick up rhyme schemes, metrical variations, patterns of assonance and alliteration, but I'll misread the poem's content—sometimes discovering, on a second reading, that the poet was saying something polar to what I'd supposed. Other readers will begin with content, and only upon a second reading may find themselves saying, "Oh my, this poem's a sonnet" or "Strange things seem to befall the meter in the final stanza." Probably it doesn't matter where you begin. The crucial issue is how fitly you wind up bringing the two strains together.

T. S. Eliot was acknowledging the reality of a bifurcated reading experience when he concluded, early in his career, that it wasn't necessary to understand a poem to enjoy it. (He also acknowledged its interconnectedness: "But I would remind you, first, that the music of poetry is not something which exists apart from the meaning.") He envisioned you entering the poem betranced by sound, and only later puzzling out a satisfactory interpretation. Actually, whatever one's initial orientation, most of us have had both experiences: reading a second time in order to let sound catch up with sense, or sense with sound. In either case, any serious poetry reader knows the precious moment when one's starting point, sound or sense, suddenly ecloses into a larger, winged clarity.

Each rereading of a good poem should bring this harmony of sound and sense into tighter connection. You're no longer reading to parse its simple meaning. Nor reading purely to assimilate sonic effects. You're coming steadily closer to seeing the poem as a whole, to absorbing the entity in entirety. As in Frost's "Directive," you're taking something into your body that ushers in a state of completion: "Drink and be whole again beyond confusion."

For most of us, it's hard on first glance to encompass the wholeness of even a short poem like a sonnet. An automotive simile may be useful here. (I was born and bred in the Motor City.) On a poem's first reading, we ordinary human readers typically find ourselves on a gravelly byway in Tennessee, deep in the Great Smoky Mountains, negotiating violent twists and turns on a foggy morning. Peering through the windshield, we see a little ways ahead; glancing into the rearview mirror, we catch some glimpse of where we've just been. But the snaking road and the morning fog prevent any comprehensive vantage. Forward and back, we see and hear only a little distance as we progress. Place a Funesian behind the wheel, however, and he is always driving in Iowa, on a cloudless day, on a straight road across an absolutely level landscape; on all sides, vistas are open to the horizon.

Pondering the Funesians over the years, I've concluded that their experience when reading a poem so differs from ours as to be a matter not merely of degree but of kind. They operate at some removes from our literary heritage. Our structures cannot be fully theirs. The poetic forms we've created please us not despite but because of our human limitations. They cater to our shortcomings, and we celebrate their suitability by continuing to employ them, century after century. How could the Funesians understand this?

Consider the most important of all forms in English-language poetry: blank verse, or unrhymed iambic pentameter. Back in the late seventies, the literary critic Paul Fussell estimated that "about three-quarters of English poetry is in blank verse." Such statistics are difficult to pinpoint, and it may be, too, that the ratio has shifted somewhat since Fussell made his judgment. Still, there can be no doubt of the primacy of blank verse. More than any other form, it defines what English poetry is.

Stately yet pliable, solid without being stolid, blank verse comprises most of Shakespeare's plays, most of Wordsworth's longer work, most of the poetry Robert Lowell wrote in his last decade. It attains a noble summit in John Milton's *Paradise Lost*, which offers us 10,565 continuous lines of unrhymed pentameter.

Unrhymed? Only deficient readers would call it unrhymed. For a Funesian, rhymes will inevitably crop up all the time, given the length of *Paradise Lost* and the finitude of syllable sounds in our language. Take the poem's opening lines:

Of man's first disobedience, and the fruit
Of that forbidden tree, whose mortal taste
Brought death into our world, and all our woe . . .

The first line finds its rhyme after 170 lines, or some 1,700 syllables: "His ministers of vengeance and pursuit." The second line looks further afield. The word *taste*—whose sound may be a more specialized taste than most—requires a full 387 lines to find a rhyme: "Between the cherubim; yea, often placed." The more gregarious *woe* (a real crowd-pleaser, that *woe*) meets up with itself in line 64 ("Served only to discover

sights of woe") and then finds a perfectly suitable mate in line
122: "Irreconcilable to our grand foe."

Obviously, Milton didn't view these as proper rhymes.
He was proceeding, justifiably, on the assumption that sounds
will fade altogether after hundreds and hundreds of syllables.
This was precisely what he was after; in his preface to *Paradise
Lost*, he describes rhyme as "an invention of a barbarous age."
He was creating *un*rhymed iambic pentameter.

But he was not reckoning with the Funesians, for whom
no monumental poem fails to rhyme. Picture your Funesian
reader making her way through *Paradise Lost*. On reaching
line 170, she grins and says to herself, "I was *wondering* when
he was going to get around to rhyming on 'fruit.' " In a poem
as long as *Paradise Lost*, virtually every line's terminal sound
will eventually find its rhyme, and the Funesians (who, inci-
dentally, have a special partiality for the rhyme of *rhyme* and
time) are nothing if not patient.

Even in much shorter poems, rhymes will spring up. At
159 lines, Wordsworth's famous "Tintern Abbey" occupies
less than 2 percent of *Paradise Lost*'s length, and yet three of
its five final lines have perfect rhyme mates buried within the
text. Bells are tolling at the conclusion. For whom do the bells
toll? For the Funesians, naturally.

Some of my readers may already have guessed that both
in their name and in their Andes homeland my Funesians
pay a tribute to Jorge Luis Borges. While thinking about the
superhuman reading of poetry, I was reminded of "Funes the
Memorious," his short story of a nineteenth-century Uru-
guayan boy left paralyzed after being thrown from a horse.
It turns out that Funes's accident has a further unseen consequence: He is suddenly gifted with total recall. Before his
fall, he had been "blind, deaf, addlebrained, absent-minded."

Now his feats of memory are preternatural, scarcely human: "Funes remembered not only every leaf of every tree of every wood, but also every one of the times he had perceived or imagined it. He decided to reduce each of his past days to some seventy thousand memories, which would then be defined by ciphers."

And when I discerned that by calling my imaginary beings the Funesians I might also pay homage to the ancient seagoing Phoenicians, who put rigging and sails to the Mediterranean imagination by inventing an alphabet, I knew I'd found for my creatures a suitable habitation and name.

Sadly, the superhuman gift bestowed on Borges's young man turns out to be oppressive. To remember *everything* winds up being an ungodly burden. Most of what Funes recalls is not merely useless but obstructive. Borges's story can be seen as a parable about insomnia—the bleakness of the brain that will not shut down. Funes turns out to be the "lucid spectator of a multiform, instantaneous and almost intolerably precise world."

So, much as I esteem my Funesians, the greatest readers of poetry the world has ever known, I don't always envy them. For all their ravishing subtleties of imagination, they are largely deprived of that primal human pleasure, rooted in inadequacy and ignorance, that arises when clarity dawns unexpectedly: the joy of enlightened surprise. To return to our automotive metaphor, the Funesians will never know what it is to follow the winding and precipitous road of a poem, through mist and fog, over rain-slicked pavement, over pounding potholes and crumbling, soft-soiled shoulders, at last to attain, abruptly, the harbor of a grand scenic overlook—and, outspread below, a comely, sunny, mist-melting valley.

▣

CHAPTER TWO

The Prosodic Contract

First, an unfortunate term: prosody.
    Unfortunate, because to high schoolers and undergrads (those in whose hands the future of poetry lies) it suggests a preoccupation with prose. Right away, they're misled. In fact, the word's Greek etymology evokes a song sung to instrumental music. A dictionary speaks of the "pattern of rhythm and sound used in poetry."

I'd offer an alternative and informal definition. Imagine you were asked to examine a poem composed in a language whose pronunciation you understood while knowing no vocabulary. (Not so fanciful a hypothetical, for this describes Milton's daughters, whom he had taught to read Italian, French, Spanish, Hebrew, Greek, and Latin to him in his blindness. They uttered syllables; he heard words.) Now, what could you tell anyone about this poem?

Actually, quite a lot. You could tell whether or not it rhymed, whether it followed a meter. You could trace clusters of alliteration and the repetition of word or phrase. You could detect the presence of homonyms, hypothesizing from there

the existence of puns and wordplay. You could pursue rhythmic variations, metrical substitutions—a whole host of things.
Whatever you could conclude about a poem whose meaning utterly escaped you? That's prosody. And in its adjectival
form, *prosodic*, it's essential to my thinking.

A **formal poem** presents its potential reader with a
deal, offer, exchange, pact. The centrality of this deal, often
remarkable for its specificity, is what most decisively distin-
guishes verse from prose, the overall experience of a formal
poem from that of a piece of fiction or a creative essay. I call
this deal or exchange the **prosodic contract.**

When I first employed the term, in an essay in *The New
Criterion* many years ago, the poet Louis Simpson objected.
To him, *contract* smacked too much of buying and selling, the
getting and spending of sullied capitalism at its most soulless.
He accused me of wishing to make the writing of poetry a
"predictable and sound investment." I guess I don't view *contract* in Simpson's exclusive way. (What of the marriage contract? Or Jean-Jacques Rousseau's social contract, providing
sanctuary to people facing "obstacles" in their "survival in
the state of nature"? What of the affable contract intimated
in the dedication to *The Pickwick Papers*, where Dickens com-
memorated the "most gratifying friendship I have ever con-
tracted"?) (Simpson might have countered me by pointing
out that you contract a disease.) Still, I suppose *compact* would
do just as well as *contract*. The point is that some variety of
exchange is tendered. In its simplest form, the poet is asking you, as reader, to demonstrate your interest: to continue
reading. In return, the poet is pledging to behave in a certain
fashion. And the particularities of his pledge are the terms of
the poem's prosodic contract.

Let's suppose you chance upon a poem dressed in skillful and witty rhyming couplets—Jonathan Swift's "A Description of the Morning," say. After six or so lines, you're confident about what lies before you:

Now hardly here and there a hackney-coach
Appearing, showed the ruddy morn's approach.
Now Betty from her master's bed had flown,
And softly stole to discompose her own;
The slip-shod 'prentice from his master's door
Had pared the dirt, and sprinkled round the floor.

I will give you witty and sophisticated iambic pentameter couplets, Swift is pledging. And what is he asking of you in exchange? The usual thing. *Please keep reading my poem to its end* is his tacit and humble request.

Prose likewise creates its own expectations, and some distinctive prose stylists can reveal a good many stipulations in a short space. Consider the opening of Hemingway's *A Farewell to Arms*: "In the late summer of that year we lived in a house in a village that looked across the river and the plain to the mountains." The reader, only one sentence in, might begin to form reasonable expectations of what will follow: a spare linguistic journey, lean on adjectives, frugal with its commas, which favors a flexible use of conjunctions and doesn't shy from repeated prepositions. But all of this cannot begin to equal a poem's specificity of expectation. Given the first two lines of a limerick, anybody can tell on what rhyme sound the poem will conclude and predict how many syllables later it will fall, and perhaps even divine the rhyme word itself. Poetry brings out the inner clairvoyant in each of us.

Having once created a formula, a pattern of expectations, most formal poems pursue it to the close. Poems that begin by sounding and looking like a sonnet wind up becoming sonnets. Most poems that begin as limericks end as limericks.

This talk of prosodic contracts may appear highly abstract and professorial—when displayed upon a page. Yet it's a concept instinctively grasped by a child of two or three. I have two daughters, and when they were toddlers, I enjoyed playing a little game rooted in the prosodic contract. I would mangle nursery rhymes for them. "One, two, / Buckle my shoe," I might begin. And maybe continue this way:

Three, four,
Shut the door.

Five, six,
Pick up sticks.

Seven, eight,
Now it's time to wash your hands, darling, and have
    some dinner.

Invariably, such mischief sparked in their faces a befuddled and lit-up expression, followed by strings of giggles. The kids knew I was messing with their heads; they understood that a vague promise had been dangled before them before being snatched away. They'd absorbed the terms of a prosodic contract whose detailed complexity they couldn't begin to articulate (I suppose what I'd implicitly promised was a string of exactly rhymed **pure stress** dimeter couplets), but whose essence they had absorbed into their bodies, causing them to respond to my words physically, almost as though being tickled.

In rumpling a nursery rhyme, I behaved like a vandal toward its pattern of expectations. I might instead have rewritten respectfully, meeting all expectations of form and content. ("Seven, eight, / Let's not wait. / Nine, ten, / Dinner again.") Either way, to my daughters the prosodic contract was as real as real could be. They found themselves both taken with it and taken in by it. For them, a Mother Goose rhyme had accomplished the loftiest goal poetry can aspire to: It had blended a flow of words with the pulsing of the blood.

A poet's handling of a prosodic contract speaks volumes about what the particular poem is like. And how she treats these patterns of expectations in the aggregate, in her collected verse, speaks volumes about what the particular poet is like.

Elizabeth Bishop (1911–1979), for instance, was an inveterate, if careful, infringer of contracts. She delighted in creating patterns that she would dishevel or distress in a penultimate stanza and restore intact in the final stanza ("Cirque d'Hiver," "Large Bad Picture," "Manners," "Twelfth Morning"). Alternatively, she enjoyed maintaining formal regularity throughout a poem and surprising the reader with some twist at the very close, as in "Sleeping Standing Up," a poem of exact rhymes that terminates with a casual off rhyme:

> . . . Sometimes they disappeared,
> dissolving in the moss,
>   sometimes we went too fast
> and ground them underneath. How stupidly we steered
>   until the night was past
>   and never found out where the cottage was.

In this regard, she resembled Philip Larkin (1922–1985). He, too, loved to rumple at the close a reigning pattern of meter or rhyme or stanza ("Born Yesterday," "No Road," "Deceptions," "Arrivals, Departures," "Water," "Talking in Bed"). In what I sometimes think is Larkin's most beautiful poem, "Cut Grass," the reader begins in a chiseled two-beat iambic line (with standard variations):

Cut grass lies frail:
Brief is the breath
Mown stalks exhale.

Yet we conclude, some eight lines later, in a larger, swinging, three-beat iambic:

Lost lanes of Queen Anne's lace,
And that high-builded cloud
Moving at summer's pace.

If this poem is about the finality of death, it is also "about" the reader's transplantation into a more capacious meter. It is "about" inducing the reader to accept and eventually to welcome the breaking of the contract's initial terms.

Sometimes the surprise in a poem lies in its pattern's *not* being broken, as with Frost's "Provide, Provide." The poem begins with iambic tetrameter triplets, the meter sharply etched and the rhymes exact:

The witch that came (that withered hag)
To wash the steps with pail and rag,
Was once the beauty Abishag,

The picture pride of Hollywood.
Too many fall from great and good
For you to doubt the likelihood.

Rhymed triplets of this sort usually come undone; they typically relax into off rhymes, simultaneously moderating their harsh hubbub and relieving the poet of the task of producing natural-sounding rhymes so close together. The surprise in this poem is that Frost never lets up. He concludes five stanzas later with all prosodic requirements duly, triumphantly, exclamatorily met:

Better to go down dignified
With boughten friendship at your side
Than none at all. Provide, provide!

On the very grandest scale, this sort of punctiliousness describes *Paradise Lost*. We know from the outset not only where the poem is going but how it plans to get there. Let's briefly suppose that Milton had died in a storm after completing only the poem's first hundred lines. (Not so far-fetched a conjecture, given that in 1658, the year he began his great epic, England was hit by its worst hurricane in centuries.) So—only a few pages survive to suggest the paths Milton might have taken with his enormous enterprise. How accurately could modern-day literary detectives make predictions?

Quite accurately. They would speculate that the poem's number of books would ultimately have totaled twelve, like the *Aeneid*, or be a multiple of twelve, like the *Iliad* or the *Odyssey*, each of which contains twenty-four. (In the end, Milton chose to follow Virgil's model.) They might hypothesize that the completed poem would usher us into the Garden of Eden before expelling us eastward, into the shelterless realm of mortality and toil and pestilence. That it would employ blank verse throughout as the ligature of an intricate and multifarious syntax. That it would frequently vary its meter by substituting **trochees** for **iambs.** But our detectives could do more than this. Given Milton's steadiness of method, they might predict quite precisely the percentages of trochaic distribution—where, over time, those trochees would likely fall over the five feet of an iambic pentameter line. In other words, they could formulate a metrical and rhythmical blueprint of the entire poem.

Paradise Lost may be the grandest contract in world literature. *Stick with me,* the opening lines exhort and pledge, *and I will steadily unroll a stately and majestic blank verse until I have managed to "justify God's ways to man."*

Sometimes a prosodic contract pleases by *not* being readily discernible. A reader supposes one thing is being pledged, only to discover it's another. Frost again provides an apt example, "Stopping by Woods on a Snowy Evening," whose opening stanza may be the most famous quatrain in American literature:

Whose woods these are I think I know.
His house is in the village though;
He will not see me stopping here
To watch his woods fill up with snow.

Imagine a sophisticated reader who somehow had never before stumbled upon the poem. At this point, having read only four lines, she'd probably suppose Frost was devising a slimmed-down variation of the Rubáiyát stanza's pentameter quatrain, whose first, second, and fourth lines rhyme, leaving

the third unmated: AAxA. (I employ a small x to denote lines
not intended to rhyme.)

Usually, the terms of a poem's contract are evident by the
conclusion of the first stanza. (A stanza could be defined as
a device for cordoning off the formal duties a poem vows to
fulfill.) But Frost's second stanza shifts unexpectedly. It picks
up in prominent fashion the sound of *here*, the word seemingly left orphaned in stanza one:

My little horse must think it queer
To stop without a farmhouse near
Beside the woods and frozen lake
The darkest evening of the year.

Only now does our prosodic contract announce itself.
Frost isn't promising Rubáiyát stanzas. He has wandered back
to the Late Middle Ages to borrow and expand Dante's terza
rima (ABA BCB CDC DED), hybridizing it with the Rubáiyát to create something exacting and interlocking: AABA
BBCB CCDC . . .

Poets often loosen contractual terms, allowing themselves
additional leeway as a poem progresses. Frost is unusual in
sometimes venturing in the opposite direction, as in perhaps
his greatest sonnet, "Design." Its first line is "I found a dim-
pled spider, fat and white."

"Design" is a Miltonic sonnet, a taxing form whose opening eight lines allow only two rhyme sounds (ABBAABBA),
rather than the four permitted the more popular Shakespearean form (ABABCDCD). Because the Miltonic sonnet provides so little maneuvering room, in inexperienced
hands it invites strangled syntax and forced rhyming. Yet in
"Design," Frost compounds his difficulties by bringing into

his concluding six lines one of his two earlier rhyme sounds: ABBAABBA ACAACC. That's a lot of A's—seven in all. The *white* of our first line provides a base for half the rhymes! There are only three rhyme sounds in total, rather than the Shakespearean sonnet's seven.

Something similar transpires in Richard Wilbur's "Mined Country." Its opening stanza suggests unrhymed quatrains:

> They have gone into the gray hills quilled with birches,
> Drag now their cannon up the chill mountains;
> But it's going to be long before
> Their war's gone for good.

But the following stanza breathes a revelation, as three of those "unrhymed" lines find partners by looking back across the white space of a stanza break:

> I tell you it hits at childhood more than churches
> Full up with sky or buried town fountains,
> Rooms laid open or anything
> Cut stone or cut wood . . .

Wilbur has buried his rhyming—as befits a poem about land mines. A reader must hike some ways into "Mined Country" before identifying the terrain: paired rhyming stanzas. Which could prompt another prediction: an even number of stanzas in all, lest too many unrhymed lines be left as loose ends.

Poems like "Stopping by Woods" and "Design" delight us by providing more than we believe we bargained for; we receive a happy surprise, a bonus. Far more common, though, is to wind up shortchanged. A challenging form will begin nimbly and then, the poet becoming overborne, slide into either forced rhymes and strained meter or the abandonment of formal requirements. Either way, we don't receive what was promised.

Poets are hardly alone in dealing with an audience whose expectations border on entitlement. It's an issue for authors working in any genre. (A genre might be defined as a clustering of readerly expectations.) If I pick up a murder mystery in an airport bookshop, I proceed on the breezy assumption that the killer will be unmasked in the denouement. Were the author to throw up his hands in the final chapter and declare, *Some mysteries go unsolved,* I'd feel more than disappointed— betrayed. Wasn't there an understanding between us, author and reader, and hasn't he let me down?

The author of a vampire novel promises bloodstained pages. A Western will set the reader on horseback. A techno-thriller will click and clank with dazzling gadgetry, chapter after chapter. The concluding pages of a Harlequin Romance will not find the heroine in bed with a malodorous and unshaven buffoon. None of these rules is unbreakable, and all allow for artful games of adherence and transgression. But the reader's expectations are real, and reasonable, and are tampered with only at the author's peril.

Still, poetic expectations are far more detailed, more open to opportunities for variation and gradation than those of any other genre. This is one reason why the Funesians, in their Andean aerie, snacking on pickled parsnips and sipping temperately from their flagons of rhubarb brandy, remain so devoted to verse. When they're not classifying cloud shapes, or flossing their teeth, or dozing, their favorite pastime is reading poetry. It hones their wits. They are enthralled by literary patterns, and no other genre matches poetry for designs ingenious and painstaking and far-flung.

To any new techno-thriller we bring the same expectations we brought to our previous techno-thriller. A new Harlequin Romance is, before you turn the first page, an old Harlequin Romance. We needn't adapt in order to assimilate. Poetry, though, is something else. *Make it new*, Ezra Pound urged his fellow poets; we look to poetry for surprises. And make it new while honorably fulfilling the contracts you've made. Well, it's a tricky medium.

To read through a volume like Thomas Hardy's *Collected Poems* is constantly to identify and evaluate new configurations. Hardy was obsessed with architecture, and his poems revel in innovative construction. His stanzaic forms often have the sturdiness of something habitable—solid little rooms for the mind. New subjects germinate new structures, designed for the occasion: so-called nonce forms. Among English-language poets, perhaps only W. H. Auden wrote successfully in more configurations than Hardy did.

Hardy could be highly repetitive in his subject matter. Haunted by ghosts, particularly his first wife's, he returned compulsively to the same vanished figures, same emotional cruxes. Structural novelty alone rescued him from monotony. A new Hardy poem asks the reader, first, to identify its form; second, to identify any variations he plays upon it; third, to evaluate how well this particular prosodic contract suits its subject matter. Frankly, I don't see how it's possible to grapple with Hardy's *Collected Poems* without recourse to some notion like the prosodic contract.

A final word about the term. One of the raggedy appeals of poetry is that it's enacted in a penurious economy. The painter, the actor, the novelist—these artists can, at least theoretically, sell out. They can go slumming for the lowest common denominator and, having found it, reap the rewards.

Real money might be made. But there is no potential payout to the perennially penniless modern poet, other than his rarefied inkling that someone somewhere someday at some point in some place might look over his words with something of the care invested in them. Mr. Simpson's objection to the term *prosodic contract* suggests that the poet *could* partake of that sullying world of commercial transactions. Wishful thinking!

In fact, the bartering between poet and reader is less like something taking place at the Chicago Mercantile Exchange than what goes on in a weekend singles bar. Money isn't the chief mode or object of commerce; it's affection, a hunger for love, or something approximating love. And, unfortunately, the poet isn't likely to be the most attractive person in the place. Painters, actors, novelists, reality-TV screenwriters—these people dependably display far more dash and savvy and cool.

Even so, *Choose me, love me,* the poet keeps urging. *I'm not sure I'm interested,* the potential reader replies. *But just look at what I'm offering,* the poet doggedly continues. *I'm offering couplets and quatrains, iambs and trochees, caesuras and enjambments, exact rhymes and off rhymes and similes galore!*

Verbal baubles, bangles, beads . . . This, too, is the prosodic contract.

CHAPTER THREE

Poetic Architecture

My book hinges on the notion that poetic structures
have a physiological aspect—they're offspring of the
body as well as outpourings of the spirit or soul. These structures (outfitted with rhyme schemes, metrical configurations,
stanzaic forms, patterns of indentation and capitalization) are
the architecture of poetry, and share with architecture a creative tension between mind and body. We ask of any building not merely *Is it functional?* But also *Is it beautiful?* And *Is it
comfortable?* Even *Is it fun?* The body's hungers and hankerings
undergird both disciplines.

Imagine some group that knows nothing about what
human beings look like and act like. (I suppose I'm asking
my reader to go one step beyond the Funesians; I'm talking
about true extraterrestrials here, antennaed creatures of the
green-skinned sort.) And further imagine our otherworldly
visitors have been presented with an empty city. By scrutiniz-
ing its buildings and furnishings, they could amass a wealth
of information about the daily desires and the extended passages of a human life. Visiting a nursery, they would per-
ceive that human beings, unlike kittens or foals or giraffes,

are not ambulatory and agile soon after birth. Entering an
assisted-living facility, they would intuit that unsteadiness of
foot characterizes old age, as well. The pitch of our staircases,
the heights of our shelves and our ceilings, the layout of our
heating and cooling systems—from such elements a detailed
prospectus could be assembled about what the human body
craves and what feels easeful. Our lobbies and assembly halls
would testify to our penchant for open communal spaces, our
bathrooms and bedrooms whisper of our taste for shuttered
sanctuaries. Our lighting systems and fenestration would illuminate the engineering of the human eye; our concert halls
and PA systems, the engineering of the human ear.

In similar fashion, our stanzaic forms both mirror and
minister to our corporeal nature. As I've noted, our rhyme
schemes reflect how precariously we retain a single sound
across intervening syllables, but further observation would
reveal that this skill develops markedly with age. Our ear
for poetry alters. Rhymes in children's verses tend to be
crowded; nursery rhymes are raucous things. As we mature,
our rhymes redistribute themselves, savoring quieter and
roomier acoustics.

What sorts of structures do poets build? Ask the man
on the street and the answer might be "Complicated ones."
Certainly they're complicated in comparison to the architecture of prose, which is largely limited to the formation of
paragraphs and chapters. But a broader view (a Funesian or
extraterrestrial prospect) might contrarily reply, "Little ones."
Even in their largest constructions, poets usually proceed by
tiny units. Most poets were members of the "small house
movement" before there was a small house movement.

A sonnet is a complex structure when compared to a
heroic couplet. But it *is* a small house: built of a mere four-

teen beams, or lines. In fact, it's a rare independent poetic form that extends beyond thirty lines. John Hollander's marvelous handbook, *Rhyme's Reason*, contains dozens of forms, but precious few (the sestina, the ballade, the canzone) are longer than a sonnet. Even when "going big," in long or very long poems, formal poets gravitate toward small building blocks.

It's easy to lose sight of how humble these components are, given the gigantism of some of the overall structures. The list is imposing of major poets who composed an opus of five thousand lines or more: Chaucer, Wordsworth, Byron, Shelley, Southey, Longfellow, Tennyson, Browning, Melville, Berryman, Walcott . . . (Wordsworth's 1805 version of *The Prelude*—the *shorter* edition—runs some 8,400 lines, but he envisioned a colossal prodigy of 33,000 lines: three times the dimensions of *Paradise Lost!*) Each of these poems is a sprawling megalopolis, but in virtually every case its neighborhoods are compounded of tiny stanzaic forms—small houses.

The pattern holds from Chaucer in the fourteenth century to Seamus Heaney in the twenty-first. It's one of the oddest and most striking things about poetry lovers: their tireless taste for metrical stability. Formally, *Paradise Lost* remains unflappably, monotonously consistent for more than ten thousand lines. While there are frequent metrical substitutions (typically a trochee substituted for an iamb), the iambic armature remains rigidly unshaken. Apparently, readers of some of our language's longest poems feel a regular need for a local metrical substitution. But no such need for a wholesale change, a global substitution of meter.

This seems extraordinary at first glance—and more extraordinary the more you examine it. I once estimated that, reading aloud at a brisk canter, a human reader conceivably might absorb fifteen lines of *Paradise Lost* per minute, which would mean getting through the poem in about twelve hours. (Given the obscurity of many of the allusions and the complex, tentacular reach of Milton's syntax, I figured my estimate was probably optimistic. But in 2008, a group of Cambridge dons, celebrating the four hundredth anniversary of Milton's birth, in tag-team fashion did read the poem aloud. It consumed twelve hours.) As a piece of music, *Paradise Lost* is some seven or eight times longer than the very longest symphonies in the standard Western repertory—Mahler's Third, say. Yet a piece like Mahler's Third is forever shifting keys (some eight times through its six movements) and tempi (everything from "Very slowly, mysteriously" to "Cheerful in tempo and cheeky in expression"). By contrast, *Paradise Lost* is effectively all in the same key and tempo. No cheekiness. Imagine if Mahler had written a "super symphony," eight times vaster than anything he'd ever composed, and the immense first movement was marked andante moderato, and the immense second movement was marked andante moderato, and the immense third movement . . . In its underlying single-mindedness, the music of poetry diverges significantly from the music of music.

Uniformity of meter characterizes Homer's *Iliad* and *Odyssey*, too, and Virgil's *Aeneid*—even Byron's *Don Juan*. The epic poem (or in Byron's case, the mock epic) is typically an extended campaign conducted through metrical invariability, and our willingness to march to a single meter over yawning miles of terrain looks less like tolerance than devotion. Seems we prefer it that way.

Poems like *Paradise Lost* and *The Prelude* lend credence to an old critical notion that the iamb's appeal lies in its affiliation with the human heartbeat. Tha-*thump*, tha-*thump*, tha-

thump, tha-*thump*. (Repeat until death ensues.) Aren't we all partial to a strong cardiac regularity? While we enjoy racing our pulses a bit, isn't it true we don't actually want unpredictability in the center of the chest? That's called fibrillation or tachycardia, and we recoil from it. Most long poems in English are steadily iambic.

We crave unfamiliarity and variety, but we also crave familiarity and regularity, and any handbook of poetic forms reveals how the latter gives birth to the former. The buildings themselves may be baroque, but the building blocks are simple. Familiarity breeds not contempt but unfamiliarity—as a handful of simple and familiar parts yield unfamiliar results.

Poetry's simplest parts really are simple. They find their way, sometimes disguisedly, into a cluster of reappearing ratios. The most pervasive and puzzling of these is the ratio of 4:3. You might say that what the golden mean is to architecture, the 4:3 ratio is to our poetry.

This ratio links a trio of polarized popular forms: folk poetry's spoken or sung ballad, whose quatrains typically alternate lines of four and three stresses; the Miltonic sonnet, with its introductory octave (eight lines) and concluding sestet (six lines); and the limerick, whose five-line appearance masks its essential 4-3-4-3 structure. (The limerick's pattern of stresses looks like this: 3-3-2-2-3. But treat the first line as truncated—missing a foot at either end—and bundle lines three and four together, and we arrive at (4)-3-4-3. Edward Lear, the recognized father, if not the inventor, of the limerick, printed his creations in quatrains.) In other words, an elementary ratio binds a startlingly motley crew. It links "Amazing grace! How sweet the sound / That saved a wretch like me" and the sonnet form of Wordsworth's "It is a beauteous evening, calm and free, / The holy time is quiet as a Nun" and Auden's "The Bishop-elect of Hong Kong / Had a dong that was twelve inches long."

Or consider the widespread popularity of the seven-syllable line. On its face, it's an anomaly. English-language poetry has overwhelmingly preferred tidy lines of even-numbered syllables, usually eight or ten, sometimes six or twelve. Traditional verse recognizes no standard five-syllable line. Or nine. Or eleven. (I'm disregarding the iambic line with a **feminine ending,** a final unstressed syllable best treated as extrametrical.)

What's the magical appeal of seven? Surely it's no coincidence that it aligns with our taste for the ratio of 4:3, or 3:4; most seven-syllable lines have a natural pause in sound or sense—a caesura—in the middle, sometimes but not always marked by punctuation. Over and over, the line's syllables break into a 4:3 or 3:4 arrangement, as heard in *A Midsummer Night's Dream*:

> When thou wak'st, if she be by,
> Beg of her for remedy.

And:

> Now it is the time of night
> That the graves, all gaping wide,
> Ev'ry one lets forth his sprite . . .

And:

> Beetles black, approach not near;
> Worm nor snail, do no offense.

Sometimes these underlying ratios may conceal themselves behind a formal ornateness. In the seventeenth century, remarkably intricate-looking stanzas flourished in the hands of people like John Donne and George Herbert. But in most cases these stanzas can be disassembled into well-known parts, familiar ratios.

Here's an opening stanza from Thomas Traherne (1637–1674). The poem's premise, simple yet grand, befits a verse baldly titled "Wonder." Traherne, like Wordsworth and Ralph Waldo Emerson and Frost, cherished the notion of the soul's preexisting the body, with childhood naturally haunted by inklings of some lost grace, infinite and irrecoverable.

> How like an angel came I down!
> How bright are all things here!
> When first among his works I did appear
> Oh, how their glory me did crown!
> The world resembled his eternity,
> In which my soul did walk;
> And everything that I did see
> Did with me talk.

The stanza looks elaborate, but, as in most of "Wonder," the thought groupings cluster into two quatrains. And each can itself be viewed as a variation on the ballad stanza's 4-3-4-3 stress arrangement. (The ballad stanza's ubiquity ensures that readers detect it wherever any semblance materializes.) Traherne's first two lines portend a ballad, only to swell into something more capacious, a 5-4 stress pattern in lines three and four (4-3-5-4). The stanza's concluding quatrain again feels balladlike, though its first line carries an extra iamb and its final line is missing a foot (5-3-4-2). As ballads go, this second quatrain concludes in an atmosphere of sparsity, of things pared down.

Conjoin these two quatrains, erecting an eight-line stanza, and you create an impression of a swelling middle, a tapering close. The two together orchestrate one rhythmic pulse—an expansion and contraction perhaps allied to breathing.

Such *small* shifts: add a foot here, subtract one there . . . Formal poets rely on what might be called one-armed arithmetic: The accounting in their verse can be done on the fingers of one hand. Couplets, triplets, quatrains—from such rudimentary parts, shifted and projected as through a kaleidoscope, a profusion of stanzaic designs glimmer into existence. More than one of my students has been reminded of a childhood toy: Legos, those little plastic building blocks for the budding boy or girl architect. To a child, it can seem a wondrous phenomenon: such a plenitude of exorbitant shapes fashioned from so narrow a box of supplies. Likewise, it can seem wondrous to the adult student of formal poetry: such a plenitude of ornate stanzas, fashioned from the simple couplet, triplet, quatrain, from the trimeter, tetrameter, pentameter.

I once read that, apart from human constructions, the tallest edifices constructed by living beings are termitary mounds. Termites? It's a delicious irony. Our chief architectural rivals are forever undermining our own structures by the most primitive means possible—eating up whatever we build. But there's also here a salutary reminder: Very small things can engineer and erect very large things.

Among truly accomplished poems, perhaps the most rococo and original small structure I know is Louis MacNeice's "The Sunlight on the Garden." Here are the first two stanzas:

The sunlight on the garden
Hardens and grows cold,
We cannot catch the minute
Within its nets of gold,
When all is told
We cannot beg for pardon.

Our freedom as free lances
Advances to its end;
The earth compels, upon it
Sonnets and birds descend;
And soon, my friend,
We shall have no time for dances.

The meter is iambic, with minimal variations, producing an accent pattern of 3-3-3-3-2-3. The rhyme scheme is ABxBBA—or so it first appears. But draw your eye closer and other schemes surface, the initial word(s) of the second and fourth lines rhyming with the concluding word(s) of the previous line. There is also a systematic alternation of two-syllable rhymes with one-syllable rhymes. Most important, the structure pays canny and handsome tribute to its subject. The poem is a miniature labyrinth, uncoiling with a subtlety that parallels the cryptic twists of human memory. And the one short line in each stanza winds up providing more than variation for variation's sake. It acts as a concentrate, establishing a summary prospect. MacNeice has given us something in addition to an ingenious pattern: an affecting attestation of friendship and love, of ruefulness and appreciation. All grows clear in the concluding stanza, the poet finding solace in recollection, which alone staves off time's devastation and desolation.

And not expecting pardon,
Hardened in heart anew,
But glad to have sat under
Thunder and rain with you,
And grateful too
For sunlight on the garden.

One can only marvel at how much fertile material, both prosodic and emotional, MacNeice has crammed into a succession of four six-line stanzas. There isn't a single word to question here. The poem seems bigger—physically—than it is. (The overall looping structure, the poem's last line replaying its first, has the multiplying effect of mirrors placed in opposition.)

I was a sophomore in college when I first came upon the mathematician Georg Cantor (1845–1918) and his proof of the ascending orders of infinity. (Perhaps not coincidentally, poor Cantor ended up a suicide in a sanatorium.) It was one of the half dozen most liberating ideas in my life. Cantor proved, in a demonstration that even I could grasp, that some infinities are larger than others. I suppose it would have been elementary news to any serious math student. Yet to me, it was a revelation.

Proofs about infinities? It all seemed but one dazzling step away from some unreckonable yet inarguable *proof,* or *disproof,* of the existence of God. The infinity of irrational numbers, it turned out, is greater than the infinity of integers. You thought infinity was big? Beyond us lie, in imperturbable ranks, everywhere and nowhere at once, infinite panoplies of infinities, one vaster than the next. Cantor seemed to be saying, Big numbers can always be bigger. Something looks sizable? Look larger, look larger. Well, with "The Sunlight on the Garden" Louis MacNeice concocted a densely ornate and rewarding six-line stanza. But how much denser, deeper, more rewarding might be its prosodic complexity had he doubled the scale? What would be possible with twelve lines? Or why not eighteen? Or eighteen thousand? What sort of music might we compose if only we had keener ears, keener intellects?

Versification is the domain in poetry where mathematics intimately intersects with highly impassioned utterance. The pocket calculator meets up with the *cri de coeur* that is the poet's stock-in-trade. And once mathematical thought inserts itself, a variety of unlooked-for potentialities comes into play. Horizons expand in every direction.

In my favorite novel, *Independent People,* by the Icelandic Nobel laureate Halldór Laxness, we meet up with a twentieth-century hero, the sheep farmer Bjartur of Summerhouses, an everyman who was "brought up on the old measures of the eighteenth-century ballads." Bjartur is steeped in Icelandic heroic literature. He admires poet-warriors, "men who needed only four lines to the verse and yet you could read it in forty-eight ways." He adds, "And were I a poet, I should see that nothing of mine was ever made public unless it was a crafty verse reading the same backwards or forwards."

Bjartur is speaking of words, not individual letters, but I'm reminded of the search for palindromes, those magical words that read the same when their letters are reversed, like *race car* or *deified.* In a language like Japanese, the creation of palindromic sentences is child's play, so common there's even a word—*kaibunka*—for the palindromic poem. But in English, with all its consonant clusters that resist reversal (*th*, *sh*, *ght*), palindromes can be fiendishly difficult to pull off. Everyone knows "Madam, I'm Adam," which, for all its familiarity, boasts a perennial freshness; in the Garden of Eden, obviously, people *ought* to speak in palindromes. (And Adam's greeting invites the perfect, the only, response: "Eve."). Another familiar one, commemorating Ferdinand de Lesseps, the man who supervised the linking of the Atlantic to the Pacific, remains an absolute marvel: "A man, a plan, a canal—Panama!" My computer tells me that someone, or someone's computer, has actually constructed a 17,826-word palindrome, but its message, alas, doesn't make a whole lot of sense. It begins: "A man, a plan, a cameo, Zena, Bird, Mocha, Prowel, a rave, Uganda . . ." It ends: ". . . a wadna, Guevara, Lew, Orpah, Comdr, Ibanez, OEM, a canal, Panama!"

Bjartur, too, has trouble making sense. The formal intricacy of the verses he would create all but guarantees an inability to convey anything of emotional or spiritual import. Still, he has a starry vision—the loftiest thing about him—of a verse at once infinitely complex and incomparably supple. At one point, he spends a disastrous day and night marooned in a howling blizzard, lost and half blinded, at death's door from exhaustion and exposure. No one knows where he is. He lacks dry clothing, he lacks food, he lacks water. He has nothing to sustain him, really, but the naked mnemonics of poetry.

The experience, as Laxness drily puts it, makes for Bjartur "rather a long night." Indeed, "seldom had he recited so much poetry in any one night; he had recited all his father's poetry, all the ballads he could remember, all his own palindromes backwards and forwards in forty-eight different ways, whole processions of dirty poems, one hymn that he had learned from his mother. . . ." The storm intensifies. Bjartur's brain begins to subside into hallucination, where words alone exist, like snow crystals concatenating into ever richer and remoter geometries. And now he isn't merely everyman but everypoet. In just such a deadly predicament, perhaps, one of my favorite characters in all of literature meets up with his Funesians.

CHAPTER FOUR

Stanzas

Poets are great partitioners. Arguably, it's their defining act, the one that makes a poet a poet: She assembles blocks of words into shapes. This assembling assumes many forms, but it typically begins with a subdividing or segmenting of phrases into lines. Poets are linear thinkers.

Admittedly, I fail to include or explain the prose poem. But all definitions of poetry, however balloonlike you attempt to make them, pop and explode under enough pressure. Poetry has been memorably defined as memorable speech (Auden), but even this seemingly all-encompassing characterization might be deemed unduly restrictive. What about a pure cry of terror? Not memorable speech? Should we define poetry as memorable human sounds? If so, many parents will tell you that nothing that will ever issue from a child's mouth can match for memorability a newborn's first cry—from which you could conclude that the greatest poets are prelingual. (Wordsworth and Coleridge might concur.) The more comprehensive the definition becomes, the more meaningless it grows. Literature might be defined as a place where all definitions fail.

So—let's stick with this view of a poem as something broken up into lines. This is the first and fundamental partition and, for some great poems, the truly distinguishing one: Line after line, rollingly, the poem unfolds in even units, the way *Paradise Lost* proceeds.

Much of the time, though, there's a second significant partitioning: a clumping of lines into stanzas. These are akin to paragraphs, with the proviso that, unlike prose paragraphs, in formal poems they're usually all the same length. Maybe they're two-line stanzas (couplets), or four-line stanzas (quatrains), or eight-line stanzas (octets or octaves), or thirteen-line stanzas (which, so far as I know, have no name). The important point isn't their length, but their regularity. (If these stanzas are of differing sizes, the phrase "verse paragraph" rather than "stanza" is often useful.)

A poet may choose to continue partitioning, dividing and subdividing. He might insert white spaces within a line, to create something called a hemistich:

> An axe angles
>   from my neighbor's ashcan;
> It is hell's handiwork,
>   the wood not hickory,
> The flow of the grain
>   not faithfully followed.
>
>   RICHARD WILBUR, "JUNK"

Or, in a longer poem, he might bundle his stanzas into cantos or chapters or books. But this initial pair of partitions—the creation of lines, the shepherding of lines into stanzas—marks the fundamental shaping. With these two actions, typically, the poem's essential contours have been cast. We can think of the poem as (depending on its size) a house or a school or a skyscraper. The stanzas, both metaphorically and etymologically, are the rooms within it.

Although one-line stanzas—single lines bordered top and bottom by white space—are possible, this is no popular form, perhaps because it often feels like no form at all; it feels like single lines, and single lines beg for company. The simplest common form is the couplet, as in these examples from Wallace Stevens. Couplets may be rhymed and metered:

> Soon, with a noise like tambourines,
> Came her attendant Byzantines.
>
> They wondered why Susanna cried
> Against the elders by her side;
>
> And as they whispered the refrain
> Was like a willow swept by rain.
>
> *"PETER QUINCE AT THE CLAVIER"*

Or metered without rhyme:

> You ten-foot poet among inchlings. Fat!
> Begone! An inchling bristles in these pines,
>
> Bristles, and points their Appalachian tangs,
> And fears not portly Azcan nor his hoos.
>
> *"BANTAMS IN PINE-WOODS"*

Or rhymed without meter:

> Let be be finale of seem.
> The only emperor is the emperor of ice-cream.
>
> *"THE EMPEROR OF ICE-CREAM"*

Or unrhymed and unmetered:

> There might have been the immense solitude
> Of the wind upon the curtains.
>
> *"GALLANT CHATEAU"*

Whichever form the couplet claims, it carries associations of symmetry and balance, of dialectic reasoning, question and response—everything you'd presume of a bipartite universe.

You might expect a simple couplet to be a thing of constancy, unchanged across the centuries. A couplet is a couplet is a couplet. . . . Yet in the world of poetry, where *everything* is writ on water, even the seeming invariables mutate over time. A poem's form is a tale of shifting expectations, and as our expectations shift, the form shifts. Wallace Stevens writing couplets a hundred years ago was working in a different form from the couplet writer today.

Confronting a batch of two-line stanzas, an eighteenth- or nineteenth-century reader would naturally be on the lookout for meter and rhyme; his reasonable supposition would be heroic couplets. Back in the 1920s, when Stevens broke on the scene with his multifarious couplets, he was playing against this still-living tradition. He was cultivating the unexpected.

Much has changed. Picking up a literary magazine today, you may chance upon verse in couplets—but the odds are tiny of its being rhymed, and tinier still of its being both rhymed and metered. Rather than declaring that the heroic couplet has altered over the centuries, perhaps it's more logical to say our attitudes have shifted. But it comes to the same thing.

We might hazard another definition of poetry, hoping it no less unsatisfactory than all the others: Poetry is a collection of words creating patterns of expectation about the sound and structure of the words themselves. As tastes shift, practices and poetic forms will shift, and as practices and forms shift, a reader's expectations will shift. We have a classic feedback loop, in which new poems alter old poems, themselves altered by what comes after. An unrhymed couplet in 1917 inhabits a different form from that of the same couplet if composed in 2017. We are back in the world of Borges. In his story "Pierre Menard," he points out, with enormous relish, the diverging implications of identical pairs of passages, one written in the seventeenth century and the other in the twentieth.

Generalizations are increasingly hard to make about contemporary poetry, for it's a garden ramifying at a dizzying rate—sprouting in the uncanny, unbounded, hydroponic pastures of cyberspace. Still, for what it's worth, my sense is that the most popular stanzaic form these days may be the unrhymed triplet. Its appeals are many.

To begin with, the triplet has the allure of asymmetry in a world increasingly at home with the irregular and uneven. If it runs the risk of superfluity (as when we feel like a third wheel), there's a welcome hint of waywardness and unpredictability. As such, in its literal oddness, it promises protection from forms of expression that seem quaint or stock or glib. The triplet carries far less outmoded baggage than the quatrain, that venerable building block of the Shakespearean sonnet and the folk ballad and canonical stalwarts like Thomas Gray's "Elegy Written in a Country Churchyard" and Tennyson's *In Memoriam*. And it takes flight readily, as though the triangle of the triplet is inherently more aerodynamic than the rectangle of the quatrain:

The palm at the end of the mind,
Beyond the last thought, rises
In the bronze decor,

A gold-feathered bird
Sings in the palm, without human meaning,
Without human feeling, a foreign song.
                    WALLACE STEVENS, "OF MERE BEING"

The number three is also, as children sense and adult lovers of fairy tales understand, the smallest number with which
we can create a pattern, only to evert it. ("There were three
sons. The first two were sensible stay-at-home boys, but the
third . . ." Or: "There were three sisters. The first two were
cruel and selfish, but the youngest, whom all the animals of
the forest adored . . .") In a similar fashion, the first two lines
of a triplet can fix a pattern, and the third line emerge to
modify it. As in Sylvia Plath's "Lady Lazarus," the pattern
may be of rhyme:

I have done it again.
One year in every ten
I manage it—

Or line length and/or repetition of phrase:

It's easy enough to do it in a cell.
It's easy enough to do it and stay put.
It's the theatrical . . .

Or meter:

> A cake of soap,
> A wedding ring,
> A gold filling.

Or the pattern may be a matter of tone or theme or syntactic structure. In any case, something often pivots and veers off in the third line.

And three-line stanzas open up the potential for an array of rhyme schemes. Let's simplify things by ignoring the possibility of off rhyme and internal rhyme, so that lines either rhyme or don't. The two lines of a couplet offer but one possible rhyme scheme. (No rhyme, no scheme.) But a triplet offers four: AAx, AxA, xAA, AAA. Formal variety begins to assert itself.

The possibilities mushroom when we turn to the quatrain: fourteen possible rhyme schemes. And something quite startling occurs when you supplement these with a small range of meters. Even if we keep meter *extremely* simple and assume that only four feet, all iambic, are possible (trimeter, tetrameter, pentameter, hexameter), it turns out there are 3,584 ways to configure a simple quatrain! Again, the precise numbers hardly matter. What matters is the underlying vastness, the abyssal depths of possibility. Of those 3,584 possible quatrains, are there some never yet employed by anyone, anywhere? Perhaps. Probably. (Something similar happens with chess. Within a mere dozen moves, two players may well arrive at a position nobody has seen in the game's millennium-long history.)

The typical quatrain runs some thirty or forty syllables— roomy enough, it turns out, to utter something at once considered and substantial, yet small enough to move swiftly in and out of speech. It's a houselike form—a basic house, a log cabin of a house—and it's no surprise that poets have made themselves so at home within it, establishing it as the most popular of all traditional stanzas.

> Sunset and evening star,
>   And one clear call for me!
> And may there be no moaning of the bar,
>   When I put out to sea . . .
>
> *TENNYSON, "CROSSING THE BAR"*

Or:

> I sometimes hold it half a sin
>   To put in words the grief I feel;
>   For words, like Nature, half reveal
> And half conceal the Soul within.
>
> *TENNYSON,* IN MEMORIAM

There is an openness and ease and trueness to the form, allowing for a hasty construction that may nonetheless feel solid and even enduring—as is true of Shakespeare's sonnets. Though their dating is problematic, some critics, Auden among them, have convincingly argued that the composition of this greatest of all sonnet sequences (all 154 of them!) was a model of inspired celerity.

The obvious adjective for the quatrain is *foursquare,* in its numerous senses: rectangular, clear, unyielding, strong. It's also—one more sign of strength—flexible. It's the shortest stanza that allows for the possibility of counterpointed rhyme. With two pairs of rhymes to manipulate, a poet can play one against the other. Maybe one rhyme will be exact and the other off, as occurs in all three stanzas of Bill Coyle's "Aubade," which may be the loveliest dimeter poem I know (and one that Frost might have admired for its deft elimination of any need for punctuation):

On a dead street
in a high wall
a wooden gate
I don't recall

ever seeing open
is today
and I who happen
to pass this way

in passing glimpse
a garden lit
by dark lamps
at the heart of it.

Or one rhyme simple, the other more sophisticated:

The little cousin is dead, by foul subtraction,
A green bough from Virginia's aged tree,
And neither the country kin love the transaction
Nor some of the world of outer dark, like me.

RANSOM, "DEAD BOY"

Or one sensible, the other antic, as in "Ogden Observation," my tribute to Ogden Nash:

Guys will be boys; you can't expect even grown men'll
    seize
On those elaborate social niceties
So nicely drawn they're all but subliminal.
    But the women'll.

We might define the quatrain as the smallest stanza whose structural possibilities outstrip our powers of assimilation.

A five-line stanza is called a cinquain, a term apparently shunned by all except prosodists. (When I typed it just now, my computer signaled a misspelling.) With the cinquain, an outbreak of rhyme possibilities occurs—seventy-six, to be precise. If you expand the stanza by adding a line, the number of possible rhymes explodes.

Jump now to the common eight-line stanza. There are millions of possible rhyme schemes—numbers to boggle the mind even of a Funesian.

Everyone registers the musical difference between an ABAB quatrain and an ABBA quatrain, as found in those Tennyson quotations a couple of pages back. And any serious reader of poetry has a feel for all fourteen of the rhyme schemes available to the quatrain. And no reader of poetry, however serious or gifted, can cope with the musical variants available to the eight-line stanza. Poets in English adore the eight-line stanza and have employed it regularly over the centuries; but the poet working in it—whether it's William Dunbar at the turn of the sixteenth century writing "In Honour of the City of London" or Byron in the nineteenth composing *Don Juan* and "Beppo" or Yeats in the twentieth constructing "Sailing to Byzantium"—is piloting a little skiff upon a horizonless ocean.

What's striking is the speed with which our capacities are outpaced. We have a grip on things—and then we don't. We succumb to an architecture far greater than ourselves when stanzas grow as long as a mere four or five lines. And we are utterly at sea by the time we reach eight lines.

Some contemporary poets feel that rhyme and meter are passé. I disagree, but I suppose my heart sinks just as much as theirs do when I meet a contemporary poem in iambic pentameter ABAB quatrains. (The poem may indeed be wonderful, but a powerful presumption of staleness must first be overcome.) Yet whatever one thinks about the viability of rhyme or meter, any serious student of literature needs to understand what a straitened formal ambit we've customarily worked in. The sheer plenitude of potential rhyme schemes ensures that any exhaustion we might feel toward a poetic form—oh, the poor, overworked quatrain!—is less mathematical than psychological. Rhyme isn't exhausted so much as we are exhausted with rhyme.

In the second canto of *Don Juan*, stanza 49, Byron originally came up with what his editors call a "defective rhyme scheme." The first six lines were expected to rhyme ABA-BAB, but his rhymed ABAABA. One might suppose he was again up to something clever, but the pattern (corrected in later editions) appears to have been an oversight. ("I am but a careless reviser," Byron himself once observed to his publisher.) After completing nearly three hundred stanzas, Byron was certainly entitled to a neglectful moment. His defective stanza is a reminder that eight lines is actually a lot to look after.

Rhyme may be dead. (I don't think so.) Meter too may be dead. (I don't think so.) But few would claim that the stanza is dead. If anything, its importance has swelled with the abandonment of other traditional tools. Even staunch free-verse advocates who shun rhyme and meter are quick to break language into similar-size clusters of lines. William Carlos Williams is a case in point. You seldom find him working with either meter or rhyme, but he adored the business of fashioning stanzas.

Admittedly, the stanza of set length makes an easy target for anybody wishing to discard or deride one more traditional tool. It smells of conformity and rigidity. It runs in opposition to the attractive doctrine that poetic form must be ever adapting to content, and that any preconceived structure is ultimately a drag on the imagination. Its opponents might demand, *Why should we regiment our thinking into cookie-cutter shapes?*

Actually, the cookie-cutter simile may be a good and useful one. For it speaks volumes about the durable appeal of stanzas. Some stanzas (observe the ornate fourteen lines of Donne's "Air and Angels") signal a rarefied taste not only through content but also through structural intricacy and subtlety. Yet the appeal of fashioning stanzas is also, at bottom, very childlike. And what child doesn't enjoy making cookies?

I think it's no accident that while the heyday of meter and rhyme lies behind us, the stanza flourishes. The child inside the poet (and once the child inside the poet is dead, his own days are numbered) relishes this process of grabbing a handful of words from the great sticky and lopsided ball of language, imposing a mold upon it, grabbing another handful, imposing the same mold . . . and when you have amassed a satisfying total, you slide them all into the oven of your brain, and wait for them to rise slightly and solidify.

CHAPTER FIVE

Enjambment

When I was a kid, growing up in Detroit, my friends and I embraced a verb now perhaps fallen out of favor: *leg*. We kept it in constant use. It sounded adult and vaguely martial, or cinematic, or at least wiseguyish. It was most commonly employed in the imperative: *Leg it*. Meaning, "Get moving," "Get walking," or "Get your butt over here."

Still a fan, I admire the little word's cogency. It's hard to imagine any coinage more directly getting the notion, the motion, across.

Although a fancier term, the prosodist's **enjambment** is equally rooted in the body's lower limbs. The definition on the poetry.com website is: "The running-over of a sentence or phrase from one poetic line to the next, without terminal punctuation; the opposite of end-stopped." The word is derived from the French *enjamber*, "to stride over" or "go beyond," and ultimately from *jambe*, "leg." You might say that an enjambed line is legging it.

A line without terminal punctuation . . . Well, the most powerful enjambment I know appears in Milton's "On the

Late Massacre at Piedmont," where the poet beseeches the Lord not to permit the martyred Protestants to go unavenged:

> in thy book record their groans
> Who were thy sheep and in their ancient fold
> Slain by the bloody Piedmontese that rolled
> Mother with infant down the rocks.

Typically, the associations of *rolled* are smooth and temperate and playful—anything but violent. But horror lies in wait for us over there, after *rolled*, on the other side of the enjambment: Oh, this is no place to encounter a mother, no place for a baby. The bouncy, gamelike *rolled* renders everything the more unconscionable, and harrowing, for this is a "game" we've come to know all too tragically over the centuries. It's called the Slaughter of the Innocents, it's called Pogrom and Final Solution and Ethnic Cleansing.

Everyone would agree that meter and rhyme are the two prime instruments in the formal poet's toolbox. But the third? A good case might be made for repetition, I suppose, the recurring refrain of line or stanza. Still, it's a technique that often looks quaint, its heyday behind us. I'd vote for enjambment. Indeed, in an era when free verse predominates, as now, enjambment often becomes the prime, the characterizing tool.

The free-verse poem, the one with no discernible meter or rhyme scheme—how to distinguish it from prose? We might answer in high-minded terms, citing differences of tradition or spirit or sensibility. But a more down-to-earth— a better—rejoinder would be that enjambment is the differentiating force. Typically, a poem is a text whose right margin isn't arbitrarily generated by a word processor. Rather, it is thoughtfully, humanly fixed. The poet establishes both margins on the page, left *and* right, determining which word shall begin and which end a line.

Actually, it's misleading to speak of enjambment in absolute, yes-or-no terms. Better to think of degree, along a continuum. We've seen an enjambed line defined as a line that isn't end-stopped—but not all end-stopped lines are alike in their pausing. Any punctuation mark at line's end will likely slacken the reader's pace, slow the flow. Such marks are the poetic equivalent of music's *ritardando* and *rallentando*. But some punctuation marks hit the brakes harder than others.

The question mark typically produces the greatest pause. It enjoins the reader to stop, to ponder, to formulate an answer. The ellipsis probably comes next, each of its three dots a miniature stop sign. The exclamation mark would follow; its breathlessness invites the reader to take a breath. After which would arrive the period, and then (in jumbled, shifting fashion) the semicolon, the dash, the colon, and the comma. Finally would appear the hyphen, which hardly slows the reader. Indeed, with its promise of completion just around the bend, it might even speed her along.

Line breaks are a procedure for manipulating space. They create a frame—a frame of air—around the poem. This frame has a visual component, shaping and isolating the poem in the mind's eye, but also a temporal element: It requests of the reader various curbs in the proceedings.

One sometimes sees *enjambment* used in this inclusive sense, to signify all decisions about where to break a line. (Though *line breaks* is less confusing, it's also clunkier.) However one describes this divvying up of language into lines, the process alters the reader's fundamental unit of absorption.

When we read prose, as we do most of the time, our fundamental unit is the sentence, and the secondary unit is the paragraph. When we read poetry, the fundamental unit is the line, and the secondary unit, the stanza.

And lines tend to be shorter than sentences. The first sentence of "On the Late Massacre at Piedmont" runs nearly eight lines. We encounter seven different line breaks before we bump up against a period. Poetry carves language into littler pieces than prose does. It operates on a tighter, smaller scale.

One of my favorite free-verse writers is Amy Clampitt (1920–1994). I remember my first encounter with a Clampitt poem. It was the summer of 1978. The poem ran in *The New Yorker*, the first time she'd appeared in a national magazine. Its title brimmed with promising sonic excess: "The Sun Underfoot Among the Sundews." Clampitt had a genius for enjambment, and the first couple of lines struck me a clarifying blow:

An ingenuity too astonishing
to be quite fortuitous is
this bog full of sundews, sphagnum-
lined and shaped like a teacup.

More than forty years later, those first two lines still seem about as brilliant as any two lines can be. Whatever her true religious feelings, they ring with a theology associated with the philosopher William Paley. Paley's famous "watchmaker analogy" hypothesized the logical response of someone on a forest hike who discovers a watch lying on the ground: "Every indication of contrivance, every manifestation of design, which existed in the watch, exists in the works of nature." This is the "argument from design" so favored by opponents of evolution: The more minutely one examines nature, the more surely a divine hand is revealed.

It's an argument whose suasions occasionally touch even those who, as Clampitt did, welcome Darwin. Most evolutionists, however staunch, experience their skeptical or disbelieving moments, when it seems impossible that mere chance and insentient mutation could engender all the natural world's extravagant excellences. (Indeed, the feeling was shared by Darwin himself, who, struggling with the devastating implications of his theories, once reported that a glimpse of a peacock's feather "makes me sick.")

In these four lines, each of Clampitt's enjambments feels athletically right. We must pause, she suggests, on *astonishing*. For something momentous is about to be voiced: a hypothesis about the world's origins. And let us pause once more on that modest little *is* (modest and assertive—like *quite*). She is saying to the scientist, to the rationalist, *Your arguments are unconvincing here, in this enchanted place.* And what an unforgettable place it is, gemmed with scores of that bizarre, blazing botanical specimen—incandescent and carnivorous—whose name sounds so demure: the tiny sundew. And concluding a line with that hyphenated *sphagnum-* feels slippery, as it should; a reader loses his footing as he descends into an "understory" that is both a sublayer of vegetation and a tale lying beneath the surface tale.

Occasionally you come upon a poem whose effect depends almost utterly on enjambment. Such is the case with that darling of anthologists "We Real Cool," by Gwendolyn Brooks (1917–2000). Let's examine two versions in entirety, the one she might predictably have written and the one she actually produced:

WE REAL COOL

> *The Pool Players.*
> *Seven at the Golden Shovel.*

We real cool.
We left school.

We lurk late.
We strike straight.

We sing sin.
We thin gin.

We jazz June.
We die soon.

And the poem as actually published:

> *The Pool Players.*
> *Seven at the Golden Shovel.*

We real cool. We
Left school. We

Lurk late. We
Strike straight. We

Sing sin. We
Thin gin. We

Jazz June. We
Die soon.

Word for word, the two poems are identical. But what a difference in quality—in artistry, in pathos—between them! "We Real Cool" consists of tiny couplets, and the first version is more "natural," more traditional, in presenting its rhymes in terminal positions. When in my classroom I've played a recording of Brooks reading the poem, most of my students have transcribed it in this fashion.

The poem contains only twenty-four syllables—shorter than a pair of haikus, shorter than a single tanka—and yet whole lives, stretching from youth to the morgue, are encapsulated within it. They come wonderfully alive, those seven boys in the pool hall.

The contemporary composer Eric Sawyer likens these line breaks to musical syncopation. Time and again, Brooks is leaping in ahead of the beat, while respecting the beat. It's another way of bringing jazz into the poolroom.

Brooks's enjambments foster an intimate camaraderie. A repeated *We* bands together into a chant, a gang of sounds, seven of them, one for each of the boys—We We We We We We We—abruptly concluding with the announcement of premature death. Each enjambment creates a lively imbalance, nudging us into the next line. Each *We* is literally on edge, the line's right edge, an edginess that captures something essential about those figures lankily banking shots on a green felt table. In addition, the pattern works a further imbalance by fashioning a first line too long—in a poem of three-syllable units—and a last line, appropriately, too short.

Whether exercised by a seventeenth-century blind English Puritan like Milton or a twentieth-century African American agnostic like Gwendolyn Brooks, the resources of enjambment are heartening to contemplate. You shift countries, you shift centuries, you shift race and gender and religion, and still the efficacy of artfully divided words burns undiminished.

Enjambment, too, presents something akin to a prosodic contract. Wherever a poet breaks a phrase or word unexpectedly, whenever an enjambment startles, there's an implicit claim that this irregularity will prove warranted. An act of violence has been committed (against syntax, or literary convention, or common sense) and the issue naturally arises: Was the violence justified? Let's take a few examples where extreme violence *does* feel justified. Here is the octet of a Gerard Manley Hopkins sonnet "Hurrahing in Harvest":

> Summer ends now; now, barbarous in beauty, the stooks
>   rise
> Around; up above, what wind-walks! what lovely
>   behaviour
> Of silk-sack clouds! has wilder, wilful-wavier
> Meal-drift moulded ever and melted across skies?
>
> I walk, I lift up, I lift up heart, eyes,
>   Down all that glory in the heavens to glean our
>   Saviour;
> And, éyes, heárt, what looks, what lips yet gave
>   you a
> Rapturous love's greeting of realer, of rounder replies?

The rhyme in line 7 looks more than peculiar. It looks like a defective member of a set: *behaviour/wavier / Saviour/ gave you a*. Gave you a? All the more odd because Hopkins so rarely allows himself the ease and relaxation of a terminal off rhyme.

But the final rhyme pair isn't actually *Saviour/gave you a.*
It's *Saviour/gave you a R*[apturous]. The rhyme reaches across
the enjambment to complete itself. Hopkins was a creator of
strange sonic spaces, with their own idiosyncratic rules, but
these rules he followed meticulously. If you know how Hopkins operates, you know that the first word of line 8 *must*
begin with an *R.*

The tone of the sonnet is exclamatory and ecstatic—as
elevated and sweeping as the skies. Addressing such grandeur,
Hopkins's impish rhyming may look and sound jarringly out
of place. But his is, temperamentally, a lighthearted truancy;
his religiosity is profound but not ponderous. In another sonnet, "God's Grandeur," Hopkins reminds us that "There lives
the dearest freshness deep down things." And in "Hurrahing
in Harvest" he reminds us that this dearest freshness is animated, at bottom, by play.

Elizabeth Bishop (whom I once heard declare Hopkins her
favorite poet) does something similar in "Arrival at Santos":

And gingerly now we climb down the ladder backward,
myself and a fellow passenger named Miss Breen,

descending into the midst of twenty-six freighters
waiting to be loaded with green coffee beans.
Please, boy, do be more careful with that boat hook!
Watch out! Oh! It has caught Miss Breen's

skirt! There! Miss Breen is about seventy,
a retired police lieutenant, six feet tall,
with beautiful bright blue eyes and a kind expression.
Her home, when she is at home, is in Glens Fall

s, New York. There. We are settled.

It's a bizarre enjambment, all the more so given that many readers, unfamiliar with the name Glens Falls, will feel utterly upended on encountering (without any hyphen to serve as warning) a solitary, lowercase *s* lodged on the ledge of the next line. But if the reader is upended, so are the imperiled passengers, who are attacked by—my goodness!—a boat hook.

Nonetheless, any threat of peril rapidly turns comical and cartoonish. Despite the five exclamation points, harm cannot possibly come to anyone in a world so jocose, so amiably ruffled and unruffled.

If surprise enjambments provide some of poetry's keenest pleasures, they also serve up many of its sharpest annoyances. Aggressive enjambments are the bane of contemporary poetry. Of course, every literary school and genre has its characteristic ways of turning out badly. The poem in a traditional form—iambic pentameter quatrains, say—frequently ushers in staleness of thought, as if the adoption of a venerable form impels the promotion of received ideas and tattered imagery. Likewise, the poem in free verse too often offers arbitrariness of line, enjambments chosen with seeming randomness or (more irksome still) chosen for their illogicality and unnaturalness. Pick up any "little magazine" and you'll find examples by the truckload of poems whose line breaks are shameless attention seekers: an overreliance on enjambment to "energize" the poem. But this is energy of a mindlessly bumptious sort—like a crowd jostling down a Jetway toward a plane whose door hasn't yet opened.

A sadly neglected poet these days, James Dickey (1923–1997) had a marvelous touch when rendering a tense, spooky world overseen by merciless predators (i.e., the natural world, the one we live in), but some of his enjambments drive me crazy. Here's the close of "For the Last Wolverine":

. . . I take you as you are

And make of you what I will,
Skunk-bear, carcajou, bloodthirsty

Non-survivor.
           Lord, let me die   but not die
Out.

He has enjambed the phrase *die out*, but to what end? What does the *Out* add, and what would we lose without *Out*? Not much. And the phrase suffers by echoing one of the greatest enjambments in our language, from Shakespeare's sonnet 116 (one of the two most beautiful sonnets ever written, according to E. E. Cummings):

Let me not to the marriage of true minds
Admit impediments. Love is not love
Which alters when it alteration finds,
Or bends with the remover to remove.

Love is not love versus *die but not die*? The first is a complex paradox; the second, an easy one.

We read *Love is not love* and we naturally await Shakespeare's inevitable qualification. But even before the enjambment is fully sprung and we drop to the next line, the paradox whispers of profundities of its own. Often we're told that all is love, but here we're told that nothing, not even love, is love. . . . And neither statement is true, and both are true, for we're contemplating that emotional maelstrom compared to which all other emotions seem clear as glass.

Enjambment is not always a matter of such gravity. With its knack for the sudden turn and capacity for surprise, it's a

darling of the light-verse writer. One of the choicest enjamb-
ments I know belongs to the underappreciated comic novelist
Peter de Vries (1910–1993). His target is Byron's "She Walks in
Beauty," which begins:

> She walks in beauty, like the night
> Of cloudless climes and starry skies;
> And all that's best of dark and bright
> Meet in her aspect and her eyes . . .

Here is de Vries:

> She walks in beauty like the night
> Watchman on appointed rounds,
> In the nursery, checking children's
> Winter respiratory sounds.

Oh, the modern housewife! What a fall from grace: from
a supernal goddess to a shuffling, overburdened mom sur-
rounded by wheezing children, and the whole comical cascade
taking place in the white space between *night* and *Watchman*.

What the double take is to the stand-up comic, the enjambment is to the light-verse poet. It's the moment between seeing and responding to one thing and then—seeing it's another
thing and struggling to respond. James Merrill (1926-1995)
was another master of enjambment. Time and again there's a
surprise, often humorous, waiting at the bright turn of a line.
This light was never brighter, and never darker, than in a couplet about atomic warfare from his *Book of Ephraim:*

> While heavy-water nymphs, fettered in chain
> Reaction, sang their soft refrain *Refrain*

While the phrase *fettered in chain* draws us one way, *chain reaction* draws us in another. Together, they point to extinction.

Enjambment is all about the manipulation of emphasis—the unlocking of nuance when choice words are paired or severed. An enjambed line effectively heightens the prominence of two words, the conclusion to one line and the start of another. It's a little spotlight or, in recurrence, a little strobe. Considering the richness of enjambment—its effects ranging through the tragic, the ludicrous, the mystical, the cynical—you might pity the poor prose writer. How ill-equipped he is, whose tools of emphasis are blunt instruments: italics, the exclamation point, capitalization. All these are available to the poet, of course. But the poet also has, by way of line breaks, a natural means of grouping and underscoring. The poet has a broader range of tools in her toolbox than the prose writer has; the result is a broader range of effects, an ampler ambit.

Lest I paint the prose writer's lot too grimly, I'd close with one more Merrill witticism, this one the opening of his introduction to *Recitative*, his collection of prose pieces. "There are after all things to be said for prose. I still read it . . ."

CHAPTER SIX

Defining and Refining

The most helpful and illuminating figure I've met in my study of versification was an elevator operator. As job descriptions go, this one delivered an appealingly decisive run of four trochees: EL-e VA-tor OP-e RA-tor. Listen more closely, though, and you'll hear four distinct levels of stress. The least stressed syllables are the second, fourth, sixth, and eighth, which I've left uncapitalized. The third and seventh (caps) carry more wallop, though not so much as that OP that has opportunistically hopped atop syllable five. More elevated still, however, is the initial EL. We might classify these as ascending stress levels one, two, three, and four. Linguists may recognize further gradations, but four levels of stress are sufficient for discussing versification.

These four levels open up the possibility of **relative stress.** Let's assume we have two linked syllables, composing one metrical foot. To create either a trochee or an iamb, it isn't necessary that either syllable attain any particular stress level. All that's required is that one syllable wield more punch or oomph than the other. It's all relative.

When Hamlet declares, "Thus conscience does make cowards of us all," the audience may hear a line containing three powerful stresses and a subordinate string of equally subdued syllables. (I've heard it so in performance: "Thus-CONsciencedoesmakeCOWardsofusALL.") But by the light of relative stress, this is, in fact, a routinely regular iambic pentameter line. I would lay out the spoken stresses like so: 2-4 1-2 2-4 1-2 2-3. Others would hear the line differently. Such interpretative variations, however, do nothing to alter its identity as a model iambic line.

In turning from metrical prototype to actual utterance—a Shakespearean pentameter declaimed to an audience—we arrive at an intersection crucial to any understanding of formal verse. This crossroads is a noisy and animated and sometimes contentious place. A scholar scans a soliloquy on a page and an actor delivers it from a stage, and what do the two actions have in common? The scholar's scansion deals with meter. The actor doles out rhythm—speech rhythm. And the confusion between meter and rhythm remains the prime source of misunderstanding in any discussion of how poems actually operate.

Again, a little math might be helpful. Assume we have a ten-syllable line composed of iambs and trochees. There are thirty-two possible ways the line can fall out metrically, beginning with da-DUM da-DUM da-DUM da-DUM da-DUM and ending with DUM-da DUM-da DUM-da DUM-da DUM-da. But only sixteen of these lines will be iambic, since the other half are predominantly trochaic. (Keen metrists, or maybe simply those feeling a little OCDish, will observe that, practically speaking, the number is even smaller than sixteen, since some metrical configurations see little use. When was the last time, reading an iambic poem, you came upon a line consisting of three iambs followed by two trochees?)

Now, take the same ten-syllable line and assign each of its syllables a value from one to four, based on how much spoken stress it commands. How many possible *rhythmic* patterns result? Over a million! From a single pentameter! In the case of a pentameter line, rhythm might be defined as the class of these million-plus possibilities.

One needn't do the math to grasp the fundamental point. Meter is a blunt instrument. Rhythm is dizzyingly subtle and polymorphous. Meter is too thick-fingered (as Frost once said of an insensitive reader) to pick up a dime. Rhythm has a violin maker's delicacy of touch. To mistake meter for rhythm is to mistake your old two-speed electric fan for a hospital air-regulation system that monitors and adjusts humidity and temperature while filtering out allergens and pollutants measured in parts per million. But let's put this in the starkest possible terms: *Meter is narrow, rhythm is broad.*

You'll sometimes see a critic saying of a line like "Thus conscience does make cowards of us all" that it has a subtle or interesting meter. It hasn't. Meters aren't subtle or interesting. That's not their job. Their job is to be simple and yet indispensable. They provide a grid or rubric, upon which speech rhythms can lavishly disport, unfolding their endless variations. Meter is an obliging enabler, making it possible for rhythm to play at counterpoint.

The clearest account I've found of all this, fixing meter and rhythm in their proper roles, is *Versification*, by the Australian poet James McAuley. The book is unusual among prosodic texts in enjoying a substantial shelf life (still in print after half a century) and it fully deserves its longevity. McAuley lays out lines of poetry in tiered fashion, as though in a musical score, marking metrical accents on one stave and actual spoken stresses on another. Where these two staves coincide, a metrically regular poem results.

In Frost's "Stopping by Woods," for instance, metrical accents and spoken stresses exactly coincide. Frost's poem, like Housman's "Oh When I Was in Love with You," is that great rarity: a wholly iambic lyric, undisturbed by metrical substitutions or nebulous rhythms. Da-DUM da-DUM da-DUM . . . On the other hand, the farther one stave diverges from the other—that is, the farther apart metrical accent and spoken stress actually lie—the bumpier and less predictable the ride.

In his essay "Reflections on *Vers Libre*," T. S. Eliot spoke of the necessity in free verse of the "ghost of some simple meter"—a sensation, fluttering in and out of the reader's perception, of an underlying framework behind or beneath what might otherwise look unstructured. The beauty of McAuley's grid is that it provides a nonverbal, visual dramatization of what precisely a poem may feel like and, in doing so, throws light on the issue of how far lines may meander from prototype without losing their metrical identity. A passage of blank verse, for instance: How many metrical substitutions can it support before it is no longer either iambic or pentameter—before it is no longer blank verse at all? How far can a ghost of a meter roam before giving up the ghost?

The American poet Theodore Roethke (1908–1963) was critically drubbed for a couple of lines in one of his late poems:

I take this cadence from a man named Yeats;
I take it, and I give it back again . . .

I recall someone accusing Roethke of stealing Yeats's meter, but this is utter nonsense. It's not Yeats's meter. It's iambic pentameter, which belongs to nobody and everybody. The *rhythm* of the first line, on the other hand, does have a Yeatsian resonance. (I hear its pattern of stresses as 2-3 2-4 1-2 1-4 3-4: five iambs.) But rhythms, as we've seen, number in the hundreds of thousands. Resisting categorization, they shift, they drift, they divagate. They come and go—as Roethke acknowledges in the lines that immediately follow:

> For other tunes and other wanton beats
> Have tossed my heart and fiddled through my brain.

Confusions of rhythm and meter insinuate themselves even down to what may be the most minute particle in poetic analysis: the two unstressed, unassertive, unassuming syllables sometimes referred to as a pyrrhic—pairings like "to a" or "in a" or "for an." We're told that a pyrrhic is a poetic foot. But it doesn't behave like other feet.

Other feet successfully mix and mingle. An iamb can follow a trochee (Dryden's "Arms and the man . . .") or a trochee an iamb (T. S. Eliot's "A cold coming . . ."). The pyrrhic is standoffish. Other feet can repeat themselves to fill a line ("Shall I compare thee to a summer's day?"). But nobody in the history of English poetry has filled a pentameter line with five pyrrhics. Ten unaccented syllables? It doesn't happen.

It couldn't happen because of the jurisdiction of relative stress. Even two adjacent pyrrhics don't happen. Four unaccented syllables? Place them together and they jostle for primacy. Inevitably, one syllable will outmuscle its neighbor, however slightly, and we'll end up with some combination of iambs and/or trochees. When critics introduce pyrrhics into a discussion, they're generally confusing rhythm and meter. They're seeking to describe a rhythmic phenomenon— a miniature decrescendo, a sudden drop in spoken stress— through metrical terms.

The pyrrhic represents only one facet of a problem traceable back half a millennium, when we adopted into English a prosodic vocabulary belonging to Latin and Greek—*ictus, iamb, trochee, dactyl, anapest, amphibrach,* et cetera. Unfortunately, these terms described **metrical systems** remote from our own, rooted in quantity (syllable duration) rather than syllable accent. The terms are, simply, maladapted to the way we talk and write.

Not all our problems can be blamed on the Greeks and Romans. We have a knack for rendering the language of versification clumsy and obfuscatory. I can recall when *poetics* was a useful term, designating an attentiveness to verse structures. But beginning in, I believe, the seventies, the word was so warmly and indiscriminately embraced by English departments ("The Self-Referential Poetics of Madonna's 'Like a Virgin,'" "The Starveling Poetics of Kafka's 'Metamor(e) phosis'") as to suffer the fate of poor little Miles in Henry James's *Turn of the Screw*: hugged to the point of asphyxiation. It's now a pretty corpse of a word.

The same could be said of *metrics*. Go to Amazon and type in *metrics*, seeking books about versification, and you'll find blueprints for tailoring children's clothing, manuals about measuring business performance, rock CDs (?), women's boots (??)—pretty much everything except what you're looking for.

·   ·   ·

For a while I considered trying to coin some prosodic terms as substitutes or supplements for the especially unsatisfactory ones. But past efforts by others have rarely gained currency. Vladimir Nabokov proposed the quite handy "scud" to designate a lightly stressed foot that nonetheless maintains its place in a metrical line (the sort of foot often labeled a pyrrhic). The term remains useful—and unused. It seemed a saner course to restrict my prosodic vocabulary to the smallest-possible pool. I'll try to limit myself in these pages to about a dozen non-self-explanatory terms: *iamb, trochee, anapest, dactyl, enjambment, caesura,* and a few others.

The unwelcoming vocabulary goes a long way toward explaining something otherwise inexplicable: how little critical attention prosody has garnered over the years. A comparison with musical scholarship is both instructive and startling. The student of versification who wanders into a good music library can only be dumbstruck by its bowed and burgeoning shelves. Music theory is an intimidatingly lively field. Any college with a decent music department has somebody teaching mechanics and forms. By contrast, it's a rare English department that has anyone offering courses in prosody (poetic mechanics and forms), let alone publishing in the field.

The contemporary poet Dana Gioia once observed: "Over the past quarter century I have slowly acquired nearly every study of English versification published since 1900 . . . [M]y entire collection occupies only two shelves on my bookcase. A similar accumulation of modern books and pamphlets on a single poet, like Emily Dickinson or T. S. Eliot, might easily fill the entire wall." This was written more than twenty years ago, but the place of versification has changed little.

In the metropolis of literary scholarship, versification remains tucked away in a small and sleepy quarter. A few years ago, Robert B. Shaw published an excellent study, *Blank Verse.* You might suppose that blank verse, as the language's dominant poetic form, would have inspired mountains of scholarship. But before Shaw's book, the last full-length study appeared in—in 1895!

One naturally inquires, What does it matter? Does a lack of prosodic scholarship harm or inhibit the poets themselves? I can't imagine it does. Poets falter for all sorts of colorful reasons, but nobody ever failed to write a poem out of discouragement at the shortage of thoughtful prosodic treatises on his local library shelf.

Still, there's something troubling about an academic world so indifferent to versification. If our teaching of poetry is imbalanced and distorted, the next generation will likely perpetuate our mistakes. Anybody making a thoughtful foray into current poetry scholarship will discover whole books in which there's scarcely an acknowledgment that the subject under examination, poetry, exists in a different guise—an independent genre—from prose observations about it. The modus operandi seems to be, Let's talk about poetry as if it were not poetry.

Poetry scholarship tends to obsess narrowly over what the poem says (or, more misguided and insulting still, with what the poet is "trying to say"), as if this were fully separable from how it is said. If, generations hence, literary historians take any interest in what went on in our criticism in the twentieth and twenty-first centuries, surely they will marvel at an explosion of explication surveying poetry from every conceivable vantage (psychoanalytic, sociological, political, philosophical, environmental, etc.) except structural. In recent years, the situation may have altered somewhat for the good, with publication of academic studies like Meredith Martin's

The Rise and Fall of Meter (2012). But most criticism of poetry continues to scant or ignore its musical aims and methods.

Of all the versification books I've come across, my favorite title belongs to John Ciardi: *How Does a Poem Mean?* Not *What,* but *How.* The title strikes me as more than merely catchy. It artfully but firmly posits its own priorities. The *what* of a poem is ultimately an issue of subject matter—the usual business. But the *how*? How rich, how mysterious is *how*! *How* transports us into that enchanted zone where a scatter of dry-looking data—metrical models, rhyme schemes, stanzaic patterns—unaccountably comes alive, there where the miracle of language germinates a second miracle: the music of verse.

We might go a step further and propose that it's the *how* that gives value and meaning to the *what.* The contemporary poet Richard Kenney, who of all the writers I've met over the years comes closest to being a Funesian, has put this quite deftly when speaking of "the miracle of transubstantiation, when a syntactic and perhaps even cerebral proposition gets cast in a succession of such sweet syllables as to precipitate its 'felt' understanding—an apprehension which though it can't logically defend itself as superior in the court of reason, nevertheless feels miles deeper."

As a teacher of fiction and poetry, I've occasionally had a conference with a vexed student who accused me of being less engaged with what he or she was saying than in the manner of its being said. Whenever such allegations arise, I feel stirrings of an unspoken admiration and sympathy. *Yes. We're beginning to understand each other. . . .* For conference time is necessarily limited, and we ought to be lucid in our priorities. I don't doubt that over the years my student's *what* will be more than adequately addressed in other classes, other dis-

ciplines. I worry, though, about the *how*. In a world out of
kilter, a teacher must sometimes swing far to the other side for
equilibrium's sake. If most poetry criticism is largely or solely
about content, let's speak insistently about form.

Reading poetry criticism, all too often I find myself being
gravely notified, after substantial hemming and hawing, that
the poet under consideration is urging us all to recognize that
love is iffy or that youth is heedless or that into each life some
cold rain must fall. But isn't it clear: Poems are hardly the
place to look for interesting messages, as the wise poet and
critic L. E. Sissman used to remind us.

If you happen upon an interesting message—marvelous.
But many imperishable poems—poems you wouldn't wish to
live without—have little to say. Their content isn't why we
preserve them and revere them. Perhaps A. E. Housman put
it best: "Poetry is not the thing said but a way of saying it."

Perhaps we all should show more sympathy with those
sullen back-of-the-classroom students who resent even the
scanty time devoted to poetry. (Oh how deadly it can be—the
"poetry unit"!) For *if* we suppose poetry is about what it says,
and *if* in roundabout fashion it often says little, why on earth
should we torture ourselves in tracing out its circumlocutions?

The concluding lines of Keats's "Ode on a Grecian Urn"
present one of the great textual conundrums in English literature, a matter ultimately but provisionally resolved by
punctuation. We are invited back to a timeless pastoral. The
numinous figures on an ancient urn inspire the poet's meditation, beginning with a flurry of questions and ending with
a categorical, if enigmatic, pronouncement. The urn itself
speaks at the poem's conclusion, followed by the poet's sum-
mation, or perhaps ratification:

"Beauty is truth, truth beauty,"—that is all
Ye know on earth, and all ye need to know.

Or should the quotation marks close not after *beauty* but after *know*? Does the urn speak both lines in full? In other words, is any portion of the final two lines attributable to Keats himself, an unmediated Keats?

In some ways, this strikes me as an issue of limited interest. Taken as philosophy, none of the possible interpretations has much to offer. Beauty is truth? *Really?* And this (you tell me) is all I need to know on earth? If so, what does our revelation clarify about numerous burning questions, like, *Is there a God?* Or, *Do people have rights, and if they do, what are they?* Or, *Is there such a thing as a just war?*

But if the student of philosophy turns disappointedly from the poem's close, the lover of poetry can only be enthralled. For here is the real thing: the heartfelt to-and-fro of a rare sensibility traversing the millennia, teetering between pain and sanctuary, between the inconclusive and the definitive, and the whole agon played out with a music of unrivaled sumptuosity and subtlety. The poem places us, urgently, in the head of somebody else—somebody of a truthful beauty, John Keats, who happens to be the most gifted prodigy in the English language.

The message of most poetry, including the greatest poetry, is usually commonplace or even banal. We treasure it not for its *what* but its *how*. Although Gerard Manley Hopkins's sonnet "God's Grandeur" is perhaps my favorite of all poems (the one, anyway, I've recited to myself more frequently than any other over the decades), I'll concede that its message could be condensed, probably without traducing its author, to a bland platitude: *Though we sully the Earth, God keeps cleaning up the mess.* Hopkins allocates the first eight lines to our besmirched human world; to heaven, six. The music of those first eight lines yammers and hammers with an internal din that subjugates syntax and sense and the architecture of its end rhymes:

> Generations have trod, have trod, have trod;
>   And all is seared with trade; bleared, smeared with
>   toil;
>   And wears man's smudge and shares man's smell: the
>   soil
> Is bare now, nor can foot feel, being shod.

Then, in the final six lines, everything eases, and we enter a new horology. Speech stresses fall away, and a different internal prospect opens:

> And for all this, nature is never spent;
> There lives the dearest freshness deep down things . . .

The poem concludes by ushering in the dawn:

> And though the last lights off the black west went
> Oh, morning, at the brown brink eastward, springs . . .

What could be more predictable and mundane than the start of a new day? And in Hopkins's hands, what could be more unexpected and otherworldly?

A poem like Andrew Marvell's "To His Coy Mistress" shares an urgent message (*Carpe diem*) with that of a thousand poems by a thousand of his contemporaries. We've discarded and forgotten those thousands, but rightly we cherish Marvell, not for what he expresses but for the nimbleness and originality of its expression:

> My vegetable love should grow
> Vaster than empires and more slow.

★ ★ ★

> But at my back I always hear
> Time's wingèd chariot hurrying near;
> And yonder all before us lie
> Deserts of vast eternity.

W. H. Auden once observed, of young aspiring writers, "As a rule, the sign that a beginner has a genuine original talent is that he is more interested in playing with words than in saying something original." A mature, consummate master may write solely, fiercely, and beautifully of heartbreak. But the wellspring of his poems properly originates decades before, in a youthful and overspilling passion. There never was, and never will be, a great poem written by someone who doesn't love words disembodiedly—for their own sake. There can be no real poetry without, deep in the background, an abounding juvenile joy. Poets who entertain a message so pressing that they needn't worry about the music are doomed to write message poetry. And the message of most message poems, often undetected by the author himself, is *This is not a poem.*

The critic who doesn't contend with a poem's music isn't writing poetry criticism. She's writing something else— a biographical or historical study maybe, in which poem after poem is superimposed upon personal incident ("Written only a month after his move to the countryside, the poem reflects . . .") or historical event ("The gathering clouds of war in Europe throw a shadow over these seemingly sunny . . .").

In sum, a great poem may or may not have interesting things to say. But if it isn't an interesting piece of music, it is no great poem, and we who aspire to be poetry critics might consider gathering up our subsidiary tools (our biographical research, our sociological insights, our critical theories, our footnoted footnotes) to look elsewhere.

CHAPTER SEVEN

The Marriage of
Meter and Rhyme (I)

It's the profoundest alliance in English-language literature: the marriage of meter and rhyme. And as marriages go, remarkably stable: It has flourished since the Age of Chaucer, and even now adheres to codes of behavior Chaucer would recognize. Without the marriage, we would have no *Canterbury Tales*. Or, for that matter, Spenser's *The Faerie Queene*, Shakespeare's sonnets, Donne's sonnets, Milton's *Lycidas*, Pope's *The Rape of the Lock*, Coleridge's *Rime of the Ancient Mariner*, Byron's *Don Juan*, Tennyson's *In Memoriam*—indeed, most of the material covered in any ambitious yearlong college survey of English poetry. Some poets were such devoted children of the marriage that their careers, their oeuvres, are simply unimaginable outside it: George Herbert, Andrew Marvell, Gerard Manley Hopkins, Emily Dickinson. . . . They stayed in the family compound.

Dickinson provides an especially pointed example. On the one hand, she's maverick and unorthodox: Her poems often look and sound startlingly idiosyncratic, modern. On the other, devoted and dutiful, she was the unquestioning daughter of the old marriage, and celebrated it traditionally.

Of the 1,775 poems in the standard volume of her work, how many forsake the partnership of rhyme and meter? None.

Like any marriage, this one embraces some mysteries. It's a union of opposites, obviously, but opposition hardly guarantees stability—usually the reverse. It helps if each partner provides something the other doesn't, or can't, which is the case here. Of the many bonds uniting them, I believe one is primary: They gaze in contrary directions. *Meter is prospective; rhyme is retrospective.* (Add this to my other six-word apothegm—*Meter is narrow, rhythm is broad*—and much about poetry is explained.)

Any poem in rhyme and meter is Janus-faced: It peers with matching intensity into future and past. A dark and brilliant short poem by Malcolm Lowry (1909–1957) should make this clearer:

STRANGE TYPE

I wrote: in the dark cavern of our birth.
The printer had it tavern, which seems better:
But herein lies the subject of our mirth,
Since on the next page death appears as dearth.
So it may be that God's word was distraction,
Which to our strange type appears destruction,
Which is bitter.

The meter (iambic pentameter with some feminine endings) behaves as meter generally behaves: It jogs steadily along. The rhyme feels less resolute, however, as is perhaps expectable in a poem about typos. Lowry leaves a word—*better*—hanging rhymeless for an extended interval. Unpartnered, it cries with the outraged indignity of a lost child.

So you, fair reader, read along, held by the advancing

meter, admiring the deft way Lowry's imagination has seized on something inconsequential—a pair of printer's errors—in order to posit, in an organic and unforced fashion, a topsy-turvy theology. The poem asks whether it's possible that some slight breakdown in communication, some celestial equivalent of printer's errors, has wound up regimenting our fates, inadvertently condemning humankind to misery. Yes, you read along—admiring, too, the turn of the thinking, the punning on *type* and *word,* the artfully offhand and jaunty tone of voice as we confront a botched universe . . . and all the while, in some ancillary pocket of your mind, you're fretting about that *better,* that lost child.

The fretting isn't necessarily conscious. Yet it's there, in the back of your head, as an unresolved issue. The more poetry you digest over the years, the keener your feel for the words likely to find rhymes in the lines ahead—for the words that are the candidates to watch (to listen to). You progress from syllable to syllable, attempting to follow the poem's argument, savoring its felicities of phrase and image, while also attempting to register what's happening with its form—to appreciate its music.

Stanzaic patterns instruct us—liberate us. When, in childhood, as new readers, we first encounter rhyming poetry on the page, we instinctively learn to embed into our short-term memory the end words: the sounds likeliest to resurface as rhymes. It's always possible you'll meet a pattern of internal rhyme, as in MacNeice's "Sunlight on the Garden," but such poems are rarities. Stanzas are, among other things, a kind of Rhyme Alert System, tipping us off about what to listen for, investing selected sounds with an air of pregnant expectancy. (As such, stanzas are of no utility to the Funesians, who require no such aids. To them, the stanza's chief appeal is visual: They savor the lacy splay of errant stanzas upon the page, the loosened dress of modern poets like William Carlos Williams and Marianne Moore and E. E. Cummings.)

The blocky but irregular appearance of Lowry's poem, with its short sharp hook of a last line, warns us to expect a dissolution at the close. Even as you're reading the first few lines, part of you is probably wondering, What's up with that final line?

As you approach it, the heretofore stable meter stumbles, in the penultimate line, where perhaps an initial syllable was dropped. And meter collapses in the concluding line, which, in addition to missing some three feet, shatters the iambic mold. Welcome to chaos.

Welcome, also, to recovery, to restored order, as *better* finds its mate and the poem's rhyme configuration is put neatly to rest. In this little poem, meter rends and rhyme mends. At the close, meter and rhyme are working in rivalrous harmony: meter marching steadily forward until reaching a point of exhaustion, rhyme thoughtfully gazing over the terrain just crossed, re-establishing connections over the burgeoning distance.

A word about that peculiar *better/bitter* rhyme. It's a special form of off rhyme called pararhyme, or **rim rhyme,** in which consonants remain unchanged and internal vowels are altered. Its unusualness functions beautifully here, suggesting one more typo, another slip involving a single letter. The entire poem might be seen as one overall act of correction, whereby the initial "which seems better" is accurately, desolately reformulated as the final "which is bitter."

The health and intimacy of the marriage of meter and rhyme lend it an air of inevitability, as though poetry behaved this way anytime and anywhere. Yet rhyme had no real role in the millennium-long tradition of classical Japanese verse—or in classical Latin, for that matter. In a poem like "Strange Type," an assumed inevitability works to disguise the partners' fundamental differences, the relationship's asymmetries.

In some ways, meter and rhyme are one more of those arbitrary pairings, often regarded as innate and unalterable, that characterize so much of our everyday life. Thinking in pairs, we tend to view the world through such couplings, such binaries. It's how we see our selection of a morning beverage (coffee people versus tea people), our pets (cat people versus dog people), our board games (checkers, chess), our condiments (mustard, ketchup), our recreational vices (alcohol, pot), our lodgings (apartment, house). Pairings like these can seem written in the stars. But they're often less logical than first appears.

Take salt and pepper—those long-wedded household gods, cosovereigns over virtually every kitchen table in America. One of them is a simple inorganic molecule compounded of two dangerous elements, ionically bonded to create a crystalline substance essential for human life. Remarkably stable, it's reliable and consistent in terms of its taste. The other grows on a bush and is woven of complex and perishable DNA, with a highly variable flavor dependent on weather, fertilizer, soil conditions.

Or take meter and rhyme. One is blunt, peremptory, essential; the other is filigreed, ambivalent, dispensable.

Meter is the salt in the marriage, far simpler in spirit than rhyme, and far more stable. Rhyme alters from neighborhood to neighborhood as pronunciations shift and metamorphose. Frost rhymed *been* with *in*—a perfect match to his Yankee ear. Other poets rhyme *been* with *mean* or *dean*. To my ear, *been* is a suitable partner for *when* or *then*. Pronunciations and perceptions can shift markedly even in oneself, over a lifetime. Early in his career, W. H. Auden, accustomed to soft English r's, rhymed *saw* and *corridor*. Later, the American Auden learned to deplore such unions.

Rhyme's fragility intensifies with the passage of decades, centuries. Reading a poem from an earlier era, you can be much more confident about how the meter rings than about whether two words were intended as exact rhymes or off rhymes. Take this quatrain from William Habington (1605–1654), which asserts death's primacy not merely over individuals but over nations:

And then they likewise shall
Their ruin have;
For as yourselves your empires fall,
And every kingdom hath a grave.

To my ear, both rhymes are off rhymes, making this quatrain an aberration, since neighboring stanzas employ exact rhyme. But did Habington hear these as off rhymes, or have the sounds mutated? Was he seeking a discordant note, or has time, willy-nilly, assigned him one?

Everything about language eventually decomposes, and I'll have more to say about what I call metrical decay and rhyme decay in later chapters. Back in 1931, when Yeats wrote a poem called "Remorse for Intemperate Speech," he included a footnote about the pronunciation of "a fanatic heart." His adjective was meant to reverberate to an old-fashioned cadence: **fan**-a-tic. Yeats was exceptionally instructive. In most cases, we don't know whether an outmoded or emergent pronunciation was intended.

Meter may be the more stable partner, but *The Canterbury Tales* offers an outstanding reminder of how meter's drumbeat, too, sometimes loses its way along time's meandering pathways. Today, we don't know what to do with the very first line of the poem: "Whan that Aprille with his shoures soote . . ." Scholars debate how the meter runs: "**Whan** that **A**prille **with** his **shour**-es **soote** . . ." or "**Whan** that A-**pril**-le **with** his **shour**-es **soote** . . ." We're less than ten syllables in, and uncertainty reigns!

The first interpretation is what prosodists call "headless"— it's missing an initial, unstressed syllable. The second interpretation is an absolutely regular iambic pentameter line. Well: Does this dawning moment in our literature, the arrival of *The Canterbury Tales*, commence with a discrepant or a conforming note? We don't know.

John Dryden (1631–1700) revered Chaucer, but he drastically misread his meters, which in Chaucer's day depended on the voicing of what Dryden assumed were silent *e*'s. Dryden kept tripping over missing syllables, though they weren't missing—they were hiding in plain sight. Metrical decay had distorted the music.

There's an enormous amount to say about the marriage of meter and rhyme—it's the heart of my book. But some background is necessary before fully taking up the subject. I'll turn to meter first, in this chapter and the two following. Then on to rhyme, the dispensable but (to my mind) far more endearing and fascinating partner. Five chapters about rhyme. At which point, we'll contemplate the marriage once more.

Meter, then . . . Meter is a form of measurement. Readers of poetry in English typically employ accents as their unit of measurement—the number of audible thumps per line. Yet pretty much anything can supply us with a meter, provided only that it can be counted reliably. We can ignore accent and tally up syllables, as in Japanese **syllabic verse,** with its haiku (5-7-5 syllables) and tanka (5-7-5-7-7). Or we can tally up words, ignoring syllable count altogether, as May Swenson does in "Four-Word Lines," which begins like this:

> Your eyes are just
> like bees, and I
> feel like a flower.
> Their brown power makes
> a breeze go over
> my skin . . .

Yet there's no reason to restrict our imaginations to procedures so commonsensical. We could whimsically, but with an equal sense of sureness, establish a rule that our poetic line immediately concludes whenever any word containing the letter *x* appears, or we have a second arrival of *the*, or we're halted by a semicolon. Meter is a key ingredient in many of poetry's most mystical moments, but it cannot in and of itself be a mystery. Disagreements will arise about which meter governs certain passages, due perhaps to ambiguities of pronunciation, but these contending meters are themselves as unambiguous as tape measures. We might argue about whether a particular line is trimeter or tetrameter, but we have no argument about what trimeter or tetrameter signifies.

You'll sometimes see critics or poets bandying talk of flexible or indeterminate meters, but this is a confusion between the object we'd measure and the tools of measurement— ultimately, a consequence of the hoary confusion of meter and rhythm. Meters are not flexible, although their application can prove problematic. Similarly, scientists may struggle when measuring the cubic kilometers of a gargantuan iceberg, but the difficulty lies with the wayward and inaccessible contours of the object, not with the notions of cubic or kilometer.

Meter has no memory. It may have a cumulative, durational effect, as with any sort of incantatory repetition, but it gazes in only one direction: forward. I've been dressing up meter in the domestic simile of tape measures, but Robert Graves (1895–1985) spoke of it in military imagery. He compared it to the unswerving march of an ancient Roman army.

Graves's metaphor is apt in all sorts of ways. It suggests meter's primeval origins, its forceful discipline, its cultivation of predictability and uniformity. In addition, it connects us to what was most formative in Graves's own life: his wartime experiences, as chronicled in his classic and harrowing memoir, *Good-bye to All That* (1929). In selecting a martial metaphor, Graves was plumbing the center of himself.

I've spoken already of meter's comforts, its role as a cardiac substitute or simulator. Tha-*thump*, tha-*thump*, tha-*thump* . . . This cadence could be your mother's heartbeat, and you folded safely in the womb. Or it could be the pumping in your lover's chest, and you triumphantly and jubilantly sprawled in a rumpled bed. Tha-*thump*, tha-*thump*, tha-*thump* . . . Or it could be a ticking clock, reminding the midnight insomniac that the tedium of present fretfulness ineluctably leads, in the emptying fullness of time, to incapacity, confusion, pain, doubt, exhaustion, regret, shoddiness, and sheer terror in the face of death's imponderables. Tha-*thump*, tha-*thump*, tha-*thump*. For there is this other aspect to most meters—an imperious and minatory atmosphere.

Poets immersed in metrical writing will likely feel occasional resentment toward its stubborn nudge and jostle. Meter
can be an unshakable companion, relentlessly present whenever you open your mouth to speak. You toss off an idle
remark to a friend and discover yourself, in the momentary
pause that ensues, mentally recasting your words, smooth-
ing them out, regularizing them, channeling them into some
metrical grid. . . .

Certainly anybody with a touch of arithmomania, the
expression of OCD commonly referred to as the "counting
disorder," will intuitively understand the doubled effects of
meter: its comforting role in taming chaos, in rescuing order
on a jumbled page, as well as its impulse to dominate all discourse, in the process squelching those redeeming little anomalies and delinquencies that are the squiggling heart of many
an insight. Language is by nature a disheveled sprawl. Artful
prose often imposes upon it a rough meter of sorts. Poetry,
with its strict meters, further tidies it up, but in the process
may denature not merely one's speech but one's thinking.

"Amazon Ants" by Peter Kane Dufault (1923–2013) offers
a martial image that would have spoken to Graves: It captures
something of this darker side to any metrical marching. The
foot soldiers are insects. Dufault's inspiration was discovered
in his own backyard, which, to his surprise, overnight had
become a battleground:

> the horde is leaderless,
> the foremost ants
> are lost and hesitate
> but then are caught up strait-
> way in the blind advance
> of those still in the press

and drawn along with them—
who in their turn
halt and are overrun. . . .
But leave to Solomon
how all step to one stern,
if infinitesimal, drum . . .

The rhyme scheme is ABCCBA. The meter is 323333. (Eagle-eyed readers will see in this metrical pattern a mirror image of "The Sunlight in the Garden." Once you start examining poetic forms, unexpected resemblances surface at every turn.) That infinitesimal drum is, in its way, more menacing and overbearing than any loud and flagrant banging. It reminds us that the call to slaughter is a universal cry permeating everything, even down to—innocent as grass?—your own backyard.

It's this despotic side to meter that fuels so much of the exhilaration found in early free verse—the dominant mode of the last century. Walt Whitman (1819–1892) was the first great poet in English to write almost exclusively nonmetrically. Though employing various traditional devices and rhythms, he jettisoned any chartable measure. The best of his poetry blazes with the easy-moving brio of someone who has just cast off a long and cumbersome burden:

I believe a leaf of grass is no less than the journeywork of
     the stars,
And the pismire is equally perfect, and a grain of sand,
     and the egg of the wren,
And a tree-toad is a chef-d'oeuvre for the highest,
And the running blackberry would adorn the parlors of
     heaven,

And the narrowest hinge in my hand puts to scorn all
   machinery,
And the cow crunching with depressed head surpasses
   any statue,
And a mouse is miracle enough to stagger sextillions of
   infidels,
And I could come every afternoon of my life to look
   at the farmer's girl boiling her iron tea-kettle and
   baking shortcake.

Actually, it's often easier to discard meter altogether,
as Whitman does, than to substitute one for another. Over
the centuries, noble and fascinating experiments have been
conducted in search of a replacement for iambics. Thomas
Campion (1567–1620) pursued a quantitative meter based on
syllable duration, as an escape from "that vulgar and easy kind
of Poesie which is now in use throughout most parts of Chris-
tendom." Coleridge, in "Christabel," retrieved an old system
of counting accents and permitting syllable count to vary
widely, from four to twelve per line; Longfellow (1807–1882)
resorted to trochaic tetrameter for *The Song of Hiawatha*. But
appealing as some of the results were, they remained experiments; none toppled the hegemony of the irrepressible iamb.

Would-be replacements face a formidable obstacle. They
require a system that can be absorbed both intuitively and
satisfyingly. Recall May Swenson's "Four-Word Lines." Let's
suppose she'd chosen eleven-word lines or nineteen-word
lines. These would be fully valid meters, no less definite and
delimited than what she actually chose. But eleven-word lines
(and, still more so, nineteen-word lines) are something that
we—unlike the Funesians—can't easily digest. Either the

meter wouldn't be perceived or it would be processed through a stop-and-go toting up, spoiling the poem's fluidity. There are, literally, an infinity of possible meters. People have written whole novels without a single appearance of the letter *e*, and it will hardly be surprising if tomorrow some poet concocts a meter whose lines all must terminate with a doubled consonant, or with some anagram drawn from the letters of *anagrams* (*magna ars?*). But the limitations of our bodies and brains ensure that only a tiny handful of meters offer the aesthetic potential to be felt unconsciously yet decidedly.

The memorization of poetry plays a dwindled role in our society, and an air of quaintness attends school recitations and ceremonial declamations. Yet there can be no question that memory loves meter. When I occasionally meet somebody who has locked away substantial amounts of verse, it's almost always metrical. He or she may adore free verse. Indeed, he or she may devote most of their creative energies to writing it. But the bulk of the internal archive will be metered.

In the end, meter may bring us full circle. At the outset, metrical verse plays the role of primordial comforter— a soothing and portable heartbeat, conveniently tucked into a slender volume. And somewhere along the way, meter may reveal a burly and bullying side, pounding and pounding, seeking to impose itself into speech where it's not wanted. It is too insistent, isn't it? It has malign intentions, doesn't it?

Yet it winds up being your servant, your obliging secretary, helping you to file in the recesses of your brain the thoughts, the images, the sonic dexterities of much that is most beautiful and truthful and trustworthy on this Earth. To have in your head "God's Grandeur" or Shakespeare's "When, in disgrace . . ." or Milton's "When I consider . . ."

or Housman's "Loveliest of Trees" or Frost's "The Master Speed"—these are talismans for the darkest times you'll ever face. You need these verses to be present for you always. And meter (how could you ever have doubted its good intentions?) is working to do just that.

◫

CHAPTER EIGHT

Iambic Pentameter

Last chapter, we met the profoundest alliance in English-language literature. In this one, we confront its greatest workhorse.

No poetic form has borne more weight—more heartbreak and more spirituality, more autobiographical confession and chronicle, more blaze and bluster, hope and fear and ardor—than iambic pentameter. And a remarkably uncomplaining beast of burden it shows itself. Reared and nurtured for the bearing of capacious loads, its ten-syllable unit turns out to provide a flexible and handy sumpter for transporting information of every stripe. The tasks assigned to it over the centuries have been almost comically diverse.

When Charles Darwin's uncle Erasmus chose to mount a natural history of the world, half a century before the appearance of his nephew's *On the Origin of Species*, he outfitted it in rhymed iambic pentameter couplets. Why not? Here he is on physiology:

In branching cones the living web expands,
Lymphatic ducts, and convoluted glands;

Aortal tubes propel the nascent blood,
And lengthening veins absorb the refluent flood . . .

The notion that weighty and detailed scientific information
might be suitably housed in metered verse may seem prepos-
terous today, but it carried a pedigree from Lucretius. Com-
mercially, Erasmus's book went like hotcakes.

Iambic pentameter is a jack-of-all-trades. It has been
employed for high school dramatic pageants and lengthy, bib-
ulous after-dinner toasts, for biblical catechizing of the young
and for political remonstration. Last wills and testaments have
been solemnized within it. So have recipes and prophecies and
Christmas lists and municipal injunctions. Unlikely though it
may seem, all English readers today commonly descend from
a literary community convinced that anything worth remem-
bering might reasonably be slotted into the handiwork of an
iambic pentameter line.

In some eras, so ubiquitous was the form as to become
synonymous with poetry itself. A number of our greatest
poets led peaceable and prolific lives within its measured
compass. If iambic pentameter is a tent, beneath which poets
have gratefully huddled, it has been less like something made
of canvas than like the Earth's atmosphere itself; you can
gather underneath it while feeling that nothing but openness
lies overhead.

If you held in your hands the standard one-volume edition
of Alexander Pope's poems (880 pages) and you excised from
it every line of iambic pentameter, your door-stopper volume
would abruptly, magically transform into an airy pamphlet.
Pope, like many a prolific writer, envisioned more than he
accomplished: an *Opus Magnum*, of which *An Essay on Man*
would be but a portion. But wherever he ventured, however

far his imagination might take him, it seems no new creative enterprise would ever repudiate his companion in arms, the iambic pentameter line.

Pope is one of the immortals, and his self-chosen interment within a single meter is less a reflection of his narrowness than a testament to the richness and resourcefulness of this bare-bones, elementary-seeming structure. Da-*dum*, da-*dum*, da-*dum*, da-*dum*, da-*dum*. It looks so simple, but this chain of five identical links happily enveloped one of England's most sophisticated literary minds throughout his lifetime.

We might suppose Pope's devotion to be mere idiosyncrasy, if so many others didn't resemble him. Apply the same test to Byron or Keats or Shelley, expunging from their collected poems every pentameter line, and again and again we would behold a miraculous dwindling, a bricklike book transformed into an airy hand fan.

Shakespeare wrote thirty-seven plays. In how many did he decide to branch out formally, to forsake iambic pentameter for some alternative meter? Exactly none. If pressed to explain why he returned so often to harvest the same field, he might have replied, echoing Bassanio in *The Merchant of Venice*, that the pentameter "works a miracle in nature." And perhaps he would have left it at that. But the critic has to go a step further, scrambling after explanations.

What is the secret behind the meter's mystical hold? Some have argued that it corresponds to the human breath, the lines somehow clumping together in coordination with our rib cages, yielding a satisfying rhythm of depletion and repletion. It's an appealing theory, but how, then, account for the French mainstay, the alexandrine, with its twelve syllables? Perhaps English poets are hyperventilators, taking shallower breaths than their unflappable Gallic counterparts? (And what of those Japanese, with their five- and seven-syllable lines—what in the world is going on with their birdlike respiration?)

It's also been argued that the pentameter is somehow fused to the very essence or genius of English. Vocabulary, pronunciation, speech rhythm—these basic linguistic elements have steadily and dramatically altered since Chaucer's day, necessitating (you might suppose) the continual fabrication of new meters. And yet the pentameter perdures. Doesn't this suggest at the core of our language some steadfast affinity with the alternating whisper and thump of a ten-syllable iambic line? This argument makes sense intuitively, even as it remains tantalizingly unverifiable.

What we can say with certainty is that the pentameter derives much of its power and charm through a numerical imbalance, an inherent asymmetry. Its structure resists neat partition. The line refuses to break cleanly.

In this it differs broadly from the French alexandrine, or the alexandrine's English twin, the iambic hexameter. The ancient Babylonians had logic on their side in espousing a numerical system rooted in base twelve rather than base ten. Cleanly divisible by two, three, four, and six, the number twelve provides a domain of happy subsets, easy symmetries. It assumes many guises. Even so, it seems our fingers (to which the brain listens closely) voted ten to nothing in favor of base ten, which prevailed and overwhelmed the mathematical world—just as the pentameter overwhelmed the world of English poetry.

Anybody compiling a taxonomy of poetic forms might well divide them first along a symmetrical/asymmetrical partition. Nothing tells you more about a form. The iambic hexameter and the iambic tetrameter are each neatly proportioned; they split nicely into matching fragments. The hexameter's twelve syllables divide into two sixes or three fours; the eight syllables of the tetrameter yield two fours, four twos. In spirit and behavior, the hexameter and tetrameter are closer than either is to its nearer neighbor, the iambic pentameter. For the pentameter is stubbornly, jaggedly asymmetrical. Try as you might to smooth it out, an irreducible spikiness juts forth.

Let's begin with symmetry, since it's easier to see and hear and evaluate than asymmetry. One needn't know much French to detect the clean, cut-in-half partition of these alexandrines from Charles Baudelaire:

Lorsque tu dormiras, ma belle ténébreuse

★

Dormir nonchalamment à l'ombre de ses seins

Or the clean thirds and fourths of Victor Hugo:

Je suis veuf, je suis seul, et sur moi le soir tombe

★

Seul, inconnu, le dos courbé, les main croisées

No English-language poet employed hexameters more fruitfully than Dryden, and similar balances proliferate in his work. In his translation of the *Aeneid*, we constantly encounter twelve-syllable lines broken into clean halves:

But shut from ev'ry shore, and barr'd from ev'ry coast.

★

Observant of the right, religious of his word.

★

Despairing of success, ambitious to be slain!

Or occasionally into thirds, or a one-third/two-third arrangement, again extremely clean:

> What heart could wish, what hand inflict, this dire
>   disgrace?

★

> With clotted locks, and blood that well'd from out the
>   wound.

The task of our hero, Aeneas, is to wrest the stability of empire
from a bedlam of warring and fractious tribes. Aeneas suffers
his doubts along the way, but we don't; his ultimate success is
presaged in every line of Dryden's versification, where order
and harmony reign.

The tetrameter line in English likewise begs to be rent in
half, as in these examples from Andrew Marvell:

> And manna falls, and roses spring

★

> Though infinite, can never meet

★

Insnared with flowers, I fall on grass

★

Mistaken long, I sought you then

But there is no bisecting an iambic pentameter line into tidy halves or tidy thirds—into tidy anythings. The line (its ten syllables the product of two primes, two and five) has some of the impregnable aloofness of a prime number: It issues a sloppy remainder when other divisions are attempted. You can split an iambic pentameter line equally in terms of syllables, as Frost does in "Never Again Would Birds' Song Be the Same" ("Be that as may be, she was in their song") or in "The Gift Outright" ("But we were England's, still colonials"). But the first of your segments will contain two accents; your second, three. They look the same, but they're not at all the same. We wind up in a semantic Wonderland of "bigger halves" and "smaller halves."

Critics have sometimes pointed out that when spoken aloud, as in a staged performance, pentameter often poses four discernible accents, which allows for a two-two symmetry. (The fifth accent, often devoted to a pair of lightly stressed words, effectively falls away.) When Macbeth evokes a knell "that summons thee to heaven or to hell," we might hear a balanced disjunction, two and two, like so: *that summons thee/ to heaven or to hell.* But this is a raggedy symmetry at best, its "unimportant" syllables failing to distribute themselves evenly. Compare the mirroring halves that spring so naturally to the tetrameter ("We slowly drove—He knew no haste"—

Dickinson) or to the hexameter ("Dead cats, and turnip tops, come tumbling down the flood"—Swift).

I once read a physiologist describing the process of walking as a state of "controlled falling." It's a truth familiar to any stouthearted toddler: Upright movement is perilous and you must constantly prepare to meet the earth. The trick, once moving, is to keep moving. At the age of two, you lunge out an equilibrium-shattering foot, and to correct your balance you lunge out another equilibrium-shattering foot. . . . Something analogous occurs as iambic pentameter amasses itself. The first line is imbalanced, and the second line helpfully steps forward, righting the imbalance but also introducing a new imbalance, to which the third line . . .

It's all kinetics, which helps to explain something otherwise inexplicable: the absence of anything like blank verse composed in iambic tetrameter. Where *are* all the unrhymed tetrameter poems? Since blank verse is much the most popular of all forms, wouldn't you conjecture that we'd have *some* substantial body of unrhymed tetrameter? Yet I don't find any such poem—not one—in The *Oxford Book of English Verse*. In a tantalizingly tossed-off footnote composed nearly a hundred years ago, Housman analyzed the limitations of his favorite meter, iambic tetrameter, declaring that "a series of octosyllables ceases to be verse if they are not rhymed." To him, the futility of the task was self-apparent—leaving the rest of us to puzzle out exactly why this might be so.

It's an "impossibility" surely linked to issues of symmetry. Controlled falling has its advantages, it would seem, over the sturdiness and self-containment of the tetrameter or the hexameter; the pentameter's imbalance provides a gentle propulsion that naturally summons another line to support it.

Things are continually tipped and righted, in a controlled falling. Walk the line? The line knows how to walk.

When one pentameter follows another and also rhymes with it, however, we do reach a resting place, one that turns out to be an extremely popular spot. In the history of English-language verse, the vogue of the rhymed couplet has no parallels. During a poetry-dominated era, it managed utterly to dominate poetry: It reigned supreme in England throughout the eighteenth century.

Two lines, twenty syllables, one rhyme—with these simple ingredients a momentary stasis is achieved. The couplet might seem a recipe for neatness and sameness. But, in fact, it turns out that the arrangement opens a sweeping array of permutations. Seeming sameness gives way, on closer inspection, to a field of variability.

The bond between a couplet's first and second lines may consist in their regularity, as when they mirror each other in an adherence to the (da-DUM da-DUM) metrical prototype:

> The tortoise here and elephant unite,
> Transformed to combs, the speckled and the white.
>
> *POPE*

Or they may mirror each other by sharing the same metrical deviations:

> Treated, caress'd, and tir'd, I take my leave,
> Sick of his civil Pride from Morn to Eve.
>
> *POPE*

Or their pairing may be rooted in disparity, one line regular and the other disheveled by metrical substitution, as in Seamus Heaney's "Blackberry-Picking":

> At first, just one, a glossy purple clot
> Among others, red, green, hard as a knot.

Or the couplet may revel in dissimilarities, meters and rhymes remote from each other, as in this passage from the same poem, which might still be described, though just barely, as rhyming iambic pentameter couplets:

> . . . summer's blood was in it
> Leaving stains upon the tongue and lust for
> Picking. Then red ones inked up and that hunger
> Sent us out with milk cans, pea tins, jam-pots
> Where briars scratched and wet grass bleached our boots.

A feat of balance in itself, the rhymed couplet is a balancing act in an additional and greater sense. Sometimes, audaciously, it weighs itself against a sizable block of lines.

In Shakespeare's sonnets, the concluding couplet frequently summarizes the preceding three quatrains. It's a huge burden to impose upon a mere two lines, and sometimes his couplets come across as glib, loosely and arbitrarily fixed to the poem's main body. Yet the result is breathtaking when the couplet artfully squares everything, elucidating and enhancing all that went before. In such moments, the final two lines and the preceding twelve seem evenly matched, perfectly partnered:

> The worth of that is that which it contains,
> And that is this, and this with thee remains.

SONNET 74

Or:

But since she pricked thee out for women's pleasure,
Mine be thy love, and thy love's use their treasure.

SONNET 20

Or:

All this the world well knows; yet none knows well
To shun the heaven that leads men to this hell.

SONNET 129

Or:

Therefore I lie with her and she with me,
And in our faults by lies we flattered be.

SONNET 138

A couplet is the briefest English form to achieve a sense of wholeness and completion. A single line, however marvelous, is not a poem; it's a marvelous line. But fuse two good lines together and you may have something satisfying and self-contained. There's genuine wit in what may be the shortest poem anyone ever wrote, Strickland Gillilan's "Fleas":

Adam
Had 'em.

The poem does in fact offer a "criticism of life"—Matthew Arnold's touchstone for poetry that addresses the "spirit of our race." Doesn't it ask, Why fuss over minor annoyances, as we fruitlessly have been doing since the beginning of time, given that complaint brings no alleviation? But more than wit is on display—there is also pathos and wisdom—in this Frost pentameter couplet:

> But Islands of the Blessèd, bless you, son,
> I never came upon a blessèd one.

Together the three forms of *bless* encapsulate a passage from youthful mythology to paternal affection to a benign valedictory oath (*blessèd* as a reverent substitute for *damned*). Herein is the arc of an extended life, and all in twenty syllables.

The last word on couplets probably belongs to Pope. To the extent that the form's essence resides in a movement from asymmetry into symmetry, in a benign conspiracy to bring everything cosmically into poised adjustment, the ideal couplet in the language may be found in his *Essay on Man:*

> All are but parts of one stupendous whole,
> Whose body nature is, and God the soul . . .

Earth and zodiac, syllable and epic, everything fits.

There's a similar fittingness in the iambic pentameter line's ability—at times almost magical—to channel a poet's wandering reflections into memorable ten- or eleven-syllable segments. The line is endlessly hospitable to summary and aphorism. To inquiry and judgment. To postulate and expostulation. It has a spaciousness about it, even while fostering condensation. It's awe-inspiring, really, to contemplate how much it has enfolded over the centuries. The very riddle of our existence takes shape in the most famous line of poetry ever composed:

To be or not to be, that is the question.

The pentameter provides a proverbial home for meditations on human trial and human weakness:

To seek, to strive, to find, and not to yield. (Tennyson)

★

A little learning is a dangerous thing. . . . (Pope)

★

For fools rush in where angels fear to tread. (Pope)

For moral injunction and theology:

To err is human; to forgive divine. (Pope)

★

Do not go gentle into that good night. (Thomas)

For the compression of heartbreak:

But one man loved the pilgrim soul in you . . . (Yeats)

★

you of my heart, send me a little word (Cummings)

And sometimes the single line delivers us to our better selves, as in Frost's "Directive," where an abandoned house inspires one of my two favorite lines that anyone ever wrote: "Weep for what little things could make them glad." This most god-like of all urgings, which embraces both tears and laughter— could it be stated more concisely, more penetratingly? How better to renew our souls but through a musical extending of empathy to the wretched, betrayed, forgotten?

Yet the pentameter's achievement exceeds even this. To my mind, it reaches its zenith in those instances where a single line presents—adequately, freshly—nothing less than a view of the world, an apt summing up of the human predicament. The final line of Milton's sonnet "On His Blindness" might plausibly be inflated into a full-blown sermon: "They also serve who only stand and wait." But honestly, do we need anything more? Milton has momentarily quelled a thousand debates about the relationship of faith to good works. He has eased the troubled spirit.

Something similar occurs in a poem we've already seen, Frost's "Design," which records an act of violence on the insect level. Was this morning's murder—the snuffing out of a moth's life by a spider—something foreordained? Did any cogitating mind envision it and engineer it and oversee it? Frost's tentative answer is yes—"If design govern in a thing so small."

The potency of this *If* lies in its branching into a pair of alternatives each more unacceptable than the other. Either we inhabit a universe whose maker exults in mayhem or, even at the minutest level, chaos and blind slaughter prevail. Which-ever path you choose, the human lot is both untenable and inescapable. In its quiet and unassertive way, the poem's con-clusion offers one of the most desolating lines ever written.

Perhaps we shouldn't close on so forbidding a note. Rays of hopefulness gild the final line of Shakespeare's sonnet 146:

But Death once dead, there's no more dying then.

It's an unlikely place to seek out hope, a line where variants of *death* surface in three forms. But the line actually addresses another topic, although the word doesn't appear within it: life, the life everlasting.

Here, too, we find a comprehending of the world in a single pentameter, a clear and hopeful message enwrapped in dark paradoxes and biting wordplay. Death is not dismissed at the close of this sonnet. To the contrary. Like the rest of us, Death must undergo a formidable and frightening experience, venturing out beyond that bourn from which no traveler returns: It has to die. Does the universe contain a stranger translation than the death of Death? What lies ahead for mere people is more hinted at than portrayed. But it must be a better place. We've been relieved of a terrible burden.

◨

CHAPTER NINE

Iambic Tetrameter

On a visit to the Serengeti some years ago, I spotted a large three-legged hyena. Creatures often lose a limb out on those sanguinary plains, but as our guide pointed out, this was something special: Although its injury was far from recent (the wound had healed and grown over), the creature was fat. He was prospering. In that sun-beaten, unforgiving landscape he was, missing limb and all, doing just fine.

You might say about iambic tetrameter that it has lost a leg—a foot anyway—and that it, too, does just fine. Some creatures are born to thrive. Given the unshakable dominion of iambic pentameter, it's tempting to view hexameter as having an extra foot, and tetrameter as having lost one. But tetrameter turns out to be in no way handicapped or hobbled. It flourishes, with a stylish fineness and fullness that belies any suspicion of shortcoming or subordination. Beloved by Marvell, Blake, Tennyson, Yeats, Frost, Housman, Auden, iambic tetrameter provides a gallery to many of the most beautiful poems in the language.

Students are often skeptical about claims of any great gulf between pentameter and tetrameter. What significance could there be in the addition or subtraction of two little syllables? Surely it's a niggling change? And yet, those two little syllables transport us across a threshold; they upend the world. Add them, subtract them, we shift realms, from asymmetry to symmetry, or vice versa, and in this journey our aesthetics are transformed.

I sometimes come across articles proposing an ideal English curriculum for undergrads. What indispensable knowledge should any English major possess on graduation day? I'd be as happy as the next professor, I suppose, if our graduate could tell me when *Lyrical Ballads* was published (1798) or Shakespeare was born (1564) or Chaucer died (1400). But the pinning of dates to books, or authors' names to titles, strikes me as a secondary concern.

My wish would be that any newly minted graduate would have a visceral feel—threaded throughout the body—for how two distinct lines of poetry behave: the pentameter and the tetrameter. If in your student days you successfully incorporate those two lines, if truly they've become a part of you, you're well on your way to being able to read any poem in *The Oxford Book of English Verse* or *The Norton Anthology of Poetry*. The bedrocks of the two meters lie kilometers apart. Yet in their union lies the beginning of mastery.

Most books should probably limit themselves to a single anecdote at the expense of dim-witted American tourists. Here's mine. I recall a sharp-voiced woman at Chartres Cathedral once inquiring of our tour guide, incredulity as well as some asperity in her tone, how it was, exactly, that those anonymous builders of the two spires—one of them ornate and Gothic and the other spare and Romanesque, one of them some thirty feet taller than the other—had never noticed, over the decades of their construction, that the two failed to match. From her perspective, it was inconceivable that such blatant, blazing asymmetry might be a deeply held aesthetic goal. At the time, I found this all quite amusing, but in retrospect I think there's something quite illuminating here: for the canyon separating symmetry and asymmetry is indeed enormous—as she was tacitly asserting.

As for the pentameter and tetrameter, our five-legged creature and our four-legged creature display radically different gaits, not surprisingly, and often move in contrary directions. The tetrameter can handle a broad variety of tasks, but it's especially adept when transmitting the muted and delicate. It provides a congenial sanctuary to a dreamy temperament like that of Walter de la Mare (1873–1956). It lends itself to watercolors and nocturnes. His effects may be magical:

> And moveless fish in the water gleam,
> By silver reeds in a silver stream.

Or quietly eerie:

> The dusk was still, with dew a-falling,
> I saw the Dog-star bleak and grim,
> I saw a slim brown rat of Norway
>   Creep over him.

Or forlorn:

> Only the evening star on high
> Less lonely makes a lonely sky . . .

All are marked by a structural lightness of handling.
De la Mare remains a marvelous and underappreciated

poet, whose entire career speaks of how far apart in spirit the tetrameter and pentameter reside.

His adroitness departed him when he shifted from tetrameter, or lines shorter than tetrameter, into pentameter-length lines. The two meters are two different instruments. An able oboist doesn't necessarily make a fine trumpeter.

That the tetrameter line prospers in a world of delicacy and nuance and decorum also means that it's especially ripe for the occasional irruption of vehemence or violence, as in this stanza from Marvell's "The Garden":

Meanwhile the mind, from pleasure less,
Withdraws into its happiness;
The mind, that ocean where each kind
Does straight its own resemblance find;
Yet it creates, transcending these,
Far other worlds, and other seas;
Annihilating all that's made
To a green thought in a green shade.

Things unfold here with a balanced, bookended composure—everything, that is, except the penultimate line, with its abrupt and uncontainable *annihilating*. Heretofore, the stanza has displayed a comportment upright and almost vertebral: an imaginary spine running vertically down its middle, four syllables typically ranged on each side. Only one word—the longest in the poem—belligerently breaks this spine. *Annihilating* shatters all protocol, arrogating more than half of the line's available space. Much like a small subway car, a line of only eight syllables fills up quickly, especially when a polysyllable enters. And, as in a small subway car, the broader-hipped seem to grow broader-hipped as the crowd increases.

Annihilating is a more voluminous word in a tetrameter line than in a pentameter line. (T. S. Eliot teased this notion to a witty extreme by opening a poem with *Polyphiloprogenitive,* a behemoth spanning an entire tetrameter.) And volume—expansiveness—is precisely what Marvell was seeking here. A tetrameter framework offered opportunities for enhanced destruction.

The stanza's final line—perhaps Marvell's most celebrated—dramatically restores our equilibrium: "To a green thought in a green shade." All has turned abstract, and all the poem's abstractions are in accordance. A model of rationing, of artful repetition of word and structure, this is the poem's most exquisitely balanced line.

Marvell's overspilling but controlled violence reached a demonic summit with Robert Lowell (1917–1977), who made fruitful use of the tetrameter's associations of temperance and tranquillity. His may be the most forceful, propulsive tetrameter ever contrived:

> O to break loose, like the chinook
> salmon jumping and falling back,
> nosing up to the impossible
> stone and bone-crushing waterfall—
> raw-jawed, weak-fleshed there, stopped by ten
> steps of the roaring ladder, and then
> to clear the top on the last try,
> alive enough to spawn and die.

This is from my favorite of his books, *Near the Ocean,* in which the technical rigor of his early style blended splendidly with the urgent clarity of his later work. It's the closest thing the twentieth century offers to the thoughtful muscularity of John Donne.

Yeats's "An Irish Airman Foresees His Death" has the most beautiful articulation of any poem I know. It's articulate in the common sense of beautifully voiced, but also in the root Latin notion of small-parted and jointed. I once heard a lecturing paleontologist speak of "gorgeous articulation." I was moved to see how moved *he* was—eyes aglow over a chance splay of bones fossilized some hundred million years ago. "An Irish Airman" has gorgeous articulation.

Presentiments of death haunt a young combatant of the First World War. As an Irishman, why should he fight at all? Why in God's name invest himself in a conflict between a distantly oppressive Germany and a more proximately oppressive England? But the siren skies over his troubled land, over all the world's troubled lands, kept calling to him, and he has heeded the call:

Nor law, nor duty bade me fight,
Nor public men, nor cheering crowds,
A lonely impulse of delight
Drove to this tumult in the clouds;
I balanced all, brought all to mind,
The years to come seemed waste of breath,
A waste of breath the years behind,
In balance with this life, this death.

One of the pleasures of Yeats's lyric is that the topic of balance (which largely defines the tetrameter as a verse form) arises explicitly. The word appears twice, and the entire poem is, like the wobbly motions of the primitive aircraft our speaker pilots, a balancing act.

Frost once declared that there are essentially two meters in English: strict iambics and loose iambics. In strict iambics, few substitutions occur, and these are mostly trochees; a pentameter line likely has ten syllables. In loose iambics, anapests sometimes replace iambs and lines are likely to be longer, baggier.

As is common in matters of versification, tiny variations spawn monumental differences; Frost's two meters are indeed miles apart, as his own poems display. Though both are in tetrameter, the difference in music between "Stopping by Woods" (strict iambics) and "The Road Not Taken" (loose) is dramatic.

But Frost might have equally sliced the world another way and remarked that in iambics there are two basic meters, the pentameter and the tetrameter. Over the centuries, the two have divvied up most of the outspread territory. And they have governed beautifully.

This isn't to gainsay the charm or utility of hexameter and trimeter. But historically these have served as complements— the hexameter as a weightier, heftier alternative to pentameter, the trimeter as a lighter, leaner tetrameter.

The trimeter didn't come fully into its own until the twentieth century, when poetry grew lighter. Not in subject matter, perhaps, but in ballast. Your average nineteenth-century poem carried more syllables per line (those stout Victorians!) than its twentieth-century counterpart. In America, the modern trimeter bloomed into little masterpieces: Louise Bogan's "Roman Fountain," Theodore Roethke's "My Papa's Waltz," Richard Wilbur's "Seed Leaves," Elizabeth Bishop's "The Moose." Still, in the overall historical scheme, rhymed trimeter is an outlier. The proximity, the tightness, of its rhymes renders it unwieldly to amateur hands. As such, the trimeter is a polar counterpart to the hexameter. If the trimeter often feels too tight, the hexameter feels too slack. Poets have traditionally felt most comfortable driving the midsize vehicles, the tetrameter and pentameter lines, rather than the subcompact or the SUV.

Despite its penchant for tidiness and composure, all is not always so calm within the tetrameter. The line has a rowdy twin that wallows in unevenness, roughness, unruliness—in asymmetry. This twin is what prosodists call "headless": Its unaccented initial syllable has been dropped. One might instead call it "heedless," for it's an engine of flaming, impulsive energy.

We've already noted that the popular seven-syllable line is a maverick in traditional versification, where lines of even-numbered syllables prevail. It was beloved by Shakespeare, who put a string of sevens into Puck's mouth at the close of *A Midsummer Night's Dream*. Puck asks the audience to suppose

That you have but slumbered here,
While these visions did appear.
And this weak and idle theme,
No more yielding but a dream,
Gentles, do not reprehend:
If you pardon, we will mend.

Prosodists sometimes feel uncertain what to do with passages like this—specifically, what to do with the lines' missing initial syllable. Shouldn't every poetic foot possess at least two syllables? If so, what of the first foot here? Sevens like these are often spoken of as trochaic meter. But this merely pushes the missing syllable from front to back: Instead of a headless, you have a tailless line.

I think it's a serious misunderstanding to call this trochaic meter. To do so is to fall victim to that unkillable confusion

between meter and rhythm. Each line may indeed have a falling quality at its outset—a trochaic texture. But the feel typically shifts in the line's middle, often after three syllables. It's
rare for a seven-syllable line to feel trochaic right through to
its end. The iamb reasserts itself.

For this is the iamb's dominant trait: domination. Instinctively, efficiently, rapidly, and wherever it can, the iamb seizes
control. Wherever there's doubt about how a line ought to be
scanned, it waits in readiness, eager to pounce. Throw some
syllables randomly together, it's startling how often they'll
assemble into iambics. Whether this occurs because a regula-
tory iamb somehow indwells in our language, or because as
readers we're trained in an iambic tradition, would be difficult
to say. But the iamb is an invasive species. It roots quickly
in the loamy soil of a coalescing poem, and it's very hard to
eradicate.

A few small acts of vandalism may elucidate the iamb's
tendency to colonize. Consider this famous passage from
Auden's "In Memory of W. B. Yeats":

And in the deserts of the heart
To let the healing fountain start,
And in the prison of his days
To teach the free man how to praise.

Clean iambic tetrameter—all very neat and simple.

This isn't what Auden wrote, however. I'm transgressing
and defacing. He wrote in sevens, actually, in a meter that
some would call trochaic:

In the deserts of the heart
Let the healing fountain start,

> In the prison of his days
> Teach the free man how to praise.

Now, if this passage of unmolested, bona fide Auden truly were trochaic, my shifting it into straightforward iambics ought to feel seismic—ought to be earthshaking. In fact, my clumsy alterations, though highly disruptive at the outset of each line, leave the ends largely undisturbed. Each version feels metrically much the same by the time you reach the close of a line. And well they might, for the two passages, the ersatz and the genuine, share an iambic meter. One version (mine) is straightforwardly so. The other (Auden's) gets there through the dynamic energies of the headless line.

True trochaic meter, all but undisturbed by mutinous iambs, is a genuine rarity. Over the years I've seen references to the "mysterious" meter of Poe's "The Raven," but there's no mystery in it. It's in trochaics. It's indicative of how seldom we see the authentic article that the meter might be deemed a mystery:

> Ah, distinctly I remember it was in the bleak December;
> And each separate dying ember wrought its ghost upon
>   the floor.
> Eagerly I wished the morrow;—vainly I had sought to
>   borrow
> From my books surcease of sorrow—sorrow for the lost
>   Lenore . . .

Poe offers four elongated lines (though on closer inspection they disassemble into rhymed tetrameters: eight trochaic tetrameter lines, two of them tailless). Trochee follows trochee follows trochee. Once you recognize what's going on, the "mysterious" meter is all too forthright. It winds up being less complex than a comparable stretch in iambics, which presumably offers variety via metrical substitution. "The Raven" sticks to its script.

Even more strictly than Poe, Henry Wadsworth Longfellow held the wheel steady in his immense tale of an Ojibwe warrior, the trochaic *Song of Hiawatha*. Virtually every line has eight syllables; Longfellow forwent tailless lines. He also forwent rhyme. (Perhaps blank verse in tetrameter is not impossible, as Housman insisted. You merely need to fashion it in trochaics.)

> From the brow of Hiawatha
> Gone was every trace of sorrow,
> As the fog from off the water,
> As the mist from off the meadow.
> With a smile of joy and triumph,
> With a look of exultation,
> As of one who in a vision
> Sees what is to be, but is not,
> Stood and waited Hiawatha.

Although this verse allows for rhythmic variation, metrical variation is prohibited. Here is one way to prevent the iamb from intruding: never deviate. Yet if there's safety in sameness, there's also stultification. The richness of any prosodic system ultimately is measured by how fruitfully its rules can be bent or broken. There is novelty in *Hiawatha*'s ever-falling cadences—it sounds different!—but little flexibility. We're boxed in. Our music, our captivating tune, discourages variation. It's hard to imagine other poets extending Longfellow's journey. On the distant shores of Lake Superior, the poem's *Big-Sea-Water,* also known as *Gitche Gumee,* Long-fellow stands tall—and yet marooned.

The suppression or exclusion of the iamb can be a tricky business, as anyone knows who chooses to write in syllabic verse. You quickly learn to avoid six- or eight- or ten-syllable lines—those the iamb finds most congenial. The iamb treats those as an open door—and before you know it, all those delicate effects you intended, your artful emplacements of clustered syllables, are lost in the iamb's hammer-stroke chorus.

Often it's wiser not to battle but to cooperate with the iamb. In practice, Shakespeare's sevens usually turn out to be sevens and eights. He adds a syllable here and there. Though the meter is steadily iambic, some lines have a trochaic propulsion at the start. He mixes it up.

Fear no more the frown o' the great;
Thou art past the tyrant's stroke;
Care no more to clothe and eat;
To thee the reed is as the oak . . .

Metrically, these four lines are mirrored in the first four lines of the third stanza of Auden's "Lullaby":

Certainty, fidelity
On the stroke of midnight pass
Like vibrations of a bell,
And fashionable madmen raise
[Their pedantic boring cry . . .]

The headless tetrameter harnesses energy. Its governing rhythm is trochaic; its meter is iambic. We arrive at a tug and pull, usually resolved in the middle of the line. The shift commonly takes place after three syllables, as with "Certainty, fidelity," whose last four syllables come across as a simple pair of iambs. In energy and spirit, this division into that favorite ratio of 3:4 produces a sense of equivalence. Placed on opposite sides of a scale, the two parts would stabilize.

How does a three-syllable word successfully balance a four-syllable word? Mostly through poetic convention. Typically, as its capitalization suggests, the first word of a line wields heightened emphasis. It carries the line's biggest syllable: a sort of syllable-plus. The reader is launching something—the reading of a brand-new line—and she brings to it a natural energy of commencement and regeneration. Hence, three syllables at the beginning of a line may "equal" four at the close.

Let's once more play vandal and metrically alter Auden's line ever so slightly, to "Uncertainty, fidelity." The result is a stateliness fit for Marvell's tranquil "Garden." Here is symmetry of a static kind. The two halves repose like items on a shelf, in harmony forever. With "Certainty, fidelity," by contrast, symmetry is of a keener variety, not literal but seeming. This is what I call "dynamic symmetry," depending for its poise upon movement. The words are on the march.

A. E. Housman made his home almost exclusively in the tetrameter. He was a master of this trafficking between static and dynamic balance, the full and the headless line, as in these stanzas from "To an Athlete Dying Young":

> Smart lad, to slip betimes away
> From fields where glory does not stay,
> And early though the laurel grows
> It withers quicker than the rose.

Eyes the shady night has shut
Cannot see the record cut,
And silence sounds no worse than cheers
After earth has stopped the ears.

When the theme calls for abruptness, the lines go short. When it calls for something more stately, long.

Now you will not swell the rout
Of lads that wore their honours out,
Runners whom renown outran
And the name died before the man.

There's a trim timeliness to the tetrameter line. Its lightness gives it adaptability. Pentameter couplets tend to announce themselves forcefully. But you'll often come upon tetrameter couplets whose modern disguise takes a moment to penetrate, as in this from Langston Hughes:

Weather and rose
Is all you see,
Drinking
The dewdrop's
Mystery.

"SNAIL"

And certainly nothing feels the slightest bit dated when Boz Scaggs, in a 2001 recording, woos his elusive Miss Riddle, who has him "playing a game I should know all about":

So cool, so clear, so nonchalant.
So absolutely what I want.

And yet how minimal is the distance—metrically, lexically—
between this and George Herbert in the seventeenth century:

> Sweet day, so cool, so calm, so bright,
> The bridal of the earth and sky . . .

In its gift for equilibrium—its athleticism, its prowess in finding poise and symmetry amid imbalance and
unevenness—the tetrameter is the most comely line in the
language. When I was in college, a mentor of mine would
regularly insist, over his Lucky Strikes and innumerable cups
of strong black coffee, that Yeats's "The Song of Wandering
Aengus" is the most beautiful poem in the English language.
Back then my friend mostly convinced me, and I remain
mostly convinced today.

> And walk among long dappled grass,
> And pluck till time and times are done,
> The silver apples of the moon,
> The golden apples of the sun.

This is early modern poetry, written in the cloaked sunset
years of the nineteenth century. And, simultaneously, this is
also timeless verse, spawned in the bare-limbed dawn before
the *Iliad* or the *Odyssey*. The lines evolve their own standard
of ageless beauty, based on lightness but sureness of step. Here
we behold the tetrameter moving the way it was meant to
move, singing as intended to sing.

◻

CHAPTER TEN

Rhyme and Rhyme Decay

Maybe every sound ever uttered is calling out for a mate. Most words never succeed in finding one, though. The ones that do, the rhyme words, are natural grandees; in the great, swirling marketplace of all speech, they occupy a post of privilege.

A rhyme arises when like calls to like and like responds. As a rhymed poem progresses, every word is inquiring, *Is there anyone out there for me?* Whitman has a phrase in *Leaves of Grass*, "a call in the midst of the crowd, my own voice." Whitman was no systematic rhymer, but it's a lovely metaphor for how rhyme operates.

Like calls to like, but difference also calls to difference. In a typical rhyme we don't seek an identical match; we're looking instead for a sibling resemblance. French poetry traditionally encouraged rhyming through identical terminal sounds: *hérédité/fécundité*, or *furtivement/lentement*. English poets refer to this as rime riche, whether the identicals are in English or in French. That we resort to a French designation for English rhymes is solid evidence of how rare and exotic these remain in our practice. For us, with our different tradition, rhymes like *excite/incite* or *elate/relate* look suspect, and rhymes like *heredity/fecundity* or *furtively/leisurely* (borrowed from Baudelaire) look positively sloppy. And while such rhymes may sometimes find artful employment, our poets usually reserve rime riche for special effects and occasions. It isn't your everyday way of pairing up.

Our typical rhyme looks like this: *slick/trick, book/crook, dump/trump*. The sounds of the paired words initially differ, then converge. There's a motion to it, which, happily, might itself be presented as a rhyme: from disparity to similarity.

There's a code that simplifies this process. C stands for consonant sound, V for vowel sound. We'll use subscripts for differentiation, so C_1 and C_2 are different consonant sounds. C_3 and C_3 are the same consonant sound or consonant blend. (Note that we're talking sounds, not letters. Hence, the divergent spellings of *tuft* and *roughed* would not affect their status as rhymes: $C_1V_1C_2$ and $C_3V_1C_2$.) Regardless of spelling, rhymes of this sonic sort—*tuft* and *roughed*, or *name* and *fame*, or *salt* and *vault*—are our prototype, though in fact both rhyming words may lack a final consonant sound, as in *slow/go* (C_1V_1/C_2V_1) or one may lack an initial consonant, as in *in/bin* ($V_1C_1/C_2V_1C_1$). None of this alters the crucial, distinguishing motion, from disparity to similarity.

We mostly take this for granted: Hey, that's what a rhyme is, isn't it? But the Funesians (nothing if not methodical) are left to ponder why our rhymes don't work the other way. Why doesn't our typical rhyme commence with identical sounds and end on a difference? Why don't we habitually rhyme *soul* with *soak*? Or *death* with *den*? It's a phenomenon we might call "reverse rhyme," further observing that the loveliest example in the language may be on display in the English proverb *Time and tide wait for no man.*

Why don't we rhyme this way? Is there something within us, constitutionally, that prefers migrating from difference to likeness? Or is conventional rhyming somehow inbred into the English language? Or is it merely ear training—and the thoughtless force of habit?

Whatever the reason, we learn from childhood to accept this as norm: $C_1V_1C_2/C_3V_1C_2$. Just as the child of two or three grasps the nature of the prosodic contract, she comprehends our rhyme prototype. A rhyme means coming together, not drifting apart. Our terminology only reinforces the notion. Rhymes failing to operate this way are off rhymes. Not variant rhymes, or some variant of *variant*. Off—as if something's wrong with them. Some poets, like Dylan Thomas and Seamus Heaney, revel in off rhyme—at times positively prefer it. But the governing assumption over the centuries has been that exact rhyme represents the preferable path, and only exigency—a shortage of inspiration or suitable alternatives—drives anyone into off rhyme.

Rhyme enacts itself through performance, realizes itself through time. The phenomenon is fleeting—no more than a few seconds, typically: the duration required to utter all the syllables intervening between two rhymes. Sounds fade in the air before us, and fade likewise in the mind, and as we've seen, rhymes rarely bridge an expanse exceeding fifty syllables. Still, fifty syllables is not nothing. Between initial call and echoing response a gratifying interval arises—often sufficiently lengthy to foster a dual sense of need and satiation.

Meter's relationship with time is far simpler than rhyme's, since meter is at home in an endless present. Evenly it slogs onward, not looking back. Recall: *Meter is prospective; rhyme is retrospective.*

Rhyme is also specific and targeted. Or call it selective,

preferential, choosy. Or even monogamous. Typically, it fixes upon a particular partner, and if not exactly forsaking all others, it does settle its principal energies on a chosen mate.

An example should make this clearer. Here is a quatrain from John Donne's most famous sonnet ("Death, be not proud . . ."):

> From rest and sleep, which but thy pictures be,
> Much pleasure; then from thee much more must flow,
> And soonest our best men with thee do go,
> Rest of their bones, and soul's delivery.

It concludes with perhaps the most common rhyme sound in our language, a long *e* (*be/delivery*). In this case, it's a feeble rhyme, since the final *y* in *delivery* doesn't carry a primary accent. In addition, an internal *thee* twice makes a stronger natural pairing with *be*. But in the larger scheme of things each *thee* hardly matters; they are subsidiary sounds. What matters is whether *be* will find a mate some thirty syllables later, for that is when we'll arrive at the quatrain's end. Our *be* has an appointment then and there—a blind date.

One could, I suppose, eliminate each *thee* by substituting a *you*, altering the poem's atmosphere but leaving unchanged the pattern of expectations. Likewise, we could pack the intervening lines with internal *e* rhymes—again changing atmosphere but not obligation. Donne still "owes" you, according to the prosodic contract of the sonnet, a rhyme at line four, and the pressing question is whether he'll provide it. He may follow the rhyme scheme respectfully. Or may startle you with an unexpected sound, in which case you're left to wonder whether to applaud or disparage his boldness, his trickery.

James Wright's "Speak" is another quatrain-based poem,

though rigged out in eight-line stanzas. The schema is clear: ABABCDCD, mostly off rhymes. But things go seriously awry within the first three stanzas. (The Liston referred to is Sonny Liston, the former heavyweight boxing champion widely accused of throwing his title fight in 1965 against Muhammad Ali.)

To speak in a flat voice
Is all that I can do.
I have gone every place
Asking for you.
Wondering where to turn
And how the search would end
And the last streetlight spin
Above me blind.

Then I returned rebuffed
And saw under the sun
The race not to the swift
Nor the battle won.
Liston dives in the tank,
Lord, in Lewiston, Maine,
And Ernie Doty's drunk
In hell again.

And Jenny, oh my Jenny
Whom I love, rhyme be damned,
Has broken her spare beauty
In a whorehouse old.
She left her new baby
In a bus-station can,
And sprightly danced away
Through Jacksontown.

If Ernie Doty (unidentified) is in hell again, we might also ask, what in hell is going on with this rhyme of *damned/old*? This is such an off rhyme as to be a defiant, self-declared jettisoning of rhyme. Wright breaks the prosodic contract in order to suggest there are things more important (heartbreak, treachery, bloodshed) than prosodic contracts. It's an artful repudiation of art.

Any assemblage of words has a natural tendency to subside into a confusing and unruly crowd, and a poem's stanzaic pattern can be an aid in maneuvering through it, guiding us by way of end words to the likeliest candidates for rhymes. On entering any formally complex poem, a wise reader concedes that much will fall by the wayside. When listening for a weak rhyme like *be* and *delivery*, we can't afford to be too distracted by intervening sounds. Our overall goal is unwavering: to hear as much as we can while not losing the primary rhyme, the supervising structure. Those who can't hear *everything* must fix priorities, and a stanzaic form is a convenient manual for indicating what these ought to be.

But, just as important, a poem is also a device for instructing the reader when to tune out. Some sounds are primary, some secondary. The formal poem, recognizing our frailties, and understanding that despite our good intentions all sounds naturally dissipate, takes upon itself the task of indicating which sounds should be deliberately and artificially preserved. It's a sort of traffic cop that sometimes overrides your readerly instincts, signaling you to halt, to turn, to ignore normal procedures, to advance with special care, or to face front and just hustle along.

The formal poem plays a wily game of apportionment, saying, *Pay less attention to that sound*, as well as *Pay more to this*.

Its structure is an ongoing concession to the reader's limitations. Even as it's formulating exorbitant demands—*Examine me more closely than anything else you look at today!*—it's seeking to be helpful. Frankly, it cannot do otherwise. Altruism, a reflexive offer of assistance, is built into a poem's architecture.

By promoting the exact rhyme, we've established a long tradition of treating rhymes unequally. But even if we restrict ourselves to exact rhymes, inequality persists. Not all words are equally good at summoning and keeping a partner. Unusual sounds are better at it, being easier to retain. A rhyme like *it/bit* has less chance of lodging in the mind than, say, *lengths* and *strengths*. Old, wayworn rhymes (*love/dove, art/heart*) pale beside similar-sounding but fresher pairings (*love/shove, art/fart*). The profane, the scatological, anything the slightest bit shocking—in their indecorousness, they make powerful rhyme words.

Rhymes are tied to syllable duration. Historically, English *meters* based on duration have foundered, largely because nobody can agree on how long a syllable lasts, given the wild vagaries of our spelling and the melting pot of our language. In the realm of *rhyme*, however, duration is formative. Simply, the more shared sounds between two words, the more conspicuous and durable their rhyme. A two-syllable rhyme (**feminine rhyme**) takes longer to utter than a one-syllable rhyme (**masculine rhyme**), and, loitering in the ear, is more prominent; we'll retain *swimmer* and *dimmer* well beyond *swim* and *dim*. Three-syllable rhymes (trisyllabic rhymes) are so egregious, calling such attention to themselves, as to risk overwhelming the rest of the poem. Thomas Hardy is almost alone among major poets in regularly employing them in moments of pathos and desolation:

Or is it only the breeze in its listlessness
Travelling across the wet mead to me here,
You being ever dissolved to wan wistlessness,
Heard no more again far or near?

Trisyllabic rhymes belong chiefly to light verse, where antic attention seeking is often the point. There, they flourish with abandon, as in these verses from Byron:

He learned the art of riding, fencing, gunnery,
And how to scale a fortress—or a nunnery.

★

But—Oh! ye lords of ladies intellectual,
Inform us truly, have they not hen-peck'd you all?

Or these from Nash:

Never has host encountered a visitor
Less desirabler, less exquisiter . . .

★

I do not charge the asp with matricide,
But what about his Cleopatricide?

Four-syllable rhymes (*particularly/perpendicularly*) belong all but exclusively to the virtuosos of Tin Pan Alley, where a lyricist can also rely upon a composer's melody to consolidate an elongated word cluster, as often arises in Rodgers and Hart: *keep to yourself / weep to yourself* ("This Funny World"), *pet her a bit / better a bit* ("Comfort Me"), *zoo with a man / do with a man* ("What Can You Do with a Man?"). But why limit yourself to four-syllable rhymes when five are available, as in Johnny Mercer's: *haggard in the morning / laggard in the morning.* Or Noël Coward's *mad about the boy / sleepless nights I've had about the boy.*

But duration isn't merely a matter of syllable counts. Some vowels outstay others in the mouth. Those called "gliding vowels," or diphthongs (Greek for "two tones"), like the *ow* in *town* or the *oi* in *coin*, persevere longer than monophthongs, like *ah* or *eh*. *Boy/toy* endures beyond *bed/head*. Likewise, tongue-twisting rhymes, like *myths/smiths*, will outlast sounds that trip off the tongue tip, like *trip/tip*.

So there's good reason behind our long-held preference for exact rhymes. They demonstrate durability; they outcompete off rhymes; they have more to share when like meets like. One of James Wright's off rhymes is *turn/spin*, two words with nothing in common but the ubiquitous letter *n*. As echoes go, *turn* and *spin* are an attenuated duo, incapable of bridging any sizable sonic distance.

Ironically, the twentieth century, when free verse became dominant, was also the great age of exploration into rhyme's varieties and capacities. Lively experiments and innovations were carried out by Wilfred Owen, Auden, MacNeice, Heaney, Dylan Thomas, Marianne Moore, James Merrill, Derek Walcott, and many others. Much of the most interesting work involved off rhyme or off off rhyme. Where a rhyme like *turn/spin* becomes not an aberration but a mode, we enter a realm of soft echoes, muted summonses. Such poems, even when outfitted like Wright's "Speak" with a rhyme scheme, often seem closer in spirit to free verse than to the crisp sturdiness of, say, Pope in full couplet regalia:

See! and confess, one comfort still must rise,
'Tis this: Tho' Man's a fool, yet God is wise.
Here then we rest: "The Universal Cause
Acts to one end, but acts by various laws."

Yet it turns out even Pope is less sturdy than he looks.
Farther down the same page in *An Essay on Man* I find four
rhymes that to my ears are off: *endued/good, sustain/again, born/
return,* and *good/food.* My guess is that only *born/return* was
an off rhyme to Pope's ear. I've spoken of metrical decay in
Chaucer's *Canterbury Tales* (largely caused by *e*'s having gone
silent), but rhyme decay is a much more widespread phenomenon. The shifting of pronunciation, rumpling the rhymes,
occurs not only over time but over geography. Imagine four
native speakers of English declaiming *An Essay on Man* today.
One is from Edinburgh, one from Mumbai, one from Trini-
dad, and I'm reciting in flat midwestern American. Doubtless,
we would each detect a different number of decayed rhymes.

What's significant isn't the precise number of rhymes
twisted or shifted over the centuries. What's important is the
overall trend, which is *always* going to devolve from exact
rhyme to off rhyme, rather than the reverse. And since we
tend, by convention, to hear exact rhyme as euphonious and
off rhyme as cacophonous, it follows that the tidal movement
of formal poetry is toward dissonance and disorder. Even
Pope's hardy couplets come undone. In the universe of poetry,
as in the universe at large, entropy is the ultimate victor.

Why is this—why does poetry over the years move toward
disorder rather than increased order?

Again, a little math offers illumination. According to our
prototype, there is a prescribed way in which two words will
normally rhyme: $C_1V_1C_2/C_3V_1C_2$. But there are multiple

ways in which two words can off-rhyme; they merely need to have *something* in common. Vowels may alter; initial or final consonants may alter; accents may alter. So while it's mathematically possible that a deliberate off rhyme in Pope's ear might, over the centuries, become an exact rhyme in mine, the opposite is far more probable. Things irregularize.

When we read an anonymous poem of the fifteenth century that begins

> Blessed Mary, mother virginal,
> Integrate maiden, star of the sea,
> Have remembrance at the day final
> On thy poor servant now praying to thee

we're left to wonder whether *virginal* and *final* once rhymed exactly. Or take "De Puero Balbutiente," by the ill-named Thomas Bastard (1566–1618). (I like the idea of his being a well-established family name.) It's a poem of six couplets, five of them exact and one of them drastically off-rhymed:

> The alphabet is searched for letters soft,
> To try a word before it can be wrought . . .

Was this once a bona fide rhyme? I suspect so. I suspect that a change has been wroft, or wrought. And that rhyme decay has affected 18.67 percent (one in six) of the poem's rhymes.

Of course I'm being pseudomathematical. But I've sometimes fantasized that we might date poems through rhyme decay much as we estimate the age of prehistoric objects by carbon testing. If a poem was written wholly or chiefly in exact rhyme, its proportion of off rhymes will increase with age (much as, with carbon dating, the ratio of carbon-12

increases at the expense of carbon-14). Needless to say, radio-
active decay is precise and gradual in a way that rhyme decay
never could be, since it may intensify in periods of turmoil.
(Historians of our language speak, rather imposingly, of the
Great Vowel Shift between Middle and Modern English.)
Still, we might come up with some reasonable estimates. . . .

Of all the great English writers, H. G. Wells surely took
most to heart the implications of entropy, both in its strict
thermodynamic sense of the dissipation of useful energy
and in the broader metaphorical notion of things running
down and out and into damned disarray. Entropy dogged
and goaded his imagination, galvanizing his masterpiece,
The Time Machine. The universe was destined to dispel and
disintegrate, indifferently, ineluctably, and what did it matter
if, as the Time Traveller discovered, there were still scrappy
vestiges of life on the Earth in thirty million years? Look at
the long-term trend! A mere thirty million years! Less than
half the distance between us and the doomed dinosaurs of the
Cretaceous . . .

One can view poems in much the same way, as devolving organisms, and rhyme decay provides a fecund notion for
those wishing to indulge in feelings of universal futility and
loss. Rhymes fall apart, and everything else about a poem
does, too. As Thomas Nashe put it more than four hundred
years ago: "Peace, plenty, pleasure, suddenly decay." We lose
the meters, the rhythms, and the wordplay, as meanings wan-
der and puns are mislaid. In a verse called "On Discovering a
Butterfly," Nabokov has a wonderful line: "poems that take a
thousand years to die."

Of course, the scholar emerges at this juncture, playing
stopgap and restorer, reconstructing the meters, the rhythms,
the wordplay. Hers is a noble task. But if Homer could be

returned to us for one command performance, placed before
the world's most erudite audience, there's no classicist on
Earth who could attend to him with the visceral immediacy
of those bright-eyed, torchlit faces once clustered around their
talebearer. Those scruffy listeners were illiterate, but also far
abler and richer than we can ever be. For they could hear
Homer, regular as breathing.

Many of us have a favorite natural image for contemplation—a slow oak fire maybe, blazing away in an antique
hearth, into which one stares and loses oneself. For Wordsworth, who once memorably wandered "lonely as a cloud," it
might well have been the variegated skyscape over Cumber-
land, as recalled in childhood memories in *The Prelude:*

> . . . drinking in
> A pure organic pleasure from the lines
> Of curling mist, or from the level plain
> Of waters coloured by the steady clouds.

James Dickey somewhere commented that the most inspiring object in the universe is a river, and he added, *any* river.
My own choice would be a waterfall. Not necessarily a large
falls, drawing tourists and hikers. But a small waterfall of the
sort you sometimes come upon in the forests in hilly New
England, a whisperer, not a thunderer—a personal-size falls,
if you will. The eye rests upon that point where there is no
rest, only an enhanced restlessness: a place of push and plash,
the junction where a stream lets go of its banks into the even
delirium of free fall.

There's something hypnotic to it, and inspiring, and also

mysteriously unnerving, and in this potent combination I'm reminded of the flow of language generally, the ceaseless and careless tumble and spill of words, words, words wherever you venture. At my local gym, as my treadmill turns and turns, I'll sometimes circle through its TV channels, creating a kind of double flow. Here's another waterfall, this one of impromptu speech, a deluge forever cascading into a bright and dotty oblivion. I'm reminded once more of my favorite novel, Laxness's *Independent People*, where we encounter a small boy, Nonni, who is obsessed with waterfalls. A portrait of the artist as a child, Nonni has begun to reflect on the nature of time. An illusory image haunts his imagination: the moment when the present's march is halted and a waterfall flows backward. Nonni doesn't know it yet, but he's obsessed with poetry.

Well, any big waterfall of language contains within it, along with pinhead pundits and preening fops and shameless pitchmen and a good many thoroughly contemptible politicians, a few poems. And as all the words of the world surge ever forward, over the lip of the cataract, the rhymes in those poems keep calling backward. They are linked to the wish Frost expressed for his daughter in "The Master Speed":

But in the rush of everything to waste,
That you may have the power of standing still . . .

Or as Nonni has it: "Mother, I saw the water blown back over the waterfall." *Forward*, says the meter. *Backward*, says the rhyme. For just a moment, indeed, time's march is stayed.

◻

CHAPTER ELEVEN

Spelling and the
Unexpected Rhyme

I once met an Italian woman whose surname was Cairoli. When I asked how she spelled it, she looked at me quizzically. "Exactly as it sounds," she replied.

In her gaze lay, besides a little puzzlement, a glinting splinter of pride, on behalf of a language whose spelling is upright and commonsensical, where to hear a word or a name is to know its spelling.

Not so with English. In America, it's never out of place to ask people how they spell their names. Is this particular Ms. Jones a Ms. Joans? This Day a much cloudier Daye? This garden-variety Mr. Root actually a transplanted Mr. Rute? This Ball a less bouncy Bawl? (You can find all four variants in the Manhattan phone book—provided you could find a Manhattan phone book in our online culture.)

Spelling is a trial and terror for anyone learning English as a second language. This isn't for lack of firm efforts by crusading luminaries (George Bernard Shaw, Noah Webster) and high-powered organizations (the Carnegie-funded Simplified Spelling Board of 1906). We seem unbudgeable in clinging to the spellings we know. Native speakers get used to such things. We don't pay much attention, mostly, though through enough thought we may get some inkling of how odd and illogical our spelling is—as illustrated by a phrase like *though through enough thought.*

But what makes an onerous burden for the ESL student provides a boon for the formal poet. From the gnarled thickets of our spelling all sorts of rhyming surprises are flushed, equally for writer and reader. Suddenly it dawns upon you: Those two words *rhyme.* They shouldn't; they look worlds apart.

Elizabeth Bishop recounted in an interview the role that rhyme played in her friendship with her mentor Marianne Moore:

> She was rather contradictory, you know, illogical sometimes. She would say, "Oh—rhyme is dowdy." Then other times when she was translating La Fontaine she would ask me for a rhyme. If I could give her a rhyme, she would seem to be pleased. She liked a ballad of mine because it rhymed so well. She admired the rhyme "many antennae."

The ballad was "The Burglar of Babylon," set in Rio de Janeiro:

> Women with market baskets
>   Stood on the corners and talked,
> Then went on their way to market,
>   Gazing up as they walked.
>
> The rich with their binoculars
>   Were back again, and many

Were standing on the rooftops,
  Among TV antennae.

It's an image to cherish: poets sharing the contraband of an unlikely rhyme. I once pointed out to the Russian poet Joseph Brodsky the near-exact rhyme of *Christmas/isthmus*, found in Frost, among others. And Brodsky's eyes immediately lit up with a sharp, grateful *Of course*. . . . Clearly, in his mind each word had just now been slightly modified. He responded by offering up his favorite rim rhyme: *Hebrews/highbrows*. Some things are too good to keep to oneself.

Such moments of recognition represent a rare and welcome triumph of ear over eye. Over the ages the trend has been steadily otherwise, until sometimes it's easy to forget that poetry began in the ear. And that poetry, for God knows how many centuries, before the birth of general literacy, to say nothing of the birth of writing, was aural. And that even literacy was aural for most of its long history. In *Capturing Music*, Thomas Forrest Kelly observes that "until well into the Middle Ages, it never occurred to anybody to read silently."

Classical scholars debate the dates of the *Iliad* and the *Odyssey*, while agreeing that generations passed before some conscientious scribes had the wherewithal—of time, education, materials—to begin the monumental and novel task of setting the world's greatest epics down on papyrus rolls. These immense poems originally had no visual existence.

The long history of world poetry might be viewed as a peremptory series of encroachments, the visual steadily supplanting and dominating the aural. Over time, alphabets grow more calibrated and efficient. Punctuation develops and publication explodes—and the role of memorization declines.

The eye reaches its ascendancy, perhaps, in those moments when a poem is read silently, at a pace far exceeding speaking speed—just the way a student of literature crams for an exam. Reading in this fashion is like listening to a 33⅓ LP at 45 rpm. You may catch all the words, and do so with magnificent rapidity, but nothing sounds right, or even quite human.

If the eye keeps blithely abandoning the ear, the ear provides a comeuppance when revealing an unsuspected rhyme. Such moments remind us that when the brain is processing poetry, the eye is the quicker, the ear the more trustworthy, faculty.

One of the peculiarities of English (pretty much unthinkable to an Italian speaker) is that two words can rhyme exactly without having a single letter in common: *glyph/tiff*, or *spew/through*, or *ticks/pyx,* or *flee/quay/prix*. They can also rhyme when it appears they must merely repeat themselves: *re-sign/resign*. (Or better still, an opening sentence I once found in a magazine article about martinis: "Begin with gin.") At such moments, when the eye and ear are at odds, the often neglected ear—blessedly—dominates. The old adage *Looks are deceiving* has a special aptness in regard to poetry. You might even argue that the poem in type or on a computer screen isn't the real poem—that the written words before you are a simulacrum, mere representations of the poem's essential sounds. (Whereas you couldn't sensibly argue, it seems to me, that the sounds are mere stand-ins for the words on the page. Here, the ear is primary.)

Some letters in English, like *b* or *m*, create a single sound, rarely duplicable by other letters. Others, though, create a multiplicity of sounds, like the chameleonic *c* (*call, cell, cello*) or the slippery *s* (*as, ass, pleasure*). Confusion naturally reigns.

It's all a delightful cacophonous morass, and when you add to it the way identical sounds can be rendered by different combinations of letters—*laugh, staff, staph*—you realize that the possibilities of disguise are endless. Poets are forever bringing together words whose sonic kinship flouts appearances: *certain/hurtin'*; *hydroponics/onyx*; *mirror/nearer*; *header/meadow* (baby-voiced Blossom Dearie: "The moon is takin' a header / A lark'll wake up in the medder"); *they'll/sail; gospel/poss'ble; ferny/attorney/journey* (gravel-voiced Tom Waits: "You'll need an attorney for this journey").

And yet, though rhyme's an aural phenomenon, it's striking how many of its effects depend on visual insignia. Typically, the more remote the spelling, the more pleasure in the union, as occurs in pointed form when one of the words is "spelled" with numbers. There's a potential wit to the rhyme of *plenty/20* that doesn't exist for *plenty/twenty*, though the ear is deaf to any difference.

Visual effects are central to Browning's "Home-Thoughts from the Sea." The poet stands upon a ship heading south from England into the Mediterranean. The sights that unfold are geographical, as he rounds Portugal (Cape Saint Vincent) and Spain (Cádiz), but they are also historically laden, evoking milestones in English history (Trafalgar, Gibraltar):

> Nobly, nobly Cape Saint Vincent to the North-West
>   died away;
> Sunset ran, one glorious blood-red, reeking into Cadiz
>   Bay;
> Bluish 'mid the burning water, full in face Trafalgar lay;
> In the dimmest North-East distance, dawned Gibraltar
>   grand and gray;

"Here and here did England help me: how can I help
   England?"—say,
Whoso turns as I, this evening, turn to God to praise
   and pray,
While Jove's planet rises yonder, silent over Africa.

What begins seemingly as a simple geographical chronicle
yields to a contemplation of empire, until at last the poet
encounters something too vast to encompass psychologically,
or prosodically: The basic rhyme scheme falls apart in the
final line.

After six clean rhymes on *a*, we're tempted to close the
poem with a final *a* rhyme. Visually, the poem's terminal
Africa obliges us, with not one but two open *a* sounds. Neither
one provides a rhyme, though. The visual linkages encour-
age us to bend the word drastically out of shape: *Ay*-frica, or
Af-ri-*cay*, or even *Ay*-fri-*cay*. But we don't. The outstretched
continent, lying beneath not a Christian but a teeming poly-
theistic firmament, is not so easily assimilated. The poet has
more than met his match, as the failure to rhyme attests.

The visual aspects of rhyme are an engaging maze. Poetry
handbooks speak assuredly of the phenomenon known either
as "sight rhyme" or "eye rhyme," as though its value and
appeal were patent, though I've never understood its attractions. Sight rhyme is the obverse of the kind of unlikely rhyme
that strikes me as charming. Instead of offering two words
that actually rhyme while looking as if they shouldn't, it offers
two words that look as though they rhyme but don't: *though*
and *through* or *eight* and *sleight*. But how much unexpected-
ness can such rhymes possibly pack? Given the vagaries of
English orthography, how much surprise, how much delight,

is derivable from the realization that—yes—two more words that ought to rhyme don't? Perhaps, too (in some overarching aesthetic system, connected to the way our brains and bodies work), unexpected likeness is simply more gratifying than unexpected difference.

Light-verse writers and lyricists expand the field of unexpected rhyme through free and whimsical contractions, as in Rodgers and Hart's "I Married an Angel":

> Have you heard?
> I married an angel
> I'm sure that the change'll be
> Awf'lly good for me

Or George and Ira Gershwin's "Sunny Disposish":

> Taking your advice, the sad and weary'll
> Have no material
> To be funereal

Or their "Bidin' My Time":

> I'm bidin' my time
> 'Cause that's the kind of guy I'm

Contractions are normally employed when we're in a hurry. Yet here we have a speaker who tells us

> While other folks grow dizzy
> I keep busy
> Bidin' my time

The kind of guy I'm? The humor lies in the contraction's seeming to be not merely wrong but willfully, *needlessly* wrong. And it's but a short step from the Gershwins to *The Simpsons* and Cletus, the slack-jawed yokel:

> Some folk'll never eat a skunk,
> But then again, some folk'll,
> Like Cletus, the slack-jawed yokel.

Pleasure in wrongness reaches a brilliant extreme in George Starbuck's "Sonnet with a Different Letter at the End of Each Line." Starbuck pulls out every trick in the book to ensure that, though it looks as though he's falling down on the job, indeed every line (once some abbreviations are unpacked) ends in an *o* sound.

> O for a muse of fire, a sack of dough,
> Or both! O promissory notes of woe!
> One time in Santa Fe N.M.
> Ol' Winfield Townley Scott and I . . . But whoa.

> One can exert oneself, *ff*,
> Or architect a heaven like Rimbaud,
> Or if that seems, how shall I say, *de trop,*
> One can at least write sonnets, a propos
> Of nothing save the do-re-mi-fa-sol
> Of poetry itself. Is not the row
> Of perfect rhymes, the terminal bon mot,
> Obeisance enough to the Great O?

> "Observe," said Chairman Mao to Premier Chou,
> "On voyage à Parnasse pour prendre les eaux.
> On voyage come poisson, incog."

(Extra credit to those readers who noticed that on the other margin, the left margin, every word begins with an ordinary, overused, on-the-job *O*.)

We don't expect a final *o* sound from words ending in a consonant. But that's how most of Starbuck's lines end, and these are, in their unlikelihood, the more satisfying rhymes. Rhyme, theoretically a purely aural phenomenon, is affected by what lies on the page, by what we see. The rhyme of, say, *kernel/infernal* is far less rich than the aurally identical *colonel/ infernal*, where a good marriage establishes itself despite irreconcilable visual differences. So, too, with *papery/potpourri*— vastly superior to *papery/popery*.

Spelling is only one of a number of ways in which rhymes surprise us. They also surprise where a single word is partnered with two or more words. For a moment, typically, there's a suspicion that bumpiness must result. The satisfaction's all the greater when the rhyme turns out to be smoothly perfect. Poets have long been fond of rhyming *minute* with *in it* or, better still, as in Wilbur's "A Grasshopper," *minute* with *within it* (where the rhyme is, to draw on the poem's concluding phrase, "busily hid"). Here are the first two stanzas:

But for a brief
Moment, a poised minute,
He paused on the chicory-leaf;
Yet within it

The sprung perch
Had time to absorb the shock,
Narrow its pitch and lurch,
Cease to rock.

Light-verse writers and popular song lyricists love this stuff. So you'll find Ogden Nash rhyming *chorus* and *bore us* or *art is* and *parties*, and Lorenz Hart rhyming *hear drums* and *eardrums*. The field of potential rhymes becomes dizzyingly large, free and open, once you begin to think not in terms of which word rhymes with which, but—as Byron saw—which syllables rhyme with which combination of syllables, irrespective of word boundaries.

It helps to view the space between two words as merely one more letter, as your keyboard encourages you to do: The space bar is simply another key. A rhyme like *passionate* and *cash in it* ("Her kisses were passionate / For there was some cash in it") might be seen as a rhyme between two "words," one of which contains a couple of spaces. Such rhymes are all the more cheering and lovely for being unobtainable through your rhyming dictionary. They ask you—you the poet, you the lyricist—to listen for unlikely combinations, to ignore boundaries and heed only the way syllable combines with syllable. You can sense the delight, the half-suppressed giggle, when Hart pairs *Greenwich* and *men itch* or *lover, let* and *coverlet* or *truly yet* and *Juliet*.

Something similar arises where rhyme binds two languages, with all their clashing tones and rhythms. Prosodists call this "macaronic rhyme," beautifully employed in Wilfred Owen's sonnet "Dulce et Decorum Est." The title derives from Horace: *"Dulce et decorum est pro patria mori"* ("It is sweet and fitting to die for one's country"). In the sonnet's octave, Owen details some of the ravages of the First World War. View war for the horror it really is, Owen advises, and

My friend, you would not tell with such high zest
To children ardent for some desperate glory

The old Lie: *Dulce et decorum est*
Pro patria mori.

The beauty of the Latin lies in how seamlessly it threads into the English, both its meter and (still more impressive) its two rhymes. Languages sing to each other across the millennia, twenty centuries drop away, as one poet addresses and challenges and incorporates a faraway forebear.

Macaronic rhyme caps the final two quatrains of Wilbur's "For the New Railway Station in Rome," in which a mysterious voice drawn from "the least shard of the world" speaks:

"What city is eternal
But that which prints itself within the groping head
    Out of the blue unbroken reveries
    Of the building dead?

"What is our praise or pride
But to imagine excellence, and try to make it?
    What does it say over the door of Heaven
    But *homo fecit?*"

That final rhyme, so dexterously conjoining the two languages, is all the more felicitous for arriving within a poem about architectural marvels.

Macaronic rhyme turns humorous where the poet mangles the foreign word, subjecting it to callous mispronunciations, as Auden does in "Letter to Lord Byron." A superb linguist, Auden takes great joy in creating buffoonish pratfalls:

So looking round for something light and easy
I pounced on you as warm and civilisé.

Or:

> And with the help of Sunlight Soap the Geysir
> Affords to visitors le plus grand plaisir.

Cole Porter does something similar in "You're the Top," in which he rhymes his exclamatory *top* with *flop* and *pop* and *blop* and eventually *de trop*:

> You're a rose, you're Inferno's Dante,
> You're the nose on the great Durante.
> I'm just in the way, as the French would say, "De trop,"
> But if, baby, I'm the bottom, you're the top!

(The joke's all the sweeter in that Porter, who for years lived an elegant expat's Parisian life, probably had the best French of all the great American popular song lyricists.)

Byron similarly romps and rips through Spanish in *Don Juan*, beginning by having *Juan* rhyme with *new one* and going on to link *Cadiz* with *ladies* and *Lopé* with *copy*. Nash rhymes *gourmet* and *sure may*. Anthony Hecht links *men's sauna* and *mens sana*. Howard Moss's wonderful "Tourists" concludes with an inspired mispronunciation:

> Humdrum conundrums, what's to become of them?
> Most will come home, but there will be some of them
>
> Subsiding like Lawrence in Florence, or crazily
> Ending up tending shop up in Fiesole.

A passionate American Italophile might well disappear into Tuscany. But never—the rhyme suggests—will he blend in like a native, to whose ear *Fiesole* is no suitable partner for *crazily.*

But you don't need a second language to re-create feelings of foreign intrusion. These arise wherever rhyming dictions clash, one argot with another. This is particularly effective when a specialized, coldly scientific term, with the precision of a hypodermic needle, inserts itself into a lyrical coursing, as in Anthony Hecht's "Japan":

> Human endeavor clumsily betrays
> Humanity. Their excrement served in this;
> For, planting rice in water, they would raise
>   Schistosomiasis
>   Japonica, that enters through
>   The pores into the avenue
> And orbit of the blood . . .

It's now been more than half a century since C. P. Snow famously bemoaned our "two cultures"—the unbridgeable gap between the sciences and the humanities. But in such moments, when a medical term sings like a troubadour, the two are one.

Rhyme likewise clashes, freshly, wherever two antonymous or antagonistic words are bridged: *sadness/gladness* or *breath/death* or *bright/night* or *cat/rat* or *cheerful/tearful.* But since such pairings, eagerly seized upon, are easily overused, any innate wit or paradox quickly becomes blunted. Surprise is lost; we've seen these rhymes before. This is another terrain where meter and rhyme differ: Meter marches on, inhumanly indefatigable, whereas rhymes soon grow tired.

Tired, and yet replenishable. One of the prime delights

of formal poetry arises when the rhyme itself is familiar—
perhaps drearily so—and yet the resourceful poet imparts
a fresh twist. Two shopworn terms come together like
ingenues.

Philip Larkin's "This Be the Verse" concludes with a
linking of *shelf* and *self*, one of the tiredest rhymes in the language. (This isn't to sneer at poets who employ it. *Self* is an
indispensable term, but what on earth to rhyme with it? If
you're Robert Frost, you may succeed in inserting a small *elf*
into your verse ["Or easy gold at the hand of fay or elf"] or
even some *pelf* ["By grace of state-manipulated pelf"]). But
such options aren't available to most modern poets. For hundreds of years, most of the rhyming on *self*, whatever the tone
of the poem, has been of a shelving variety:

When true love broke my heart in half,
I took the whiskey from the shelf,
And told my neighbors when to laugh.
I keep a dog, and bark myself.

ROETHKE

Or Langston Hughes in "The Weary Blues":

I heard that Negro sing, that old piano moan—
    "Ain't got nobody in all this world,
    Ain't got nobody but ma self.
    I'se gwine to quit my frownin'
    And put ma troubles on the shelf."

Any real poetry lover has come upon this rhyme dozens,
perhaps hundreds of times. But Larkin's use is different. I first
encountered "This Be the Verse" in my twenties, and still

recall the liberating, down-sweeping expansiveness of its final
stanza:

Man hands on misery to man.
It deepens like a coastal shelf.
Get out as early as you can,
And don't have any kids yourself.

While this may look like the same old rhyme, it isn't at
all. Larkin isn't rhyming *self* with *shelf*, but with *coastal shelf* (a
rhyme I'd never seen before), a colossal and integral object
whose oneness might logically be notated as *coastal-shelf* or
even *coastalshelf*. Here was a reminder that we mustn't allow
the spaces between words to obscure the unities subtending
them. In other words, the old rhyme felt new. In this delight-
fully misanthropic stanza, the unexpected springs from the
expected. The stanza remains for me a bright, dark, miniature, and haunting symbol of what the formal poem tirelessly
aspires to do.

◻

CHAPTER TWELVE

Rhyme Poverty, Rhyme Richness

English is often called "rhyme-poor," a lament trace-able back to Chaucer, who complained of a "skarsete" of rhymes to work with. Many of our profoundest words, those engaging the poet with greatest urgency and intimacy, are painfully rhyme-deficient. We've already seen how *death* is often paired with *breath*. The two make a handsome and believable couple, but the truth is they're all but handcuffed together; *death* simply doesn't offer many other choices. (That's the thing about death: so few alternatives.) I typed *death* into rhymezone.com and discovered seventeen possible one-syllable mates, nearly all highly unpromising, to say the least. (*Breth? Creath? Cheth?* Or what about *greth*—which turns out to be a Shetland Islands slang term for a piss?)

And the situation worsens. *Death* seems to be shedding potential rhymes for each new generation. (Another thing about death: It discourages company.) A Victorian might per-haps have rhymed *death* with a host of those antiquated verbs carrying an *eth* suffix: *sorroweth, offereth, suffereth.* But these make tough grist for the modern poet's mill wheel.

True, in recent years *death* has picked up a newsworthy

partner in *meth*. And, given the drug's ravages, the two make a promising pair. Still, *death*'s pickings remain slim and grow slimmer. For lack of alternatives, the hungry *death*-bound poet may gravitate toward the pantry of off rhyme, but even there, the larder is meager and it's a bare-bones diet.

Actually, *life*'s prospects are no brighter. This time, the rhmezone website provided fifteen one-syllable alternatives, but I have yet to encounter the poet who could dispatch *greiff, pfeiff,* or *phyfe*. There's *wife*, of course, and this lady is apt to be embraced all the more passionately for lack of other options. Those in a darker state of mind may brandish a *knife*. Eliot's marvelous "Rhapsody on a Windy Night" closes with the *life/knife* pairing:

> The lamp said,
> "Four o'clock,
> Here is the number on the door.
> Memory!
> You have the key,
> The little lamp spreads a ring on the stair,
> Mount.
> The bed is open; the tooth-brush hangs on the wall,
> Put your shoes at the door, sleep, prepare for life!"
>
> The last twist of the knife.

True, we end with a familiar and predictable rhyme—yet it's a hard-hitting couplet in a poem that contains few couplets. Honed, fragmentary, the last line comes at you with a sudden stabbing thrust. In the right hands, old rhymes can be strikingly potent. Still, it's no rhyme to rely upon. Its blade blunts quickly.

Love preoccupies us in life and, according to some, actually conquers death, but as a rhyme word it's the most barren of the three. The rhmezone website offers only five one-syllable alternatives. Desperate for rhymes, poets constantly wind up terminating a line with a preposition, which can feel awkward and arbitrary. (What were they thinking *of*?) And how many times has the lovelorn poet summoned the moon or stars *above*? (Where else would they be?)

Money is no better, encouraging all sorts of sunny or honeyed comparisons (most of them unfunny). And as for *God*—oh, God . . . It's one of the many triumphs of my favorite poem, Hopkins's "God's Grandeur," that he seems, without straining, all but to exhaust God's potential: *rod, trod, shod.*

Death, life, love, money, God . . . In English, the fundamentals of our existence collude to hamstring the rhyming poet. Rhyme poverty may initially present an aural problem—a monotony of sound. But ultimately the problem becomes imaginational, since paucity of rhyme fosters straitened thought. If *self* is unfailingly to be coupled with *shelf,* the poet's range of thought—images and objectives—itself is shelved. Far better to be soaring through the *heavens,* to be bobbing on the *ocean,* to be trekking through the *jungle,* but none of these words comes close to providing rhymes for the demanding *self.*

So familiar is the *moon/June* pairing as to become a jokey password for the poetaster. Yet it's not an exact rhyme in other European languages (Finnish being an exception, a Finnish friend informs me), and my guess is that poets in those other languages probably find fewer occasions to bring June and moon together. Who knows? They may prefer July. Rhyme is an independent-minded yet nostalgic steering wheel. It drives us to old haunts.

Similarly, rhymes on the suffix -*ation* usually fail to satisfy. They arrive too easily, and look and feel too much alike: *nation, elation, relation, ovation, oration* . . . The static -*ation* portion of the word—five letters, two syllables—often overbears and eclipses the rest. That said, I do remain fond of the earliest dirty joke I remember hearing. It was something of a sensation. Perhaps it was the first one I ever understood:

> A man's determination
> Is to stick his boneration
> Up a woman's separation
> And increase the population
> Of this ever-growing nation!

I must confess this still hits the bone—the little boy's funny bone. It's somehow fitting that the poem's one moment of inspiration arises when confronting the delicate, indelicate task of coining a term for a man's "thing."

Every rhyming language is going to have its *June/moon* equivalents. Nabokov deftly amplifies the point in "An Evening of Russian Poetry," whose poet-speaker is a lecturer on Russian literature introducing an American audience to the character and quirks of his native verse. Nabokov, too, speaks of rhyme poverty, though his Russian examples differ from ours:

> The rhyme is the line's birthday, as you know,
> And there are certain customary twins
> In Russian as in other tongues. For instance,
> Love automatically rhymes with blood,
> Nature with liberty, sadness with distance,
> Humane with everlasting, prince with mud,

Moon with a multitude of words, but sun
And song and wind and life and death with none.

Italian is frequently described as a rhyme-rich language,
and if we take our five key terms, the contrast is pointed. An
Italian rhyming dictionary gives me thirty-seven companions
to *death* (*morte*), including the Italian equivalents of *strong, comfort, report, stocks, contort, cakes, sort, piano* . . . And *life*? The possible companions to *life* (*vita*) number in the hundreds, perhaps
thousands. And still more for *amore* . . .

How is the rhyming English-language poet, or the English language itself, to compete with *la bella lingua*? Only by
venturing in a contrary direction. If we're no match for quantity, we must look to quality: to the existence of particularly
rewarding sets of English rhyme. We've already seen how the
complexities of English spelling offer an unexpected boon,
providing a trove of hidden rhymes. But spelling is only an
offshoot of a larger phenomenon: our language's hospitality
to new vocabulary from all over the globe, tuned to its own
distinguishing sounds and structures. In some now-forgotten
poem I once came upon the rhyme of *yep* and *schlep* and
thought, There's something appealingly American in that.
(And it's American as well that *schlep* can flexibly be spelled
shlep, shlepp, or *schlepp.*)

In particular, our rhyme is enriched by our language's
hospitality toward dense consonant clusters, which breed
quirky sonic effects. My students are skeptical when I tell
them that they all know a word of nine letters that contains
eight consonants. The word is *strengths*. These consonant clusters regularly allow for an extraordinary closeness of rhyme
that isn't, quite, exact rhyme.

If, desperate for a fresh rhyme for *death*, I seize upon

breadth, one can only marvel at how near to rhyme the two are. So lightly, so smoothly, the *d* in *breadth* glides by—and yet it wrenches the two words apart, ever so slightly. The letter *d,* like the letter *b* in *breadth,* is what phoneticians call a "voiced consonant," meaning its utterance sets the voice box reverberating, so that while *death* sets up a single tingle, *breadth,* with its *b* and *d,* provides a pair. It is, physiologically, a different sort of rhyme. *Breath* and *breadth* may be separated by only a hairsbreadth, but it's a vibrating hair.

Something similar happens in Ira Gershwin's lyric to George's marvelous "Someone to Watch Over Me":

> Though he may not be the man some
> Girls think of as handsome
> To my heart he carries the key

Man some/handsome . . . It isn't an exact rhyme—or is it? Again, we have a gentle, insistently insinuating *d*—tugging apart the rhyming pair. On the other hand, you might say it *is* exact, a reflection of how we actually speak. When talking rapidly, most people say *hansome* rather than *handsome*—as though, like a good Victorian, you were summoning a hansom cab. If it's an exact rhyme, it's one to which an asterisk is attached, and it turns out that (a) English offers many, many rhymes with asterisks attached and (b) quite a few are among the most interesting rhymes the language supplies.

Just how close can two words come to rhyming without rhyming? Here are the first stanzas of Auden's "Carry Her Over the Water":

> Carry her over the water,
> And set her down under the tree,

Where the culvers white all day and all night,
   And the winds from every quarter,
Sing agreeably, agreeably, agreeably of love.

Put a gold ring on her finger,
   And press her close to your heart,
While the fish in the lake their snapshots take,
   And the frog, that sanguine singer,
Sings agreeably, agreeably, agreeably of love.

It's a complex little structure, making use of off rhyme (*water/ quarter*), internal rhyme (*white/night*; *lake/take*), exact rhyme (*finger/singer*). Except . . . except that *finger/singer*, if you listen closely, isn't truly exact. The *g* in *finger* gets fully sounded; the *g* in *singer* doesn't, disappearing into an *ng* combination that phoneticians call an "eng."

To my ear, none of the following pairings exactly rhyme, though it's hard to imagine how they could come much closer: *nation/Asian*; *myths/widths*; *beginner/win her*; *crowns/ pounds* ("Give crowns and pounds and guineas, / But not your heart away"—Housman); *holy/solely*; *various/marry us*; *boast to/ close to* (Doris Day singing, "Someday I'll find / Someone I can boast to / Somebody to hug, a bug in a rug / To snuggle up close to"). There is a slight tension to all such pairings. Having grown up in a tradition of exact rhyme, the reader may seek to smooth out and "perfect" irregularities by minimally bending pronunciation. Meanwhile, since poetry also brings out the precisionist in us, encouraging us to enunciate more sharply, we're contrarily tempted to heighten and exaggerate all such minor discrepancies.

Poets love small tensions—thrive on them—and are forever contriving ways to exploit them for subtle effect. Minor variations of this sort are a godsend.

Look at the opening of "To My More Than Meritorious Wife" by John Wilmot, Earl of Rochester (1647–1680):

> I am, by fate, slave to your will
> And shall be most obedient still.
> To show my love, I will compose ye
> For your fair finger's ring, a posy,
> In which shall be expressed my duty,
> And how I'll be forever true t'ye.

Our earl is pushing his luck—pushing his reader—in asking you to turn *compose ye* and *posy* into an exact rhyme, but you can pretty much do it. Then, in spirited fun, he goes himself one better, with *duty* and *true t'ye*. Really?

Something similar is unfolding, not with phonetics this time but with stress, in the final stanza of Hardy's "I Look into My Glass," in which the poet laments how age strips his capacity for romance even while leaving his ardor intact:

> But Time, to make me grieve,
> Part steals, lets part abide;
> And shakes this fragile frame at eve
> With throbbings of noontide.

Again, we have an exact rhyme—or nearly so. A desire for tidiness encourages us to mispronounce *noontide*, laying the stress on its final syllable. But meaning and convention tug us otherwise, and the result is a rhyming tussle mirroring the tumult within the breast of the poet.

It's in moments of small tension like these, whether the agitated rhymes are larky, as in Rochester, or deadly serious, as in Hardy, that we glimpse the compensation our language offers us for its rhyme-poor alternatives: a surpassing opulence of shading, an array of exquisite subtleties along the rhyming continuum. Rhymed English naturally fosters minuscule variation, gradational nicety.

Our prosodic vocabulary does us no favors, typically dividing the world all too bluntly into exact and off rhyme. The Funesians, of course, have separate terms to distinguish phonetic difference (*duty/true t'ye*) from metrical tension (*abide/noontide*). They have coinages for a broad range of auditory phenomena for which we lack nomenclature. And the existence of such terms makes it easier for them to analyze poetry in detail. To their minds, the rest of us remain trapped in a painful paradox: *not properly hearing words because we lack the words to describe what we hear.*

One task of the reader of English rhymed poetry, then, is to overcome our shortage of critical language, and to register distinctions for which we lack terminology. Assume tomorrow you come upon a poem rhyming *drive* and *derive*. On the one hand, you could call it an exact rhyme, and yet there's something distinctive and odd about it. And if the same poem were to rhyme *prayed* and *parade* and *blow* and *below*, we might begin to hypothesize that the poet had a weird and wonderful bug in his ear; he was after something particular and peculiar, in this case a rhyme in which the second word seems forcibly stretched or twisted out of the first. For purposes of this chapter, let's call this "stretched rhyme." Some more examples: *plight* and *polite*; *sport* and *support*; *crowed* and *corrode*; *slightly* and *so lightly*. (Readers of a Funesian sharpness of ear will note that I slipped *slightly* and *so lightly* into the same sentence a few pages back.) It would be possible, I suppose, to compile a poem exclusively in couplets of stretched rhyme. I don't know how much sense our poem would make, but its music would be unlike that of any other poem you've ever read. Or one could reverse the process, with the shorter rhyme word arriving second, so that instead of sounds being stretched, we'd create a music of condensation: *filet* and *flay*, *succumb* and *scum*, *terrain* and *train*. Let's call this "compressed rhyme."

My point is, we have far more possibilities of rhyme than we have names for, or systematic examples of. It's one of the primary reasons why the Funesians are so fond of poetry in English. With rhyme, as with meter, our poets have traditionally worked within a narrow purview. But around the murky peripheries of the traditional canon, where much less mapping has been done and the winding streets are a tease and a tangle, overheard whispers go round and round in an intercourse queer and charismatic.

The poet aspiring to work in either stretched rhyme or compressed rhyme would immediately hit a substantial obstacle: Most words are not amenable either to stretching or to compression. The poet would face rhyme poverty of the severest sort. Yet this image of the experimenting poet is so appealing, so promising! He crystallizes our intricate relationship with rhyme, with its frustrating, fertile combinations of poverty and richness.

In the history of English rhyme, Byron is the great pioneer. He's best known for his exaggerated or outlandish rhymes: *apartment/art meant* or *Paris/war is*. This sort of rhyming was hardly his invention, and it's instructive to see, a century and a half before, a staid personage like John Milton in one of his sonnets rhyming *Tetrachordon* with *pored on* and *word on* and *Gordon*. But to my mind, Byron was the first to make brilliant use of the great discovery referred to in the last chapter: Rhyme might best be viewed not in terms of words but of syllables.

Byron regularly trampled over lexical boundaries, ignoring the spaces between words: *welcome* and *hell come, prided* and *I did, luck holds* and *cuckolds*. He regularly spotted hidden resemblances among differences, endlessly testing whether one clump of sounds came close enough to another to posit a rhyme. His rhyming of *bewildering* and *children* looks like a bit of a stretch, though he may well have heard someone say *bewild'rin'*, in which case he was pretty close to an exact rhyme. He kept his ears out. (Ira Gershwin committed still greater violence against *children* in *Porgy and Bess*'s "It Ain't Necessarily So": "They tell all your chillun / The devil he's a villain.")

Others before Byron had done this sort of thing, too, but nobody had pursued it with his thoroughness and ferocity of purpose. He seemed to be testing the potential for rhyme in every word that came his way, not merely for its terminal sound but also for the music of its entrails. A host of brilliant light-verse writers (William Mackworth Praed, Arthur Guiterman, Ogden Nash) and song lyricists (W. S. Gilbert, Johnny Mercer, Stephen Sondheim) can fairly be seen as Byron's progeny.

Working with the flexible, fundamental building block of the syllable, he was hearing the great flow of language as no predecessor quite had perhaps, pure sound all but independent of meaning. Compared to his peers, Byron was a Funesian, hearing what others did not. I envision him, on social occasions, suddenly turning vacant and abstracted when a word materialized whose rhyming potential he hadn't explored. Someone in his company would say *philosopher* and a light would go on inside him: *loss of her.* Or *individual,* and he would hear *widow all.* Or *bodices* and *Odysseys.* These rhymes, and so many more, are scattered through the roughly sixteen thousand lines of *Don Juan.* To read it aloud in entirety is to feel yourself in the presence of someone gripped by a marvelous obsession, a passion for disassembly and recombination.

Don Juan is perhaps the greatest emblem we have of both the richness and the poverty of English rhyme. The poem is written in ottava rima, which consists of eight pentameter lines rhymed ABABABCC. On the one hand, Byron is forever spinning out creative pairings. On the other, he's only forty-eight stanzas into the first canto when he reuses the B rhymes of his first stanza, *new one/true one/Juan,* and he reuses them again, in the same order, a few pages later. Throughout the seventeen cantos, rhyme repetition is rife. Again and again Byron reaches for close-at-hand, dependable pairings. But if inspiration frequently flags, Byron had an astonishing gift for revitalization; I don't know of another long poem that so continually falters and recharges.

In the poem's infectious air of compulsion, *Don Juan* seems not merely a great rhymed poem but the great monument to English rhyme itself. Seventeen sizable cantos—and Byron's tale clearly was nowhere near finished. Oh, he wanted to go on matchmaking forever: linking up another rhyme, and another, and another, pair by pair, while the world stormed and thundered around him. He would lodge every discoverable rhyme creature in the shelter of the vast ark of his epic. The search was intended to be exhaustive. Had he only had his way, had he lived forever, he wouldn't have left a single creature behind.

CHAPTER THIRTEEN

Rhymes, and How We
Really Talk

Natalie Cole had her biggest hit, "Unforgettable," back
in 1991. It was a semiposthumous duet, her voice over-
lain upon a track her father, Nat King Cole, had recorded
forty years before. When his daughter's single emerged, he'd
been dead for a quarter century. Many critics felt unnerved by
this electronic resurrection—or professed to feel so. I wasn't
bothered by it. I was bothered, though, by the song's rhymes:

> That's why, darling, it's incredible
> That someone so unforgettable
> Thinks that I am unforgettable too

The careless blurring of *d*'s and *t*'s—well, the purist in me
disapproved. The song was first published in 1951, melody
and lyrics by Irving Gordon. It belonged to a Tin Pan Alley
tradition of scrupulosity about rhyme and pronunciation, and
Gordon was letting the side down. (What would Cole Porter
say?) Admittedly, this tradition was doomed to dwindle and
fade with the ascendancy of rock and roll—but why hasten

its departure? Gordon loathed rock, which he claimed was built not of "melodies but maladies." So why was the lyric so sloppy?

Over the years, my opinion reversed. The humble truth (I eventually conceded) is that I don't pronounce the *t*'s as *t*'s in *unforgettable*. And as I listen to those around me, it seems nobody else does, either. We all say *unforgeddable*. When, for experimentation's sake, I tried pronouncing those *t*'s crisply, I winced. How stilted and pretentious and (I'd like to think) un-me I sounded!

Bowing to this reality, I was pointed to another of the boons of rhyme. Pay close attention, and it discloses what we really sound like. Forget how the letters of a word suggest we *ought* to speak. Rhyme is a realist. Rhyme is an expansive rapper. Rhyme is a restless testing ground, continually thrusting random syllables together, just to see how they get along, and it operates with few preconceptions. The wag who in the 1980s came up with *fuhgeddaboudit* as a reflection of New York speech was demonstrating a cunning keenness of ear. Riding the subway in Brooklyn, climbing out of a cab in Manhattan, waiting in a deli line in the Bronx, do you hear the King's English? Fuhgeddaboudit. It's a coinage sprung from life, and appropriately it rhymes—almost—with *crowded*.

We arrive at one of those small tensions so enriching to the poet: rhyme in practice versus rhyme in theory, the recurrent gap between daily speech and our expectations about how a poem's words should be voiced. The other day a painted truck rumbled past me, touting protection from identity theft: *Don't Sweat It—Shred It*. The truck belonged to a paper-shredding business—and perhaps to a language-shredding business as well. Were they rhyming exactly, or inexactly, and did they care? The slogan was once more sparking a lively question: How do we really talk?

Or take *identity*. (It's what cyberthieves do: They take identity.) Has the word's pronunciation been stolen from it over the years? If writing a poem, I might well rhyme *identity* with *entity*, and feel by doing so I'd laid down a perfect rhyme. But in everyday speech, especially of the rapid sort, I don't pronounce *identity* with two snappy *t*'s. I'm more likely to say *idendidy* or even *idenidy*. And yet for reasons appearing wholly illogical, but perhaps reflecting the relative rareness of *entity*, I wouldn't, even in quick conversation, say *enidy*. Two words ideally rhymed on the page wind up less than perfectly partnered in everyday discourse.

There are a host of good reasons for avoiding a stranger's poetry reading, but three come most readily to mind. The first and second are the extreme likelihood that you'll hear the poet declare either that (a) while ebooks are all right in their way, they're no substitute for holding an actual, you know, physical book in your hands or that (b) he/she became a poet because he/she wasn't competent to do anything else. Odds are pretty good you'll hear both. In any case, these observations will be offered as though formulated for the first time.

The third reason for not attending is much the gravest: the probability that what you'll hear will have no discernible link to the way that you, or anyone else you have ever befriended, actually speaks. Welcome to the fearsome "poetry voice" or "poet voice." There are a number of good dissections of it on the internet, including a perceptive and funny piece by Rich Smith ("Stop Using 'Poet Voice'"), though I think he's mistaken in characterizing it as "lilting," with all its dictionary connotations of *spirited, cheerful, pleasant, buoyant*, et cetera. I would describe the voice as one of dry, incurious inquiry: the intonation periodically lifting (not lilting), as though to shape a question, but without the vigor of feeling necessary for any sincere interrogation or investigation.

Yet a serious issue lurks here. The contemporary poet indulging in poet voice might laugh derisively on hearing ancient Ezra Pound reciting verse. (Pound in those scratchy recordings is bardic and expansive and exhortatory, thumping away in a voice seemingly meant to awaken a band of medieval troubadours.) Or might likewise laugh on hearing Tennyson, the first great poet whose voice we have in recording, declaiming in the airy, otherworldly gallop of an unusually excited Houyhnhnm, "Half a league, half a league, half a league onward . . ." Yet the three voices share a core assumption.

Both Pound and Tennyson are insisting that poems deserve a special pitch and timbre. ("God *damn* it all," you can hear Pound saying, "this isn't a newspaper account.") And so is tonight's poet, orating in poet voice. All three are many removes from, say, Marianne Moore, in whose public readings one may occasionally mistake a casual prose aside for her verse: It's all one intonation, odd and offhand and outlandishly wonderful.

How closely does or should poetry live to workaday speech? Schooled as we are in egalitarian notions of the primacy of the man or woman in the street, we may insist, reflexively, that poetry must be rooted in the daily and the demotic. As recalled by Marianne Moore, Pound himself (a great one for issuing potent fiats he himself didn't follow) regularly advised poets "never, NEVER to use any word you would not actually say in moments of utmost urgency." But such notions, however compelling or even self-evident they appear to us, didn't always prevail in the past—perhaps especially in the golden past.

The classicist Bernard Knox regularly reminded his readers that the language of the Homeric epics was miles from everyday utterance. Its unnaturalness extended to word order and formulaic phrasing and a vocabulary that was a holdover from the Bronze Age. The hexameter meter itself operated at a vast remove from its hearers: It was of divine origin, the meter of the gods and the Delphic oracle. The miraculous preservation of the *Iliad* and the *Odyssey,* over some three millennia, is a testament to how profoundly these tales were cherished in, and no doubt for, their artificiality.

Jacques Barzun makes a similar point in *An Essay on French Verse.* In a "severe handicap for the versifier," some of the commonest of all French phrases, including stalwarts like *il y a* and *tu es*, were impermissible in neoclassic verse. The two adjacent vowels were deemed dissonant and displeasing. A poet might remark to his neighbor, in conversation, *"Il y a un poème"* (putting three vowels adjacent), but never to his reader, on the page. Where everyday speech clashed with prosody, and with general perceptions of what was poetically harmonious, everyday speech was duly squelched. An unaffected speaking voice was hardly the poet's goal.

Compilers of dictionaries engage in an endless debate about description versus prescription. Unquestionably, their job is to chronicle usage. But shouldn't they advise us, as well? What does it mean to employ a word incorrectly, and how many people must subscribe to the same error, adopting and embracing it, before we can normalize (itself a word of questionable acceptability) its usage?

Rhyme, too, has a complicated relationship with description and prescription. When Irving Gordon links *unforgettable* and *incredible*, rhyme's role is essentially descriptive. The song is saying, *These two words rhyme in a love song,* or more acutely, *Here's how your average Joe might speak in his infatuation,* or less acutely, *Who cares if the thing rhymes?* But the song has little to say about whether the two words *ought* to rhyme.

Yet there are cases where rhyme assumes an adjudicating role. To my ear, *petal* and *pedal* are not quite homonyms, and in a poem of exact rhymes they should be paired up, respectively, with *metal* and *medal.* Any indiscriminate blending of petals and medals, pedals and metals strikes me as irresponsible and sloppy. At times, surely, careful rhyming consists in determining how words are properly pronounced. If I'm rhyming *glory* with *dormitory,* or *very* with *sanitary,* on some level I'm protesting that muddling British tendency to clip the penultimates off words: dormit'ry, sanit'ry. Sometimes, poets are taking a stand even when they don't realize it. The rhyming poem can serve as a vote, endorsing this or that manner of talking.

Meter, like rhyme, can play a prescriptive function, effectively insisting that we accord each syllable in a polysyllabic word its full articulation. John Updike cited a choice example when reviewing a book of Max Beerbohm's poetry:

On the copyright page of his first book, *The Works of Max Beerbohm,* Max found the imprint

London: john lane, *The Bodley Head*
New York: CHARLES SCRIBNER'S SONS

Beneath it, he wrote in pen:

> This plain announcement, nicely read,
> Iambically runs.

The effortless a-b-a-b rhyming, the balance of "plain" and "nicely," the need for nicety in pronouncing "Iambically" to scan—this is quintessential light verse, a twitting of the starkest prose into perfect form, a marriage of earth with light, and quite magical.

The little joke here is that the word inducing us to read iambically is *iambically*, insisting on wearing the formal attire of its full five syllables. But meter is just as likely, in the process known as elision, to clip a syllable from a word, shortening rather than elongating, as when *heaven* becomes *heav'n* or *over* becomes *o'er*.

A kindred joke arises in a celebrated couplet from *Don Juan*:

> What men call gallantry, and gods adultery,
> Is much more common where the climate's sultry.

A double knowingness leers through the lines. Byron is having fun with an England whose sexual mores he found hypocritical and confining. And also having fun (as Irving Gordon did in "Unforgettable") in reminding us of how we really talk. *Adultery* becomes *adult'ry*, and the couplet would be less appealing if the rhyme were not slightly besmirched.

More than any other poetic device, rhyme attunes us to the marvels and idiosyncracies of the alphabet, the sibling relationships among letters, the tight and tricky cliques they form. We've already seen how proximate *t* and *d* are. The same is true of *m* and *n*, and *f* and *v*. Even the punctilious Alexander Pope occasionally allowed himself to treat them as interchangeable.

The terminology of linguistics—beguilingly colorful, off-puttingly remote—would categorize this rhyming of *m* and *n* as linked nasal occlusives, of *s* and *z* as linked sibilant fricatives, and of *k* and *g* as linked velar plosives. But an ignorance of the terminology hardly impedes an understanding of their functioning. Just as the two-year-old toddler instinctively grasps the nature of the prosodic contract, the rock lyricist, the composer of folk ballads, and the rapper all recognize this network of audio kinships. Lennon and McCartney were forever interchanging *m* and *n:*

Would you believe in a love at first sight?
Yes, I'm certain that it happens all the time.
What do you see when you turn out the light?
I can't tell you, but I know it's mine.

Of all the poet's tools, rhyme is the one that encourages us to listen most attentively. By singing to us of its complexities, it provides ear training. I began this book with Dylan Thomas's "Prologue," where the farthermost rhymes lie more than a hundred lines apart. The poem's motto might be: *Hear Farther, Hear Finer.* And do so via rhyme.

I keep emphasizing rhyme's delicacy, but it can be hardy as crabgrass. Weed it out, it creeps back in. It's forever springing up where it supposedly doesn't belong: in pointedly unrhymed poems. Philip Larkin's "Born Yesterday" is a pretty example, in which the birth of a friend's daughter inspires him to wish for her "an average of talents." Here's the poem's conclusion:

Not ugly, not good-looking,
Nothing uncustomary
To pull you off your balance,
That, unworkable itself,
Stops all the rest from working.
In fact, may you be dull—
If that is what a skilled,
Vigilant, flexible,
Unemphasized, enthralled
Catching of happiness is called.

Throughout, the poem's twenty-four lines play a teasing game with rhyme, including a quiet amassing of *l*'s, but none of its internal workings portend the hefty contented thump of its concluding couplet. (Free-verse poets often resort to rhyme at the finish line—or resort to strict iambics, as T. S. Eliot's "ghost of a meter" rises from the crypt for the closing scene.)

Though Milton banished rhyme at the outset of *Paradise Lost* ("invention of a barbarous age"), with satanic pertinacity it keeps slithering back into his lines:

This horror will grow mild, this darkness light,
Besides what hope the never-ending flight
Of future days may bring . . .

Or:

Allegiance to the acknowledged power supreme?
And thou, sly hypocrite, who now would seem
Patron of liberty . . .

Delicate, hardy; impoverished, opulent; subordinate, primary; natural, artificial; dismissible, indispensable—rhyme is the regal riddle of formal poetry, the gonging gong whose reverberations extend to the farthermost chambers of the palace. It both invites and resists generalization, characterization. Itself a mystery, it partakes of other, broader mysteries. One sometimes sees Tennyson praised as having the finest ear of any English poet. His excesses—his susurrus sumptuosities— aren't to every taste, but for those attuned to his music, his treatment of rhyme is especially gratifying. I know of no other poet whose rhyming so consistently arrives with a sense of rightness and welcome.

Sometimes, the arrival of a particular rhyme pair may seem extra felicitous—over and above its value as wordplay or imagery or sentiment. No, the delight feels purely sonic. It's as though you'd been unconsciously awaiting *these* specific vowel and consonant combinations. As though hoping to meet rhymes that sounded precisely like these.

I'm talking not of individual pairs of words, but of pairs working in conjunction with other pairs, across a stanza, across stanzas. This is the higher harmonics of rhyme, the way pairs of words pair up with other pairs.

Tennyson's "The Lotos-Eaters" is a marvel of individual rhymes conjuring a collective magic, its rhyme clusters singing beautifully to and against each other. It opens this way:

"Courage!" he said, and pointed toward the land,
"This mounting wave will roll us shoreward soon."
In the afternoon they came unto a land
In which it seemed always afternoon.
All round the coast the languid air did swoon,

Breathing like one that hath a weary dream.
Full-faced above the valley stood the moon;
And like a downward smoke, the slender stream
Along the cliff to fall and pause and fall did seem.

Why *are* these rhymes so fulfilling? Why does the arrival
of *dream*, rapidly succeeded by *stream* and *seem*, resonate so
gorgeously?

Thirty lines later, Tennyson closes this section with a
stanza refracting the initial stanza, some rhymes unchanged
and some altered:

They sat them down upon the yellow sand,
Between the sun and moon upon the shore;
And sweet it was to dream of Fatherland,
Of child, and wife, and slave; but evermore
Most weary seemed the sea, weary the oar,
Weary the wandering fields of barren foam.
Then someone said, "We will return no more";
And all at once they sang, "Our island home
Is far beyond the wave; we will no longer roam."

Again, the rhymes satisfy not just singly but collectively.
Books about versification sometimes offer extensive scansions
professing to show why a poem's rhythm is so successful. But
I don't know of any systematic attempts to chart or catalog the
broader ways in which rhymes collaborate.

After all, where would one start? It appears an impossible task, for rhyme is a shape-shifter. It isn't as though an
eam necessarily sounds wonderful when following an *oon*,
though certainly in "The Lotos-Eaters" *dream* is wonderful
after *swoon*, just as *foam* is wonderful after *oar*. All one can say

with confidence is that when reading long swaths of Tennyson it's remarkable how often a rhyme will (I take my image
from "The Lotos-Eaters") break over you in a kind of retar-
dive drug rush.

One word pairs with another to form a rhyme pair. A
rhyme pair pairs with a rhyme pair to form a rhyme cluster. A rhyme cluster mingles with a rhyme cluster to form
harmonics wider still—the sort of comprehensive music you
experience in "The Lotos-Eaters." And what principally
moves and inspires you escapes analysis. The critic is forced to
resort to mere exhibition and summary: "Isn't this a fine passage?" Or, "And what about this one?" Some pleasures simply
don't systemize, normalize, finalize, or submit to any other
izing by the world's *izers.*

Those lotos-eaters could be dismissed as a bunch of drug-
gies, I suppose, destined to accomplish nothing throughout
their endless, ongoing afternoon. Yet in their fecklessness
they inspired a magnificent poet, who pitched all his indefatigable industry into memorializing the charms of languor and
lassitude. The poem is a parade of paradoxes.

When it comes to some of the greatest poems in our language, not even the Funesians, for all their love of system and
pattern, have a way to discuss these broader varieties of auditory behavior. From their Andean fastness, contemplatively
sipping their rhubarb brandy, the Funesians regard those
distant cousins of theirs—the lotos-eaters—with a grateful
befuddlement.

▣

CHAPTER FOURTEEN

Off Rhyme:
When Good Rhymes Go Bad

I'm tempted to observe that all exact rhymes are alike, and all off rhymes are off in their own off way. Off rhyme supplies the poet with a wild assortment of effects—discordancy, slovenliness, attenuation, unpredictability, silliness—rarely open to the more decorous exact rhyme. Action picks up when good rhymes go bad.

Philip Larkin once wrote a lament about employment. (This preceded his longtime tenure in a library in the not notably chic northern English city of Hull.) He titled the poem "Toads," and defiantly inquired, "Why should I let the toad *work* / Squat on my life?"

Some years later, now an irreproachable librarian, he composed "Toads, Revisited." This time around, the pathway of steady, routine employment looked more palatable. After all, how on earth would he fill his days without a job? He thoroughly disliked travel—as well as exercising, meeting new people, and any societal phenomenon likely to be described as an "advance." As a depressive, Larkin was unnerved by the prospect of any stretch of idle days.

Though he might fantasize about chucking everything and venturing to a tropical Pacific where "native girls" teach you how "to execute / Sixteen sexual positions on the sand," this daydream yielded only to "Nippers; the widowed mum; having to scheme / with money; illness, age." Start where you will, you wind up in the same fix.

Reality was no tropical idyll. It was, in fact, the urban idle of "Toads, Revisited," those seedy fellows found in chilly city parks who have nothing to do, nothing to wish for. Did he really want to become

> one of the men
> You meet of an afternoon:
> Palsied old step-takers,
> Hare-eyed clerks with the jitters,
>
> Waxed-fleshed out-patients
> Still vague from accidents,
> And characters in long coats
> Deep in the litter-baskets . . .

He tried putting himself in their position:

> Think of being them!

> Turning over their failures
> By some bed of lobelias . . .

Well, here is one of my favorite rhymes anyone ever came up with: *failures/lobelias*. The pair of them denote and exemplify failure: incompetence, laxness, ill-fittingness. Just imagine how much less gratifying the lines would be if *lobelias* turned a crisp and efficient exact rhyme, rather than a lame and limp substitute. Sad and pathetic though you now may appear, reader, whoever you are, you'd hit a new low if characterized by *failures* and *lobelias*.

Something similar occurs in one of Anthony Hecht's poems about the Holocaust, " 'More Light! More Light!,' " which presents a nightmarish account of a Polish Gentile commanded by a Nazi to bury alive a pair of Jews. The poem opens with clean, perfect xAxA rhymes, but something goes amiss at the close:

> No light, no light in the blue Polish eye.
> When he finished a riding boot packed down the earth.
> The Lüger hovered lightly in its glove.
> He was shot in the belly and in three hours bled to
>   death.
>
> No prayers or incense rose up in those hours
> Which grew to be years, and every day came mute
> Ghosts from the ovens, sifting through crisp air,
> And settled upon his eyes in a black soot.

As the atrocity deepens, the rhymes turn remote and harsh. That *soot* falls with a sticky, ineradicable ugliness.

Off rhyme burgeoned in the twentieth century, presenting itself as a simple variant or alternative to exact rhyme. Historical associations clung to it, however. It still retains an air of inadequacy, associations of incompetence or shortcoming—associations Larkin and Hecht seize upon.

Something similar occurs in Robert Graves's "Love Without Hope," perhaps my favorite four-line poem:

Love without hope, as when the young bird-catcher
Swept off his tall hat to the squire's own daughter,
So let the imprisoned larks escape and fly
Singing about her head, as she rode by.

We don't expect melodiousness from our rustic. It's a raggedy
rhyme, *bird-catcher* and *daughter*, as we'd expect, for his is no
debonair top hat he doffs in besotted veneration. It's a thing
of shapeless homespun, besprinkled with soil and grass and
bird droppings. We offer our goddesses not what they grandly
deserve but what we meagerly possess, and the faulty rhyme is
all the more touching for its humility.

Exact rhyme is positive, solid, *good*, and off rhyme negative, shaky, questionable—so are the assumptions explored in
George Herbert's lovely "Denial." You might even say the
poem's true subject (or most interesting subject) is off rhyme.
There are six five-line stanzas, each but the last marred by a
discordant terminal line left hanging, awkward and unpartnered. Here are the first two stanzas:

When my devotions could not pierce
Thy silent ears,
Then was my heart broken, as was my verse;
My breast was full of fears
And disorder.

My bent thoughts, like a brittle bow,
Did fly asunder:
Each took his way; some would to pleasures go,
Some to the wars and thunder
Of alarms.

Yet everything is rectified in the sixth and final stanza. The first five are essentially a report or account, a chronicle of spiritual disconnection. The sixth stanza is something else again: a prayer, a positive stride of faith and exhortation and renewal.

> O cheer and tune my heartless breast,
> Defer no time;
> That so thy favors granting my request,
> They and my mind may chime,
> And mend my rhyme.

Herbert's prayer is answered tacitly, internally. All will be well, surely, now that rhyme is reestablished in its proper station. The journey of the entire poem is encapsulated in the closing word of the first and final stanzas: we progress from *disorder* to *rhyme*. Through God's grace we are mended, both spiritually and prosodically.

Emily Dickinson was the first great English-language poet to place off rhyme front and center in her verse. At times, often in her best poems, off rhyme seems not merely an equal companion but the dominant partner, as in this little gem:

> The Bustle in a House
> The Morning after Death
> Is solemnest of industries
> Enacted upon Earth—
>
> The Sweeping up the Heart
> And putting Love away
> We shall not want to use again
> Until eternity—

Dickinson's promotion of off rhyme was a surreptitiously bold move—the act of a venturesome recluse. In the literary culture she grew up within, off rhyme suggested lack of polish, lack of education, lack of a well-tuned ear, even the lack, as Herbert's "Denial" suggests, of moral uprightness or fitness. Even so, she embraced it. The negative connotations of off rhyme were painfully demonstrated in the editorial efforts, both during her lifetime and posthumously, to repair her verse. Of these, perhaps the most notorious, or at least humorous, arose with the poem "I taste a liquor never brewed," which appeared during her lifetime in the *Springfield Republican*. Here is the poem's first stanza as she wrote it:

> I taste a liquor never brewed—
> From Tankards scooped in Pearl—
> Not all the Frankfort Berries
> Yield such an Alcohol!

And here is the newspaper version:

> I taste a liquor never brewed—
> From Tankards scooped in Pearl—
> Not Frankfort berries yield the sense
> Such a delicious whirl!

In one abstemious, though quite intemperate, stroke, Miss Dickinson was doubly smartened up: rescued from any unwomanly taint of "alcohol" and liberated of the impurities of off rhyme.

There are times when her verse passes through the looking glass into a complementary domain where off rhyme is the norm and exact rhyme the anomaly. New vantages on

English-language poetry open up: a domain where exact rhyme strikes with the force of rarity, as in one of her most haunting poems, here in its entirety:

I heard a Fly buzz—when I died—
The Stillness in the Room
Was like the Stillness in the Air—
Between the Heaves of Storm—

The Eyes around—had wrung them dry—
And Breaths were gathering firm
For that last Onset—when the King
Be witnessed—in the Room—

I willed my Keepsakes—Signed away
What portion of me be
Assignable—and then it was
There interposed a Fly—

With Blue—uncertain—stumbling Buzz—
Between the light—and me—
And then the Windows failed—and then
I could not see to see—

It's not until the final line that one of her quatrains offers an exact rhyme, though when it comes, it comes with the brilliant pummeling redundancy of *see to see.*

Yeats published almost no sonnets in his lifetime, but—Yeats being Yeats—"Leda and the Swan" is one of the best we have. The swan is almighty Zeus, festooned in feathered disguise: He is determined, incognito, to have his way with the lovely mortal Leda. Their copulation is sometimes depicted as seduction, but in Yeats's hands it's rape. The poem leaps right in: "A sudden blow."

The myth has numerous variants, but Leda is generally depicted as the mother of both Helen, whose beauty triggered the Trojan War, and Clytemnestra, who, after the war's successful conclusion (speaking from a Hellenic perspective), conspired to murder her husband, Agamemnon, commander of the Greek forces. Here is the sonnet's conclusion:

> A shudder in the loins engenders there
> The broken wall, the burning roof and tower
> And Agamemnon dead.
>   Being so caught up,
> So mastered by the brute blood of the air,
> Did she put on his knowledge with his power
> Before the indifferent beak could let her drop?

In one quaking moment of coitus, we have the birth not merely of legendary beauty (Helen) but of—so much vaster, so much more beautiful—the *Iliad*, the *Odyssey*, the *Aeneid*, all rooted in the Trojan conflict. As much as any single event could be said to do so, we confront, in a rapt display of violence, Western culture in the climacteric of its conception. And how does the poem conclude? With an off rhyme, a deficient rhyme—I'm tempted to call it, borrowing from the poem's vocabulary, an indifferent rhyme.

Again, imagine the poem in an altered state, with an exact rhyme at the close. We wouldn't need to modify that ravishing final line. We'd need only to locate a clean partner for *drop*—an easy-enough task. *Stop? Prop? Top?* Each might

plausibly be worked into some substitute phrase for "Being so
caught up." Yet how much more satisfying, with a casualness
truly breathtaking, is Yeats's portrayal of a godly and careless
postcoital satiation, content to let the world's fate fall where it
may. I don't know of a more affecting use of off rhyme.

Even now, when off rhyme has supplanted exact rhyme as
the contemporary norm, a vestigial sense of deficiency may
inspire a desire to "fix" its imperfections. Over the years,
many of the phrases that have stubbornly haunted my inner
ear are those in which we're seemingly verging on an exact
rhyme that never, in fact, emerges. I've long loved Theodore
Roethke's miniature "The Young Girl," whose subject pos-
sesses some of the fragile and indomitable jeunesse of Degas's
sculpture *Little Dancer Aged Fourteen*. Here's the poem's conclusion:

> Today I skipped on the shore,
> My eyes neither here nor there,
> My thin arms to and fro,
> A bird my body,
> My bird blood ready.

It's those last two lines that have haunted my head. They
seem to be mustering themselves toward the resolution of an
exact rhyme, but—chime after time—they happily refuse to
resolve.

Refusal is much the point and spirit of MacNeice's "Bag-
pipe Music." The poem keeps summoning conventional wisdom, only to disdain it. But the more interesting refusal is not
thematic but prosodic. There are thirty-four lines, seventeen
clangorously rhyming couplets, but not a single exact rhyme.
Its modus operandi seems to be: any rhyme but a clean rhyme.

The poem's a smithy, where weird and wonderful sounds are hammered out:

John MacDonald found a corpse, put it under the sofa,
Waited till it came to life and hit it with a poker,
Sold its eyes for souvenirs, sold its blood for whiskey,
Kept its bone for dumbbells to use when he was fifty.

It's the caterwauling music of bagpipes; or the caterwauling music of Gaelic strife; or just the thump and screech and yammer of something determined to remain incongruous and impure.

For all the poem's tone of cynicism and resignation, it winds up being a celebration, a far-flung display of the untapped vivacity and variety of off rhyme. How many ways there are to get things wrong!

It's no go my honey love, it's no go my poppet;
Work your hands from day to day, the winds will blow
   the profit.
The glass is falling hour by hour, the glass will fall
   forever,
But if you break the bloody glass you won't hold up the
   weather.

So many ways to get things wrong . . . The other day I read *retinue* and heard *retina*. I began wondering whether there were other off rhymes of this odd and particular contour: two dactyls in which the first two syllables are identical and only the third, an open vowel sound, differs. It turns out there are: *radio/radii*; *curio/curia*; *canopy/canapé*; *enema/enemy*; *manitou/manatee*. (The inexhaustibility of our language seems to guarantee that if you can identify something to search for, however idiosyncratic and obscure, you can find it.)

Just as exact rhyme has a particular music, each individual species of off rhyme, whether common or highly abstruse, creates its own acoustic reality. And just as the music of exact rhyme and off rhyme differ, so does the music differ between one sort of off rhyme and the next. I can't imagine that *retinue/ retina* and rhymes of a similar structure have any prominent place in the future of English poetry. No, this sort of sound lies on the peripheries of the peripheries, and that's the point: There are, out there, far more musical effects than we know how to assimilate.

Of course, the Funesians would have a term for the rare species of dactylic off rhyme represented by *retinue/retina*, and a different term for its mirror image: *epochal/apical*, or *aliment/ element,* or *idiom/odium*. When the lover of poetry opens herself fully to the music of off rhyme, the possibilities do not double or triple: They expand unreckonably.

How distant can two rhymes be and still be called a rhyme? It's a question raised at this book's outset, with Thomas's "Prologue": How many syllables apart can two rhymes lie and still meaningfully address each other?

But distance is not merely a matter of space on the page. It's also a matter of sonic structure. How dissimilar can two words sound and still be musically linked? How "off" can off be and still be deemed a rhyme?

While reading Housman one day, I came to the counterintuitive conclusion that two words could rhyme without having a single sound in common. But didn't rhyme mean resemblance? I'd always assumed that rhyme meant having some minimal phonetic connection, some unit of sound in common.

Housman was fond of rhyming in quatrains, rooted in the ballad stanza, whose rhyme scheme is xAxA. They might look like this:

"Is my team ploughing,
That I was used to drive
And hear the harness jingle
When I was man alive?"

Or this:

From far, from eve and morning
    And yon twelve-winded sky,
The stuff of life to knit me
    Blew hither: here am I.

He wrote some thirty poems in this form (a high proportion of his scanty total) and they are remarkably uniform in structure. The rhymes will be one-syllable masculine rhymes. The unrhymed lines will always conclude with an unstressed syllable, a feminine ending.

In other words, stickler Housman is no less strict about unrhymed lines than about rhymed ones. The unrhymed lines create a pattern of sonic expectation as firm and dependable as rhymed lines. Read all thirty poems, and it grows dawningly obvious that the unrhymed lines are echoing each other just as surely, if far more quietly, than the rhymed lines:

Now Dick lies long in the churchyard,
    And Ned lies long in jail,
And I come home to Ludlow
    Amidst the moonlight pale.

Or:

> Her strong enchantments failing,
>   Her towers of fear in wreck,
> Her limbecks dried of poisons
>   And the knife at her neck . . .

Or:

> In the morning, in the morning,
>   In the happy field of hay,
> Oh they looked at one another
>   By the light of day.

Or:

> Because I liked you better
>   Than suits a man to say,
> It irked you, and I promised
>   To throw the thought away.

The effect grows sharper with time. Clearly, the first and third lines, no less than the second and fourth, are echo mates. And what is a rhyme if not an echo? If this isn't a rhyme, how shall we speak of the way lines one and three, no less than two and four, musically address each other? Lines one and three create a pattern of expectations, a waited-for sound. Midway through the poem, a reader can predict how all four lines of the next stanza will fall out. We have a prosodic contract.

The second and fourth lines can be depended upon to rhyme exactly. (Among the English greats, few eschewed off rhyme so strictly as Housman when an exact rhyme seemed called for.) But Housman was equally careful to ensure that lines one and three do *not* rhyme; typically they are not off rhymes in the traditional sense, but what we'd normally think of as an unrhymed pair. What lines one and three have in common is nothing but a vague rumble that goes DUM-da. That's all. DUM-da. If we think of musical instruments, this isn't the sound of strings or woodwinds or brass. It's the bang of percussion.

And so the thirty poems proceed: as strict as strict can be in lines two and four, and strictly loose, so to speak, in lines one and three. Housman is consistently taking rhyme out to its liminal outskirts. Off rhyme wanders further off, and off still further, becoming less a sound than an acoustical nudge, a scratchy rumor. And if you're fortunate, it awakens you.

CHAPTER FIFTEEN

Rim Rhyme

Of all exact rhymes in English, which one is funda-mental? Which the most popular or emblematic or prominent—the one to represent rhyme in general? A num-ber of plausible candidates declare themselves, but no clear victor. *Moon* and *June* have come to symbolize the comfy clamor of old-fashioned rhyming. *Breath* and *death* may be the neatest way we have of distinguishing the quick from the dead. *Life* and *wife* have the dual advantage of evoking either the centrality of spousal living or—especially in the hands of the satirist—the suffocations of matrimony.

But turn from the sprawling empire of exact rhyme to the modest principality of rim rhyme—that variant set of rhyme, like *light* and *late* or *sickened* and *second*, where consonants are held steady while internal vowels are shifted—and we do find a basic, an ur-rhyme: *live* and *love*. It holds clear pride of place. "Come live with me and be my love," Christopher Marlowe invites us in the first line of one of the best-loved poems in the English language, "The Passionate Shepherd to His Love." The poem inspired Sir Walter Raleigh's rejoinder, "The Nymph's Reply to the Shepherd," which concludes

Then these delights my mind might move
To live with thee and be thy love.

The rhyme is potentially all the richer because *live* is so
flexible—so lively. It offers dual pronunciations, and comes
in various permutations: *relive, alive, outlive*, et cetera. If we
needed a pairing to characterize the human condition, bundling together earthly burdens and celestial ambitions, how
could we improve upon *live* and *love*? (The French might reply
that their prime rim rhyme is even richer than ours: *l'amour*
and *la mort*. And richer still for, in the background, the mur-
murs of *la mer*, and the ministrations of *la mère*.)

We've already seen that English rhymes often run scarce
in the fields of greatest ardor for the poet. *Life, death, money,
sex, beauty, loss, work, youth, verse, passion*—all are rhyme-poor.
But the shortage is still more biting when we turn from exact
to rim rhyme. Rim rhymes for *work* or *youth*? For *verse*? For
passion? (I predict a love *potion*.) Stymied, the rim rhymer may
be driven into silence.

One noble exception is *love*, which comes alive with possibilities (*alive* being but one). If *love* lacks exact rhymes, it
abounds in handy rim rhymes. And something similar happens with *God*, whose exact rhymes are few and impractical.
But with *guide* and *goad* and—especially—*good*, God wel-
comes a new and logical and pliant set of partners.

Rim rhyme in English has a puzzling history. Why did
it take so long to come into its own? It has been around forever, or thereabouts (Marlowe's "Passionate Shepherd" dates
back to the sixteenth century), tolling like a bell (ding-dong)
or a clock (tick-tock) across the pastoral landscape of English
verse. But it wasn't employed regularly and systematically
until Wilfred Owen's poems of the Great War.

Owen's work offers a prime example of poetic innovation coinciding with transformations in the world order. Our
planet had never seen anything like the Great War, both in its
global outreach and its bizarre, terrifying weaponry (crawling
armored vehicles, poison gas, aerial bombardment). Nor had
it heard anything quite like Owen's music:

It seemed that out of battle I escaped
Down some profound dull tunnel, long since scooped
Through granites which titanic wars had groined.

Yet also there encumbered sleepers groaned,
Too fast in thought or death to be bestirred.
Then, as I probed them, one sprang up, and stared
With piteous recognition in fixed eyes . . .

These odd rhymes burn and blazon. The poem, "Strange
Meeting," recounts a ghostly encounter between two soldiers,
one alive and the other dead. As the living man's victim, the
deceased has final say:

"I am the enemy you killed, my friend.
I knew you in this dark, for so you frowned
Yesterday through me as you jabbed and killed.
I parried; but my hands were loath and cold."

But the title might equally invoke the encounter between
audience and text. It was a strange meeting indeed when readers first came upon English poems that made extensive and
systematic use of a rhyme sufficiently unfamiliar that Owen
felt justified in giving it a fresh name: pararhyme. (The name
has not lodged deep: Though found in the *Concise Oxford Dictionary*, it doesn't appear in *Webster's*.)

I've never been able to determine who coined the alternative term rim rhyme, which is a shame, for some anonymous wordsmith deserves our applause. Neatly embodying the concept it would convey (as *trochee* does, by being trochaic), rim rhyme is much the most nimble and ingenious of all prosodic terms. Notwithstanding the Owen examples above, it works best, I think, when its effects are soft-spoken, as in his brief two-stanza "Futility," to me the most affecting lines he ever composed:

Move him into the sun—
Gently its touch awoke him once,
At home, whispering of fields half-sown.
Always it woke him, even in France,
Until this morning and this snow.
If anything might rouse him now
The kind old sun will know.

Think how it wakes the seeds—
Woke once the clays of a cold star.
Are limbs, so dear-achieved, are sides
Full-nerved, still warm, too hard to stir?
Was it for this the clay grew tall?
—O what made fatuous sunbeams toil
To break earth's sleep at all?

Rim rhyme was embraced by Auden (the greatest of all magpies in English verse, his capacious nest a brilliant weave of others' plumage), but it came into fullest finery with James Merrill. No other poet in English took rim rhyme so close to his heart, distributed it more broadly and suavely.

Rim rhyme is fiendishly difficult to employ with any

sense of naturalness. Yet it seemed to bloom effortlessly for
Merrill. The world is overstocked with iambic pentameter
quatrains, and here is another, but note the crucial rhyming
difference:

> The last chord fades. The night is cold and fine.
> His master's voice rasps through the grooves' bare
>   groves.
> Obediently, in silence like the grave's
> He sleeps there on the still-warm gramophone . . .

(One must commend, in passing, Merrill's panache in going
himself one better with the additional, internal *grooves'* and
groves.)

I've had students who sally right past such rhymes—who
fail to hear them. They're deaf partly through lack of previous
exposure. Rim rhymes are rare in children's verse and nursery rhymes, with the notable exception of Betty Botter, who
bought some butter:

> "But," she said, "the butter's bitter;
> If I put it in my batter
> It will make my batter bitter;
> But a bit of better butter
> Will but make my batter better."

Typically, when rim rhymes do appear in children's verse,
their arrival seems more happenstance than design. And
they're rare in the standard anthologies of adult poetry; other
than Owen's verse, there isn't a single poem in the two most
recent editions of *The Oxford Book of English Verse* in which
rim rhyme predominates.

At bottom, the rarity may be a structural issue. Rim rhyme is architecturally peculiar. As we've seen, traditional rhyme moves from difference to similarity, and the paradigmatic exact rhyme looks like this: $C_1V_1C_2/C_3V_1C_2$. Rim rhyme follows a different arc. It moves from similarity to difference and back to similarity: $C_1V_1C_2/C_1V_2C_2$. Or if the mathematical look of these figures is off-putting, think of a rim rhyme as a pair of sandwiches in which the bread stays the same but you change the filling. However you envision it, rim rhyme has a different feel and sound from exact rhyme. You might say that Owen was introducing into the orchestra of English-language verse a new instrument, liberating new sonorities.

But what sort of instrument was it, exactly? What was the young Owen (dead at the age of twenty-five, killed at the Battle of the Sambre, a week before the armistice) so brashly introducing? Rim rhyme is innately quieter than exact rhyme, as a consequence of the engineering of the human ear. In an exact rhyme, the shared content is typically a vowel (*my/why*) or a vowel and consonant (*might/white*). The shared content in a rim rhyme is purely consonantal. The difference has consequences. Vowels speak more distinctly, more forcibly, than consonants.

As hearing declines, aging folks learn to distrust consonants as evasive and tricky. Consonants are far more likely to foster mistakes—potentially embarrassing mistakes—than the more trustworthy vowels, which hang in the air. Vowels can sing in a literal sense; lyricists understand that long musical notes favor open vowels. Most consonants disappear as soon as spoken, and attempts to extend them can be painfully comic. No singer, however profound his passion, wishes to stand onstage belting out his lovvvvve; he'd much prefer to declare that he loves youuuuuu.

If rim rhyme is exact rhyme's weaker, paler sibling, it compensates, as younger and weaker siblings often will, by cultivating cunning. It carries a hint of cleverness and polish, endearing it to admen, journalists out for catchy headlines, Hollywood producers (*King Kong, Legally Blonde*), popular songwriters ("Begin the Beguine"), junk-food confectioners (Kit-Kat bars, Fiddle Faddle, Jim Jams).

Rim rhyme settles itself subtly, often on-site when you don't quite realize it's there. It emerges slowly—last but not least. It can be as furtive, and as abiding, as the man in the moon.

There's pleasure, too, in tracing how rim rhyme reflects and irregularly refracts the much larger class of exact rhyme. Their two worlds are and are not the same.

They behave similarly as regards spelling. With rim rhyme, as with exact rhyme, we savor the pairing whose spelling diverges, so that linked words don't immediately announce a rhyme (*feign/phone/fine*). A woman student in one of my classes once complimented another's blouse: "It's a killer color," she declared, and suddenly *I* liked the color better.

Things are similar, too, as regards ironic opposition: the joy we take in rhymed antonyms and words of inimical association. Just as there's pleasure in rhyming *night* and *bright*, or *cat* and *rat*, there's fun in *fit* and *fat*, *soul* and *soil*, *rich* and *wretch*. Rim rhyme opens to the poet a playground for fresh recreation.

The two schools part ways, however, when we look to the use and overuse of rhyme. Rim rhyme isn't currently threatened, as exact rhyme is, by a weary tide of repeated rhymes. The waterways of rim rhyme are far less navigated. If exact rhyme is a voluminous freighter, to which familiar pairings have barnacled themselves over the centuries, rim rhyme is

a slim kayak, whose hull is uncluttered. Clichés, predictable
chains of metaphor, stock responses—those stubborn growths
eventually affixed to any vessel plying the Seas of Poetry—
haven't yet lodged and colonized it. Rim rhyme remains ship-
shape. For those who like words for words' sake, it offers new
games to play. For example, how many consonant clusters can
you think of where the insertion of each of the five vowels
produces a word? *Bag, beg, big, bog, bug.* Or—better, because
longer by a letter: *last, lest, list, lost, lust.* Or still better, at five
letters: *plank, plenk, plink, plonk, plunk* (though *plenk,* which
doesn't appear in *Webster's* but only in online dictionaries,
feels like a bit of a cheat). Or six letters: *massed, messed, missed,
mossed, mussed*—though the use of an *-ed* prosthetic seems
another cheat. (Is there a seven-letter combination? My computer already knows the answer to this puzzle, but I don't
want it to tell me, since I want to keep looking.)

Our modern world is chockablock with internally rhym-
ing objects: *grandstands* and *picnics* and *snack packs, Fitbits* and
titbits and *mai tais, mukluks* and *nitwits, stun guns* and *moptops.* I
find such words appealing, but still more so the verbal bric-
a-brac of *knickknacks* and *flip-flops, food fads* and *flimflams,* the
survivalist's *bug-out bag,* the data processor's *stop step,* the *widow's weeds* and the lovely, self-dramatizing *look-alike.* Kudos to
Larkin's slap at the idle rich ("the shit in the shuttered cha-
teau") and to Sondheim's *poodle/piddle/puddle.* I have a particular affection for *hellhole.* Fiery old Hell, a place where pain
is paramount, and unremitting, and eternal, might seem the
sort of location where wordplay would collapse. But no.

Hellhole doesn't appear in *Paradise Lost*—or anywhere else
in Milton. But it ought to, perhaps as a throwaway by Milton's fallen angel, Lucifer, the greatest of all wordsmiths in
English. Abject Satan serves as a reminder, as *hellhole* does,

that when all else is forfeited—God and comfort and harmony and starlight—we retain a pleasure in words of artistry
and unvanquishable irony.

The most beautiful of all rim rhymes—the belle of the
ball—has to be James Joyce's "grace-hoper." Suddenly it is
revealed to us what that strong-legged insect of meadow and
field, leaping from perch to perch, has been up to all these
years: he is a pilgrim in search of the divine.

A gorgeous rim rhyme arises at the close of "Dusting," a
contemporary sonnet by Daniel Hall. It's from his first book,
Hermit with Landscape, and it opens the book's first section.

> Beautiful, visitors used to say
> absentmindedly, glimpsing the figurine
> (courtesan, bronze) ensconced in the fine
> bay window. And it was, in a way
> that the irises swaying outside
> would never be, multitudes driven
> unresisting from season to season,
> year after year. When the old man died,
> his favorite weathered the neglect
> indifferently. The pose she held
> had taken a lifetime to perfect,
> would take a lifetime, at last, to comprehend.
> Dust fell, and her hand was filled,
> awaiting the touch of a human hand.

Another poet—maybe quite a good poet—would have
selected *understand* rather than *comprehend*, thereby perfecting
the rhyme. But how much more perfect is imperfection! In
this lovely meditation on the loftily permanent and the exquisitely ephemeral, Hall cultivates the sly and rarefied music

of rim rhyme (present, too, with *fell* and *filled*). What is the connection between the bare bronze effigy and the doomed, wind-tossed, tissue-papery gesturing of the irises? Ultimately, it's the human hand—the poet's hand, at his desk—that conjoins them.

And I'd hate to leave the poem without praise for Hall's daring to open a book with that tiredest of all poetic words, *Beautiful*. The word is all but unusable unless given a twist, as Richard Wilbur recognized with his first book, *The Beautiful Changes and Other Poems*. (*His* twist materializes at book's end, when the title poem arrives. *Beautiful* isn't an adjective, as expected, but a noun, and *Changes* not a noun, but a verb.) In Hall's case, everything is wonderfully rectified with that *absentmindedly*, which shows up *Beautiful* for the vacuous stage gesture it usually is; the poem is in quest of another species of beauty, not so easily named or summoned.

Exact rhyme, rim rhyme—each branch offers its own puzzles and peculiarities. Why does rim rhyme so often move from a short *i* to a short *a*, and not the reverse? (*Mishmash, riprap, riffraff, pit-a-pat, wigwag, flimflam, knickknack, bric-a-brac, zigzag*.) Why so often employed to suggest dithering and indecision? (*Shilly-shally, dillydally, flip-flop, wishy-washy*.) Why so little employed in rhymed aphorisms, for which it would appear ideally suited? (Typically, these migrate to exact rhyme: *An apple a day keeps the doctor away; Man proposes, God disposes*.)

Satisfying as rim rhyme can be, for me there's another category, or uncategory, more appealing yet. I'm thinking of those rhymes that are not quite rim rhymes but almost are, like *kissing cousin*, or *brains over brawn*, or *nature versus nurture, or gin joint*. (Bogart in *Casablanca*: "Of all the gin joints in all the towns in all the world, she walks into mine.")

As the distinctions get very fine, we tiptoe into the

realm of the Funesians. What of the two-syllable rim rhyme in which the first vowel remains the same but the second is altered, as in *weekend* and *weakened*, or *meter* and *meteor*? Or the other variant, where you alter only the first, as in *playwright* and *plowwright* or *curried* and *carried*? The Funesians have mapped these remote byways, and how much more lengthy and complicated and scenic they turn out to be than first appears! Language shortchanges language; rhyme is infinitely subtler than our terminology.

I've long admired a rhyme in Paul Muldoon's "Why Brownlee Left": *famous* and *farmhouse*. Is this a rim rhyme? Yes. Sort of. The same might be said when Merrill pairs *eros* and *warehouse*. The reader comes away sensing that unlikely connections are forever fusing out in the sonic hinterlands, unlikely combinations are finding voice. When the Russian poet Brodsky, writing in English, rhymes *window* and *into*, you get a feeling that he's apprehending things in our language that the rest of us may be deaf to.

All such "imperfect" rhymes can be swept under the rubric of off rhyme. But in doing so, you lose track of how many exciting ways there are to be "off," so distressingly few ways to be "on"!

Rim rhyme is a symbol of the tongue's welcoming fecundity—the more the merrier—and it seems only appropriate that the universe itself originated with a rim rhyme. Or, better still, with a near rim rhyme. In the Beginning was the Words: a pair of them. Big bang.

◻

CHAPTER SIXTEEN

The Marriage of
Meter and Rhyme (II)

You're lying in a sleeping bag in Michigan's Upper Peninsula, where nights are growing sharply cool. If you were in Detroit now, full summer would still reign. If you lived in Baltimore, or Shreveport, you'd be running your AC nonstop. But this time of year, up here, autumn grows teeth—an aggressive bite—and silence has descended upon the companionable chorus of crickets that has nightly sung you to sleep.

No, not quite, not wholly. Off in the wooded distance, a solitary creature is holding forth, serenely serenading, just as though the weather were lovely—just as though the passage of time had no reality.

And while you're lying there, attending to a cricket, and feeling quite forlorn, really, and somewhat despondent perhaps, and maybe even a little self-pitying, since the passage of time *does* have a reality and your single songster must soon fall silent, something unexpected happens. The sound opens up. A second cricket jumps in—chirp, chirp, chirp—and the lifting of your spirits is more thoroughgoing than anything you might have foreseen. Nature is never spent, Hopkins reminds us, and the diminutive creatures of this world have found a way to contend with the passage of time. Here is poetry, for the two of them have invented a complicated music. . . .

The poetry of Earth is ceasing never, Keats likewise reminded us, as he contemplated a cricket's song. And, though generated by a humble and unhandsome insect, what a rich school of poetry this is, evoking both the percussion of meter and, its pliant upper wing bowing and scraping across the stiff ridges of its membranous lower wing, the string section of rhyme.

Chapter after chapter, I've pulled the two apart—meter and rhyme—in an effort to clarify each. But at day's end the formal poem is a marriage of the two, a nuptial ceremony warmed by a host of celebrants. Any just appraisal of poetry must meditate on unity. At their best, rhyme and meter syncretize in the creation of a whole whose disparate parts plunge and dissolve into each other.

There are days when I think the most beautiful poem ever composed is Frost's "Stopping by Woods on a Snowy Evening." Every line so clean, so perfect! As we've seen, its iambic tetrameter is stringently regular, the rhymes exact. And yet the poem feels fresh and innovative. It inhabits a form unglimpsed before Frost invented it. And yet could anything be simpler than its penultimate stanza:

He gives his harness bells a shake
To ask if there is some mistake.
The only other sound's the sweep
Of easy wind and downy flake.

Easy to dismiss Frost, damning him with faint or even respectful praise that weighs his simplicity against him. What's harder is to pay justice to the pleasures of a rounded repletion found only in these instances where you can't imagine changing anything. Immutability is the flip side of its simplicity.

Perfection in any language flourishes primarily on the level of the individual word. In fact, I just employed a word I think of as perfect: level. It's a lovely thing to look at and to hear. In its casual heft, its trig contours, its palindromic reversibility, and the poising suspension-bridge arch of its contours, the word is ideally housed: so neat, so pared, so *level*. (Actually, the word is less than perfect when italicized; its faint rightward lean throws it off from the true. When this happens, it becomes unlevel.)

One must similarly praise *kayak*. Surely the most seaworthy and unsinkable vessels, those fittest to deal with any capsizing, ought to be palindromes.

Or what word could possibly be better than *murmurousness*? In the language of typography, the word has no ascenders or descenders, no portions of a letter that extend above the mean line or below the base line of the font. So steadily restrained does it keep its voice, so modulated its turnings, that all of its letters are exactly the same minimal height.

I sometimes think *inarticulacy* is the cleverest, winningest word in the language—evincing, in its gently anapestic six syllables of two letters each, a grace and wit and splendid superfluity of engineering. I love it for its trim excesses. In dual senses, the word so effortlessly, ironically embodies its own antonym. In the root sense of *articulate* (small and fine-jointed), *inarticulacy* is so handsomely articulated. And in the everyday sense of being no good with words, *inarticulacy* is so arrestingly eloquent, so damned *good* with words. (The word finds a kid sibling in *ambulatory,* which walks with such sturdy steadiness on its two-letter syllables.)

Fine discriminations of this sort can easily descend into whimsy and ostentation. But they point us toward an enlightening conclusion: Perfection grows less and less likely as we move from the very small to the very large. (Recall Randall Jarrell's definition of a novel as a "prose narrative of some length that has something wrong with it.") Many lines of poetry strike me as perfect in this sense: wielding a nimble finality that leaves you unwilling to dispute a syllable. There are many fewer such whole poems. Far more typical is to find the perfect stanza in the larger poem.

Coleridge's "Kubla Khan" is one of the strangest and most marvelous poems I know. Here is perfection of a sort—a fragmentary sort. Affixed to the poem is Coleridge's apologia, seeking to justify or explain away its peculiarities. He reports that the poem arrived virginally intact, in a vision, far more complete and coherent than the fifty-four-line, ever-shape-shifting fragment left us today. He was transcribing this larger poem when an acquaintance from a neighboring town, the fateful though faceless "person on business from Porlock," paid a disturbing visit of nearly an hour, in whose wake Coleridge discovered that the poem had "passed away like the images on the surface of a stream into which a stone has been cast." (Or passed away like the clouds of a pipe dream. Coleridge liked his opium.) The poem strikes me, in its very essence, as a thing of shifting glimmers, requiring no intruder from Porlock to bundle it away. The poem's perfection seems infrangibly linked to its incompletion. I can't imagine any world, any alternative reality, in which a much-expanded "Kubla Khan," undisturbed by visitors, assumes the logic of organic growth and maturity.

"Kubla Khan" is structurally eccentric, taking the form of a double expansion. In the opening lines, a reigning tetram-

eter yields to a pentameter dominant throughout the body of
the poem:

> In Xanadu did Kubla Khan
> A stately pleasure-dome decree:
> Where Alph, the sacred river, ran
> Through caverns measureless to man
>> Down to a sunless sea.
> So twice five miles of fertile ground
> With walls and towers were girdled round;
> And there were gardens bright with sinuous rills,
> Where blossomed many an incense-bearing tree;
> And here were forests ancient as the hills,
> Enfolding sunny spots of greenery.

In the closing thirteen lines, as if our poet has just now paused
for breath, we experience a second expansion, surging from
trimeter to tetrameter:

> Could I revive within me
> Her symphony and song,
> To such a deep delight 'twould win me,
> That with music loud and long,
> I would build that dome in air,
> That sunny dome! Those caves of ice!
> And all who heard should see them there,
> And all should cry, Beware! Beware!
> His flashing eyes, his floating hair!
> Weave a circle round him thrice,
> And close your eyes with holy dread
> For he on honey-dew hath fed,
> And drunk the milk of Paradise!

The febrile poet here is both source and vehicle, the subject of the poem and its executor.

Much of the reader's delight resides in the fiery contrast between the delirium of the message and the tidiness of the form. Seven of the last eight lines are sharply etched iambic tetrameter, of a level and measured sort usually signaling tranquillity and composure. From a prosodic standpoint (exact rhymes, metronomic meter), we're not so far from Frost's "Stopping by Woods." But in matters of the spirit, there are miles and miles to go between them. Together, the two poems stand as signposts testifying to the breadth of voice open to this most fundamental of poetic forms.

There are days, as I say, when "Stopping by Woods" seems the most beautiful poem ever written. Or Housman's "Loveliest of Trees." Or any one of a dozen verses whose beauty is synonymous with simplicity and impeccability of finish, verses of a sufficiency so tranquil and surfeited as to declare on its face the folly of adding or subtracting anything.

On most days, though, I prefer the poem that trails sensations of something unfinished or unresolved, the presence of what I think of as the right sort of wrongness. Such poems leave you restless, eager to tinker, to amend and to placate. Consider Byron's beautiful miniature "So We'll Go No More a Roving":

> So we'll go no more a roving
>   So late into the night,
> Though the heart be still as loving,
>   And the moon be still as bright.
>
> For the sword outwears its sheath,
>   And the soul wears out the breast,

And the heart must pause to breathe,
And love itself have rest.

Though the night was made for loving,
And the day returns too soon,
Yet we'll go no more a roving
By the light of the moon.

The concluding line sheds a restive afterglow. Something feels wrong—the only line of the twelve without three clear stresses. Readers can amend the fault by thumping the initial word—**By** the light of the moon—but in doing so they forfeit the charming anapestic lilt waltzing throughout the three stanzas. Easy fixes do volunteer themselves, whether predictable ("By the light of the silver moon") or less so ("By the light of the waning moon").

But such fixes fix nothing. It's striking how much emotion Byron implies not through content, but metrics—metrical shortcoming. The speaker's heart is a sore and sorry organ, and qualities elsewhere a virtue—sensations of harmony, satiety, ease—are inappropriate here. Wonderful days are being recollected, but Byron's isn't the voice of someone contentedly summoning the past. ("Boy, didn't we have some marvelous times . . .") His is the unreconciled voice of somebody suffering a grievous forfeiture, registered wordlessly by failing to provide the additional syllable or syllables to satisfy prosodic demands. The final line hangs irresolutely—gorgeously.

Something analogous occurs in the closing stanza of one of America's best-loved poems, Frost's "The Road Not Taken." Laid out in four cinquains, the poem sports a loose iambic tetrameter—but never more loose and indeterminate than in its final line:

I shall be telling this with a sigh
Somewhere ages and ages hence:
Two roads diverged in a wood, and I—
I took the one less traveled by,
And that has made all the difference.

When I've asked students to read the poem aloud, they diverged most while delivering the last line. It was sometimes read: And **that** has **made** all the **diff**e **rence**. And sometimes: And **that** has made **all** the **diff**e **rence**. And sometimes: And **that** has **made all** the **diff** erence. (The problem with this last interpretation is that rhyme is pulling you contrariwise, urging you to land prominently on the last syllable.)

The poem deposits us into a familiar zone, indeed a wonderful zone: an arena where rhyme and meter are in constant and fertile contention. In his old age, Frost crystallized his life as a "lover's quarrel" with the world. But isn't the phrase equally applicable to Frost's dual apprentices, rhyme and meter, in their behavior here? They come into full fruition only when challenging each other. How to read the final line? Rhyme is voicing its demands. And so is meter. And you are a couples therapist, vainly trying to reconcile them.

As reader, your task is humble: How do I read the final line of Frost's "The Road Not Taken"? And your task is dauntingly immense: What do I do when my medium to the universe, language, is caught here and there, betwixt and between? Frost in "The Road Not Taken" is summing up his life, and if there are notes of contentment and self-congratulation, we lack the fixity necessary for complacency; prosodically, we seek in vain some sort of stable perch and purchase.

Ironically, all these challenges and ambiguities can be

made to disappear with one flick of the poet's wand. Let's rewrite the line: *And that has made the difference.* With the erasure of one tiny word, the problems associated with the final line—of sense, of metrics, of music—vanish on the instant. Here now is our final cinquain:

> I shall be telling this with a sigh
> Somewhere ages and ages hence:
> Two roads diverged in a wood and I—
> I took the road less traveled by,
> And that has made the difference.

But if the difficulty in the stanza has been removed, so has much of the beauty. It pleases me to think that in a hundred years, two hundred, long after anyone alive today who loves the poem still walks the planet, new readers will find themselves wondering why these simple lines are so uneasily haunting.

Likewise imperfect—likewise perfect—is Charlotte Mew's brief "Sea-Love":

> Tide be runnin' the great world over:
> 'Twas only last June month I mind that we
> Was thinkin' the toss and the call in the breast of the
> lover
> So everlastin' as the sea.

> Heer's the same little fishes that splutter and swim,
> Wi' the moon's old glim on the grey, wet sand:
> An' him no more to me nor me to him
> Then the wind goin' over my hand.

It's a poem in dialect—usually a mistake for anyone like Mew not native to it. I would tentatively place the speaker in northern Britain, perhaps in Scotland, where *glim* has the additional meaning (along with "source of illumination" and an obsolete sense of "splendor") of "scrap" or "little bit." In any case, our speaker is unlettered—and wise, wise beyond her years.

It's a humble voice that appears to be saying, *I'm no poet and mine is a modest observation.* Certainly, "grey, wet sand" is about as flat and uninspired a description as anyone could contrive. But look closer. The "toss and the call" is a peculiar pairing, rendered fully logical only when, a line later, the restless sea appears. And if *swim* is the world's most predictable word (what else would fish do?), *splutter* seems a queer, undersea oddity; the submerged reader has plunged into a breathless medium.

And listen closer. What is the meter? Anapestic, you might say confidently after the third line. Iambic, you might say, reconsidering, after the seventh. The poem slides about, as free-ranging, as free-metered as the ocean.

To seekers of consistency, everything here must seem wrong. The rhymes are inconsistent (both exact and off), the meter is inconsistent (anapestic, iambic, and everything in between), and even the diction is inconsistent.

Then again, the very subject of the poem is inconsistency: the capriciousness and unaccountability of eros and the human heart. We're used to reading poems about unfaithfulness— the pathos of unreturned passion and faithless love. But this is something else again.

For this isn't a poem about unfaithfulness—unless we say it's about double unfaithfulness. The speaker isn't heartbroken. Nor is her former lover. The tone is a marveling, wondering tone: *Where did it all go? What happened to a passion recently as monumental as the sea?*

The poem is the best brief example I know of the heartbreak of nonheartbreak: a sorrow, indeed, truly heartbreaking. At the end of Proust's *Swann in Love*, after hundreds of pages of what the poet Howard Moss called the greatest portrait of the anguish of unrequited love in world literature, the reader meets a disinfected Monsieur Swann, cured of passion. Swann observes, "She was never my type." Yet the recuperated man seems somehow sadder than the lovesick one. An unrequited love affair is not so loveless and forlorn as the affair whose love has mutually disappeared, tracelessly. To ask *Where did my love go?* is to ask *Where did my life go?* As Mew's poem reminds us, a dead love is a dead life.

And yet, and yet . . . There's satisfaction for Mew's speaker in seeing the world lucidly at last. In addition to all the heartbreak, there's an almost gloating wonder in the casual, throwaway, here-one-moment-gone-the-next description of "the wind goin' over my hand." (Mew shares a number of potent peculiarities with Housman, not least that the most powerful image in poem after poem is invisible: a creeping breeze, the breath of the unknowable.)

A fondness for the poem with something "wrong" in it may extend to those where virtually every line presents a problem, as in Roethke's "Wish for a Young Wife." One reason I so love this poem is that it's such a mistake-ridden triumph over itself:

> My lizard, my lively writher,
> May your limbs never wither,
> May the eyes in your face

Survive the green ice
In envy's mean gaze;
May you live out your life
Without hate, without grief,
And your hair ever blaze
In the sun, in the sun,
When I am undone,
When I am no one.

My lizard? An unappealing association for a woman we're presumably meant to favor. Is the poem about to embark on a show of raillery and contempt? And what about *writher*? A raw coinage, evoking those squirming grubs that surface, both to their dismay and yours, when you flip over a wet log. And *May your limbs never wither*? As affectionate wishes go, this seems comically clinical and literal-minded. And what about *the eyes in your face*? Where the hell else would you find them?

But in the middle of the poem we experience a shift. Clearly the poet isn't intending satire or censure. The intent is loving and valedictory. One senses in this prayer of departure a longing for a better, securer morrow. May you, the poet pleads, be less afflicted by hate and grief—by all the basest emotions—than I in my troubled life have been. Oh, and let me add, my darling, that I adore that hair of yours (which, given its bright blazonry, is presumably red). Meanwhile, you the reader intuit what the put-upon poet understandably ignores: The flame of the young wife's hair inevitably will subside into an ashen gray. The wish extended to a young wife is a futile wish. And all the more touching, more magnanimous, for being so frail and futile.

It's the last two lines of the poem that immortalize it

for me. The first is relatively simple: The poet, in common with the world's veterinarians and hedge-fund operators and waste disposal–management consultants and named professors (emeriti) and National Guardsmen and beloved local barkeeps, is destined eventually to pass away. Okay. But in this case, the poetic transition fails to proceed smoothly. Our meter poses a sizable problem, in a poem that, line by line, has been nothing but problems. Naturally, we seek to exit the poem on a clean, smooth note. We'd like to conclude with a ringing rhyme, securely linking the last word, *one*, with *sun* and *undone*. But in this case our little *one* (so little, so comprehensive) remains stubbornly uncooperative.

Readers wishing to rhyme it exactly will struggle. And in that struggle, the true beauty of the poem resides. When I am **no** one? Or: When I am no **one?** Or: When am I **no one?** The last line inquires of you, *How do you exit from this poem?* The last line asks you, *How do you exit from this life of yours?*

I've made a distinction between the perfect poem, the timeless and tranquil and unalterable one, and the one creating a tension in the reader, an urge to see things polished or amended. But even the poem I've chosen as a symbol of immobilized perfection, Frost's "Stopping by Woods," presents its own tensions, its own inconsistencies. In that storehouse of errant brilliancies that is *Pale Fire*, Nabokov takes up "Stopping by Woods," calling it "one of the greatest short poems in the English language." He turns to the closing stanza:

> The woods are lovely, dark and deep.
> But I have promises to keep,
> And miles to go before I sleep,
> And miles to go before I sleep.

He extols "that prodigious and poignant end—two closing lines identical in every syllable, but one personal and physical, and the other metaphysical and universal."

It's a tonic reminder of the complexity of even the most transparent poetry. Two identical lines—but not at all identical. One is local, one global. One is ephemeral, one eternal. Context, location—they alter everything. X is X today and here, but X isn't X tomorrow and there.

I've felt a lifelong penchant for the math of poetry: syllable counts, recurring ratios, the effects produced by minimal additions and subtractions. But all the math is useless if you fail to understand its limitations. Early in his career, E. E. Cummings mysteriously titled one of his books *Is 5*. In a foreword he noted that "nonmakers must content themselves with the merely undeniable fact that two times two is four." The poet, on the other hand, has the "priceless advantage" of inhabiting a realm where even the simplest components sometimes fail to add up, or to act like themselves. Where calculated effects yield to constant surprise. Where two identical objects may differ from each other. Where two times two is five.

▣

CHAPTER SEVENTEEN

Wordplay and Concision

Wordplay is an embellisher. It prettifies poetry's architecture. If rhyme and meter are its beams and joists, wordplay is the artfully chiseled balustrade, the pillowed window seat, the foliated mantel frieze, the coordinated hues adorning the interior walls. Choice of paint is a crucial decision—potentially elevating a room from the merely functional to the inviting and comely. But it won't keep your walls and ceiling from coming down.

Still, poetry is a tricky enterprise, routinely upending generalizations that would contain or confine it. It turns out there are moments when wordplay, taking on a structural element, does hold things together. These occur mostly within light verse.

Because the modern-day limerick belongs so firmly to the comedian, especially the bawdy comedian, we've come to expect the delivery of a (wink, wink) double entendre at its close. This wasn't always the case. When Edward Lear published *A Book of Nonsense*, in 1846, the final line of his limericks usually repeated the first. The denouement wasn't simply unsurprising; it was wholly predictable. Lear wasn't angling

to startle or shock. Rather, he sought to leave us with tremo-
los of wistful eccentricity. He'd lead you to marvel at the
upthrust oddness of the world:

> There was a Young Lady of Norway,
> Who casually sat in a doorway;
> When the door squeezed her flat, she exclaimed, "What
>   of that?"
> This courageous Young Lady of Norway.

Or:

> There was an Old Person of Ischia,
> Whose conduct grew friskier and friskier;
> He danced hornpipes and jigs, and ate thousands of figs,
> That lively Old Person of Ischia.

These constructions are miles away from the modern-day
"dirty limerick," the sort one used to encounter with dependable regularity on the unwashed walls of public men's rooms.

(To speak of men's room graffiti is to raise a nettlesome
inquiry: where on earth did they go? These days, unlike the
days of my youth, you very seldom find a men's room stall
darkly scribbled with lubricious verses. I suspect the cause
is—somehow—the internet. But this does raise the distressing
question of whether our computers have become our toilets.)

Some of my favorite limericks are those that are meant to
be doubly provoking, transgressing not merely decorum but
also grammar or spelling or, in this case, pronunciation:

> To his friend, Ned said, rather blue,
> "My wife Edith just told me we're through

For she says I'm too fat."
And his friend told him that,
"You can't have your cake and Edith too."

But back to the sad and self-exiled Edward Lear, one of my great heroes, whose fertile imagination sprang from an overfertile mother. (He arrived at the tail end of her twenty-one children.) Lear was the unquiet possessor of a shameful secret (a gay sensibility) and, to him, a yet more shameful secret (epilepsy). Some of his creations strike me as just as assured of immortality as those of *his* great hero, Tennyson. I feel as confident about the lastingness of Lear's owl and pussycat as I do of Tennyson's kraken or eagle, of Lear's Uncle Arly as of Tennyson's Ulysses. Yet I take little interest in Lear's limericks. Much more is lost than gained with that final repetition.

Repetition in comic verse works best when what's repeated isn't quite the thing repeated. Consider the charming, nubile Nan from Nantucket of an anonymous American limerick that first appeared in The Princeton *Tiger* in 1902. The poem plays wittily on a Learlike repetition. As in a Lear limerick, we begin and end with a place name, but the final *Nantucket* is a different locale from the first:

There once was a man from Nantucket
Who kept all his cash in a bucket.
But his daughter, named Nan,
Ran away with a man
And as for the bucket, Nantucket.

This pawky little gem plays games with our expectations. Given the raw materials here—a limerick, a spirited young

girl, and *Nantucket* serving as a rhyming word—we naturally
assume we know the down-and-dirty precincts where it plans
to venture. But the obscene rhyme fails to materialize. Light-
fingered Nan remains virginally untouched. The poem might
belong to some old-fashioned, run-down pantomime show,
with a brilliantined emcee wagging an extended index finger at his squirming middle-aged male patrons: "Ooh, you
naughty boys, what *were* you thinking?"

The unspoken obscene likewise animates "Verse for a
Birthday Card," by Wendy Cope:

Many happy returns and good luck.
When it comes to a present, I'm stuck.
If you weren't far away
On your own special day,
I could give you a really nice glass of lager.

These are verses where wordplay infiltrates structure. It's
built right into the poem, so that a failure to pun, or to arrive
at a particular bawdy rhyme in a particular place, feels less like
a thematic and more like an operational failure.

I was prepared for Wendy Cope when she arrived in my
adulthood, because in my elementary school days some literary sophisticates among my chums introduced me to Miss
Susie, whose adventures can be found in nineteen variant epi-
sodes in *Wikipedia*. A young woman of questionable character
but undeniable verve, Miss Susie got around, clearly. Wikipedia's Michigan version, dated 1950s, differs slightly from the
account I learned in Detroit a few years later, perhaps now set
into type for the first time:

Miss Susie had a steamboat
The steamboat had a bell
And when she pulled upon it
She led us all to

Hello, operator
Give me number nine
And if you won't connect me
I'll kick you right in the

Behind the 'frigerator
There was a piece of glass
Miss Susie fell upon it
And hurt her little

Ask me no more questions
I'll tell you no more lies
Miss Susie told me all this
The day before she died.

What binds together Miss Susie's escapades isn't, Lord
knows, meter or rhyme, but wordplay in a structural sense;
a naughty play on words staples each stanza to the next. A
firm prosodic contract governs here, no less than if this were
a sonnet or a sestina.

This is likewise true of the goofy, pun-overrun quatrains
of a number of light-verse poems by Thomas Hood (1799–
1845). An idiosyncratic contract is quickly drawn up, whereby
the reader is promised a pun—the more flagrant the better—
in the last line of each quatrain. (Others may materialize—
the more the merrier—but the contract all but guarantees a

concluding pun.) Here's the final stanza of "Faithless Sally Brown," whose fickle heart drove a poor sailor to his end:

> His death, which happened in his berth,
>   At forty-odd befell:
> They went and told the sexton, and
>   The sexton tolled the bell.

And here's another unfortunate military man, this one a soldier, once more done in by a femme fatale:

> Ben Battle was a soldier bold
>   And used to war's alarms;
> But a cannon-ball took off his legs,
>   So he laid down his arms.

> Now as they bore him off the field,
>   Said he, "Let others shoot;
> For here I leave my second leg,
>   And the Forty-Second Foot."

Though many will groan at a bad pun, the existence of wordplay—punning in the broadest sense—is unavoidable, inextinguishable. It seems to exist independent of us. Punsters often have an inkling that their creation was present from the outset, waiting for them. (Samuel Beckett: "In the beginning was the pun.") The gestation can be lengthy. In the 1200s, in northern Italy, along the Arno, an ambitious tower was steadily erected on unsteady ground. From that moment on, it was inevitable that, many centuries later, scattered across a sprawled continent utterly unknown to the medieval artisans of Pisa, various Italian American restaurants would spring up called The Leaning Tower of Pizza. This had to be. Unbeknownst to anyone, once the tower began to lean, the creative ovens were fired.

Puns are pushy, pullulating in a fen of ambivalence. By definition, a pun says two things at once. Much legal writing, especially the writing of contracts, is devoted to stripping language of ambiguity, uncertainty. The attorney's aim is to arrange a desired result (as defined by his client, however undesirable societally) in the face of every conceivable contingency. And of course such attempts to craft a language free of ambiguity, rendering a contract's terms incontestable and inescapable, and hence immune to all vagaries of interpretation and intervention, are invariably doomed; even the most straightforward words, set out in the most straightforward fashion, engender mist and smoke, shadings and concealments. What perhaps most sharply separates the poet from the lawyer is an embrace of, rather than a frequent struggle against, linguistic squishiness.

Anybody who has ever taught a poetry class has encountered the exasperated student inquiring, *"Why can't poets just say what they mean?"* Or: *"Why all this double talk?"* It's easy to dismiss such questions as naïve, but the truth is that everyone, poets and poetry lovers included, occasionally entertains the feeling: a gathering annoyance with poetry's indirection, its saying while not quite saying.

So you'll sometimes behold the poet expressing through words (the only trusty tool she has) an impatience with words. You feel this powerfully in the closing lines of Bishop's "One Art." The poem, a villanelle, begins with a confident nonchalance:

The art of losing isn't hard to master;
so many things seem filled with the intent
to be lost that their loss is no disaster.

But the tone has shifted dramatically by the last few lines:

It's evident
the art of losing's not too hard to master
though it may look like (*Write* it!) like disaster.

The concluding injunction may be parenthetical, but it is doubly emphatic, both italicized and exclamation pointed. Say what you mean! the author is enjoining herself. Life's losses are catastrophic, and any whitewashing of the tragedy is a cowardly evasion.

But while bewailing poetic artifice, Bishop has kept her poetic house in tidy order: The line is regularly iambic and the rhyme scheme is preserved. What's more, even in this plainspoken moment, doublespeak may have insinuated itself with a buried pun: (*Right* it!).

The poem stirs the ghost of Sir Philip Sidney (1554–1586), who closed a sonnet with a similar self-injunction:

Thus great with child to speak, and helpless in my
throes,
Biting my truant pen, beating myself for spite:
"Fool," said my Muse to me, "look in thy heart and
write."

In Sidney, too, we find a cry for simplicity housed within an elaborate construction: an exactly rhymed sonnet in iambic hexameter. Even as his Muse's words reproach him, they respect and embrace the form's prosodic requirements. *Keep it simple,* the poem says explicitly. *Keep it complex,* the poem says implicitly.

Why this clinging so fervently to indirection, to double-speak, to the sort of wordplay that seems to undermine the clarity and power of every assertion? One is tempted to answer, *That's just the way poets are,* and leave it at that. Or: *They enjoy making things difficult.* Or: *They're drunk on their own voices.*

All useful explanations. But the habit of wordplay is also rooted in a love of concision, of compression. To say two things at once is potentially to double one's efficiency. It's also to traffic in a language of ambivalence more emotionally authentic—truer to one's own forever irreconcilably mixed outlook on life—than any simpler utterance.

There's a modest brilliance at the heart of Emily Dickinson's credo: "Tell all the truth but tell it slant." For it seems the deepest truths, those of the heart that are the poet's lifeblood, are often incompatible with straightforward expression. In other words, indirection is more direct. At the end of the day, more honest.

Marilyn Monroe reportedly once remarked that she enjoyed reading poetry "because it saves time." I enjoy this quotation so much that I've never dared to confirm it; how lovely to think that words so wise, so helpful and constructive, issued from the mouth of somebody who back in the fifties was regularly referred to (without irony or self-consciousness) as a "sex bomb."

Poetry can invest the emotions far more rapidly and potently than prose. The language of doublespeak turns out to be doubly moving.

Consider this famous "short story" of a half-dozen words:

"For sale: baby shoes, never worn." It's usually attributed—mistakenly, the evidence suggests—to Ernest Hemingway. Whoever it was who condensed it down to six words did something masterly; the little announcement speaks not merely of the heartbreak of an infant's death but also of harrowing poverty and human resilience. The shoes weren't buried with the child. They retained some minimal financial value, which couldn't be overlooked; thoroughly downtrodden souls, even in the face of unspeakable tragedy, cannot afford to ignore the stringencies of the everyday.

Prose has, the story reminds us, its own gorgeous and powerful concisions, but nothing to compare with the reach belonging to verse. The most haunting short short story I know belongs to Somerset Maugham:

Death speaks: There was a merchant in Bagdad who sent his servant to market to buy provisions and in a little while the servant came back, white and trembling and said, Master, just now when I was in the market-place I was jostled by a woman in the crowd and when I turned I saw it was Death that jostled me. She looked at me and made a threatening gesture; now, lend me your horse, and I will ride away from this city and avoid my fate. I will go to Samarra and there Death will not find me. The merchant lent him his horse, and the servant mounted it, and he dug his spurs in its flanks and as fast as the horse could gallop he went. Then the merchant went down to the market-place and he saw me standing in the crowd and he came to me and said, Why did you make a threatening gesture to my servant when you saw him this morning? That was not a threatening gesture, I said, it was only a start of surprise. I was astonished to

see him in Bagdad, for I had an appointment with him
tonight in Samarra.

As an illustration of the folly of anyone's seeking to avoid
his fate, how streamlined this looks. But how long-winded
it appears when set beside another brief meditation on death,
Housman's "Here Dead We Lie":

Here dead we lie because we did not choose
    To live and shame the land from which we sprung.
Life, to be sure, is nothing much to lose;
    But young men think it is, and we were young.

Here, too, is a story. The deceased have come to appreciate
that death is a trifling matter. Grown clear-sighted with time,
they now recognize that life's ultimate rewards are few and
fleeting. But they once felt otherwise, wholeheartedly.

The dead are mourning not their lost lives but the loss
of this conviction that life is a priceless gift of radiance and
beauty and consummation. They are mourning lost youth's
lost illusions, and with this realization the poem broadens
until it encompasses all of us in our aging bodies, including one melancholic elderly poet. (Housman was in his sixties when this little verse was published.) On the other hand,
Housman did have the compensation (not given to the rest of
us) of knowing he'd composed one of the most heartbreaking
tiny poems in the language.

Wordplay is perhaps best understood as one of the tools
that make possible poetry's extraordinary concision. Partnered with meter and rhyme, it works beautifully to compress
a wealth of feeling into a compact stanza. One of the reasons
why the genre of the extremely brief short story in prose, the

short short, interests me so little is that, to my mind, poetry does this sort of thing so much better. Here's Frost again:

> The old dog barks backward without getting up.
> I can remember when he was a pup.

A mere twenty-one syllables, and two lives illuminated! It seems the ailing dog, in all its debility, continues to own its responsibilities; it still aims to safeguard the household. And the poet, aging himself, marvels at the speed of time's transformations: Surely just yesterday it was that this beloved creature's energy was boundless.

The poem could hardly be simpler—so simple, indeed, that you might suppose that the murk and mirrors of wordplay have no place within it. But look once more. Consider the couplet's one rather peculiar phrase: *barks backward*. Over his shoulder, yes—and perhaps we ought to leave it at that. But the throaty echoes are reverberative, and it's hard not to hear here a sense of calling backward, across the accumulating valleys of time. *I was here and I am still here*, the dog is saying in the one language it knows. *Don't count me out—I'm still in the game.*

This is, to modify Auden's phrase, memorable canine speech. And our Mr. Frost was wise enough to get it down just as spoken, in all the rich brevity that it deserves.

◻

CHAPTER EIGHTEEN

The Look of Poetry

Take the long view—the *long* view—and the look of a poem, its appearance on the page, shows up as a Johnny-come-lately phenomenon. Fad of the moment. Frills and frippery.

Go back to the *Epic of Gilgamesh*, some four thousand years, and march steadily forward. Over the millennia, what percentage of poets around the world had the opportunity to read their work in published format, whether upon a stone tablet, a papyrus scroll, an animal skin, a typeset page? And what percentage of poetry's audience encountered poems by reading them—or, for that matter, *could* read them? Historically, they're privileged parvenus, the people absorbing poetry visually. Poetry begins and ends as an aural medium.

It's tempting, then, to disregard as inessential the look of a poem, and indeed this book perches upon the premise that sound is paramount—often subordinating even a poem's meaning, and certainly its exterior dress. Even so, most contemporary poets fuss endlessly over a poem's looks. To them, its appearance matters hugely.

Of course being *able* to fuss is a great luxury. For the contemporary poet, one of the computer's prime virtues is its ability to bundle verses instantly into type, into *types*— hundreds, if not thousands, of fonts. Talk about instant gratification . . . You've just written a sonnet? How does it look in Courier? What about Helvetica? Would you prefer it in *italics*? Or **bold?** Does this particular sonnet look better in twelve- or ten-point type?

Consider two poems by May Swenson. Both are called "Out of the Sea, Early." Here's the first, published in *The New Yorker* in 1966:

A bloody egg yolk. A burnt hole spreading
in a sheet. An enraged rose threatening
to bloom. A furnace hatchway opening,
roaring. A globular bladder filling
with immense juice. I start to scream. A red

hydrocephalic head is born, teetering on
the stump of its neck. When it separates,
it leaks raspberry from the horizon down
the wide escalator. The cold blue boiling
waves cannot scour out that band that

broadens, sliding toward me up the wet sand
slope. The fox-hair grows, grows thicker
on the upfloating head. By six o'clock,
diffused to ordinary gold, it exposes
each silk thread and rumple of the carpet.

And the poem as it appeared in book form, in *Half Sun, Half Sleep*, in 1967:

A bloody
egg yolk. A burnt hole
spreading in a sheet. An enraged rose threatening to bloom.
A furnace hatchway opening, roaring.
A globular bladder filling with immense
juice. I start to scream. A red hydrocephalic head is born, teetering on the stump of
its neck. When it separates, it leaks raspberry from the horizon down the wide escalator. The cold blue boiling waves cannot
scour out that band that broadens, sliding toward me up the wet sand slope. The
fox-hair grows, grows thicker on the
upfloating head. By six o'clock,
diffused to ordinary gold,
it exposes each silk thread and rumple in the carpet.

The same child who once called out the emperor for having no clothes might now declare them the same poem—
identical, word for word. But Ms. Swenson didn't see them as
the same poem. I don't, either.

As it happens, Swenson was one of the bellwethers who
guided me into contemporary verse, in my high school days in
the late sixties. I'm forever grateful for poems like "Out of the
Sea, Early," "The Centaur," "Naked in Borneo," "A City Garden in April." In a double sense they fostered in me new forms
of observation: opening up what I might choose to see and
how I might translate seeing into language. I met her some
fifteen or twenty years later, in my thirties, and was still young
enough, I suppose, to announce that I much preferred the earlier to the later "Out of the Sea, Early." A long pause ensued.

And did I interpret aright her penetrating, enigmatic expression? (In a verse self-portrait, she boasted of her "pugnacious eye.") I'm thinking she was both irked to be told she'd mishandled the poem and flattered to meet somebody keen to argue about revisions made decades before.

I didn't get to have that argument, but what I would tell her now is that, yes, there's much to be said for the later, sculpted poem. It's as though she took to heart Marvell's "Let us roll all our strength and all / Our sweetness up into one ball." On a first reading, there's a frenzied jostle to its quirky hybrid shape, at once orbic and (at the very close) emphatically linear. I admire how the final line arrives so directly, so matter-of-fact flatly. But aren't five broken, hyphenated words, to say nothing of two adjacent lines concluding with *the*, too high a payment for the poem's strict rondure?

The earlier version offers quieter but more durable surprises. It looks so tidy and tranquil—those orderly cinquains, as similarly shapely as stacked loaves of bread—and yet the poem is an incendiary device, ingeniously contrived to blast its stanzas apart. The gorgeous, minatory imagery is startling in the way some of Monet's glazy sunrises are permanently startling. Pugnaciously, Swenson is out to make your eyes wince.

I like those aggressive participles (*spreading, threatening, opening, filling*) beetling over the first stanza. And the way the poem's one intimate statement ("I start to scream") gets quietly buried mid-line. The way none but the first line opens with a capital, since in this off-balance poem all beginnings of sentences are tucked into the interior. At the end of the day (or the end of the dawn), the earlier version seems more satisfyingly violent and uncontainable than its more dramatic- and dynamic-looking partner. (I must in good conscience give Swenson the last word here, with the brilliant rationale for her peculiar poetic shapes: "I wanted to make my poems do what they say.")

I probably couldn't have convinced Ms. Swenson of this, nor perhaps my reader now. Yet whichever version you prefer, the larger point is that the two would be interchangeable in a poetry reading. Perhaps there are recordings of Swenson reciting one or the other. (I haven't been able to locate any.) Surely these non-look-alikes would sound the same, and yet the overall experiences they offer stand miles apart.

Over the centuries, the composing of poetry has known a good many continuities. The search for a rhyme, for example, probably feels and behaves much the same whether taking place inside the head of John Milton or in the head of tomorrow's undergrad, constructing a formal poem on assignment. You might suppose that rhyming dictionaries—those handy modern appliances—have transfigured the process, but in fact they're hardly modern: They predate Shakespeare. The challenge of rhyming in a natural fashion, without sounding as though your poem's sound and sense were piloted by a reference book, is ages old. It's been speculated that Edmund Spenser's *Shepheardes Calendar* (1579) was unduly influenced by Peter Levins's pioneering *Manipulus Vocabulorum* (1570).

Yet the *visual* aspects of poetry and poem creation truly have metamorphosed in the modern age. If you examine that touchstone Christopher Ricks's *The Oxford Book of English Verse*, it's striking how many contributors never saw their scrawled manuscript converted into a published book. George Herbert's sole volume, *The Temple*, appeared posthumously. At his death, his fate as one of literature's Immortals reposed as a handwritten sheaf in the custody of his friend Nicholas Ferrar, who was instructed to burn it if he considered it

unworthy. Gerard Manley Hopkins provides a similarly tantalizing account of posthumous riches, teetering at the dark
precipice's edge. Or consider Emily Dickinson, who was a
very occasional local poetess at the time of her death (but
something altogether other, after).

But even for those poets who succeeded in steering a
book into print, the process was remote from our own. Many
of their poems, perhaps all, might be materializing in type for
the first time. Until her work emerged in full-blown publication, the poet would have little inkling of what it would look
like on the literary stage. Back then, to the poet, it must have
seemed a miraculous feat of theater: one's homely, flimsy,
individual cursive spun into a universal script.

Much of Swenson's poetry is that modern thing (or, these
days, semimodern thing): work effectively born on a typewriter. I don't mean this dismissively (as in Truman Capote's
famous put-down of Jack Kerouac: "That's not writing, that's
typing"), but admiringly. Her particular prankishness seems
to spring from typed, rather than cursive, script. It reflects
the sharp angularities and regularity and coolness of a typewriter's metallic outlook. Here's the first half of "The Universe," which opened *To Mix with Time: New and Selected
Poems:*

What
is it about,
the universe
the universe about us stretching out?
We within our brains
within it
think
we must unspin

the laws that spin it.
    We think *why*
because we think
because.
Because we think
    we think
    the universe about us.

There's a naïve quality throughout, the poet essentially asking, as any child might, *Why am I here?* But the naïveté is
belied by an eccentric, ingenious construction erected upon a
drumming tattoo of four words (*about, universe, because, think*),
aligned in those precisely vertical columns so congenial to a
typewriter, repeating themselves in a predictable thumping
placement. There's also some teasing wordplay with *about*, a
jack-of-all-trades word that can suggest approximate amount
(*about a dozen*), physical proximity (*walk about the house*), ultimate significance (*a book about forgiveness*), and egotism (*always
about you*). Swenson puts the word through its paces.

    Poems of this sort take some getting used to. And they're
troublesome from a reviewer's standpoint, refusing to be
excerpted easily or compactly; they demand a considerable
amount of territory in which to demonstrate and vindicate
their unorthodox methods. In Swenson's collections you find
poems shaped like wedges and poems shaped like pyramids;
there's a poem riven by lightning and a poem about a fountain
in which *water* bobs at the ends of sixteen of its thirty lines.
There's a poem that begins:

Kick
Kick
Kick

Kick
Kick
Kick
Kick
Kick
Kick . . .

There's another that ends:

             melted
       in   cheese
      flounder   or
  We
     candle-droppings.

As if aiming to test and bedevil her typesetter, she shifts and tinkers with font size, margins, the spacing between words, the axes of symmetry—upending all the familiar, domestic architecture of poetry.

But consider another poem, an untitled poem, by E. E. Cummings, here offered in entirety:

l(a

le
af
fa

ll

s)
one
l

iness

The poem has two sharply divided parts: the first is the bracketing term *loneliness*, and the second is *a leaf falls*, which is its core. As Helen Vendler has pointed out, here's a poem that cannot be read aloud. Cummings has done a peculiar thing: He has so deracinated poetry from its aural origins as to create something that, aurally, doesn't exist. One is tempted to declare that any text lacking an aural presence isn't poetry—and yet the little Cummings construction is, undeniably, a thing of wit and beauty.

The visual aspects of poetry are an immense topic, fully deserving a book of their own rather than the brief chapter I'm according them here. Cummings's poem is a species of calligram, defined by *Webster's* as "a design in which the letters of a word (such as a name) are rearranged so as to form a decorative pattern or figure." One thinks of illuminated medieval manuscripts, of Blake's watercolored renditions of word and image, of Edward Lear's "picture poems." One thinks also of Saul Steinberg's buoyant ink drawings (cartoons), which are rooted in and riddled with language. In one Steinberg drawing, a HELP! teeters and—in Humpty Dumpty fashion—falls off a wall; in another, a NOT YET appears whose *E* and *T* are sketchy and unfinished. In one of my all-time favorite cartoons, we find ourselves in an office where an applicant (supplicant?) meets a smiling authority whose eloquent, elegantly filigreed verbiage gathers, balloonlike, in the air above to form a simple and unyielding NO.

Steinberg, who not surprisingly was a favorite of Nabokov's, described himself as a "writer who draws." If this seems hyperbolic (can a drawing that includes one or two words be called writing?), it's worth noting that Cummings's loneliness poem consists of only four words. We seem to edge ever

closer to Ralph Waldo Emerson's observation that every word
was once a poem.

May Swenson and E. E. Cummings seem to me the two
American poets whose experiments with poetry's appearance
display the greatest invention. Not surprisingly, Cummings
was a serious painter (a painter who poeticizes?), who naturally took pains when dabbing syllables onto the canvas of an
empty page. And in Swenson's most radical book, *Iconographs*,
she seems almost as much visual artist as poet. One of the
poems begins like this:

```
   !    !           !  !
Catbird in the redbud this morning,
      !   !   !
No cat could
      !        !    ! !
mimic that rackety cadenza he's making.
```

Those floating, crisp exclamation marks adorn every *d* sound
and *c* sound in the poem. In an afterword to *Iconographs*, she
describes her wish to "cause an instant object-to-eye encounter with each poem before it is read word-after-word."

Here is another brief Cummings poem in its entirety:

un(bee)mo

vi
n(in)g
are(th
e)you(o
nly)

asl(rose)eep

I think I can offer a plausible account of what's happening here. Things are in a drowsy state. The sleepy speaker is wondering whether a companion is awake. The companion is invisible, swaddled in blankets, evoking the picture of a bee so deep in a flower as to be concealed by its petals. The two strains of thinking unfold simultaneously. One is a question: *unmoving—are you asleep?* The other is an imaginative fragment: *bee in the only rose.*

What I can't figure out is any satisfactory way to recite the poem, so that a first-time hearer might intuit not only meaning but structure.

Cummings and Swenson were lifelong innovators, quite a few of whose experiments strike me as too easy or too gimmicky. Others seem visually arresting but not really verse: more poster than poem. And others seem thrilling—quirky new sorties into hearing and seeing and thinking about poetry. I feel that way when I come upon a Swenson poem that opens like this:

> A world of storm   A life of waves
> Raging circles form   Tides and icy caves
> Wind loops the globe   Sun scorching palms
> Blizzards in the brain   Or deadening calms

Or even like this, from "How Everything Happens (Based on a Study of the Wave)":

>   happen.
>   to
>   up
>   stacking
>   is
>   something
> When nothing is happening

And here's a little Cummings poem that has haunted me for
decades:

> Me up at does
>
> out of the floor
> quietly Stare
>
> a poisoned mouse
>
> still who alive
>
> is asking What
> have i done that
>
> You wouldn't have

Eccentric—yes—but this one *could* be recited. If we blunt its
oddities by paraphrasing it prosaically (*A mouse I poisoned gazes
up from the floor wondering, "What act am I guilty of that you
wouldn't have committed?"*), we realize how the little poem is
presenting a large-souled inquiry. It's contemplating cosmic
justice.

If you heard rather than read the poem, you'd lose many
choice details, including its queer capitalizations and punctuation (or lack thereof). Cummings rarely capitalized pronouns,
and his unwonted *Me* and *You* leap off the page in seeming
opposition. But it turns out both refer to the same creature:
a human being (or inhuman being, as Cummings sometimes
would have it). If it's a towering Me and a towering You, this
elevation seems only fitting and right, for he's omnipotent,
godlike, the belatedly reflective man peering down upon

his minuscule victim. But which of the two creatures shows greater humanity?

If the poem arrived by ear rather than eye, you'd also lose that baleful, eloquent, upper-case *Stare*, whose accusations are not to be silenced or conquered by death. And you'd miss the generous outlays of white space that aerate the poem's boxy little rooms.

But you *would* be able to detect the neat underlying structure: iambic-based dimeter quatrains rhyming ABBA ABBA. The poem is one more vivid example of the occasional superiority of off rhyme to exact rhyme. Its music, suitably, is as muted as the scamper of a mouse across a floor.

Perhaps visual variety can't be pushed much further than Swenson and Cummings pushed it. (After them, what major threshold remains uncrossed? What passage more radical than the one separating traditional verse from the literally unspeakable?) Yet their focus on a poem's *look* carries us well beyond their own particular experiments. Each of their sizable bodies of work awakens us to a broadened reach of optical possibilities; the pair of them enhance our appreciation of the raiment of any poetry, drawn from any age.

Consider Malcolm Lowry's mad monologue sonnet "Delirium in Vera Cruz," which concludes:

> . . . Is this the ghost of the love you reflected?
> Now with a background of tequila, stubs, dirty collars,
> Sodium perborate, and a scrawled page
> To the dead, telephone off the hook? In rage
> He smashed all the glass in the room. (Bill: $50)

Hearing the poem aloud, you'd have no way of knowing whether the invoice was written in letters or numbers. You'd have no idea that a diminutive symbol—$—was responsible for adding two full syllables to the line. (O, almighty dollar!)

But *seeing* the poem, the italicized number has an effect at once sobering and riveting. We've been on a hallucinatory alcoholic bender, which comes to a crashing end with the curt reality of an inarguable, unbudgeable numerical sum. (For younger readers, who conceivably write their poems on a cell phone, we've gone and shifted keyboards, from the one marked ABC to the one marked 123.) Everything about the close—the quiet parentheses, the italics, the dollar sign, the Arabic numerals—feels absolutely awful, absolutely right.

Having opened this chapter with a sunrise, I'll close with a sunset. Here's Cummings again, in one of his gorgeous miniatures. This is another eight-liner doled out in somewhat concealed quatrains:

who are you,little i

(five or six years old)
peering from some high

window;at the gold

of November sunset

(and feeling:that if day
has to become night

this is a beautiful way)

The initial line recalls one of the most familiar openings in American literature (Dickinson's "I'm nobody—who are you?"), but the poem is very distinctively Cummings's own. The little child is entertaining big thoughts. He or she is speculating that if day must end in darkness, a showy sunset is an appropriate finale, and he or she is but a single step away from musing that if *life* must end in darkness, it, too, ought to blaze at the close.

Were you to hear the poem recited, you would miss the queer punctuation and spacing. (I'm not sure what, if anything, to make of the semicolon.) And you probably wouldn't suspect that half the lines are parenthetical; or that the poem in its open-endedness contains no question mark or period; or that the "i" is neither *I* nor *eye*.

But were you first to hear the poem, listening closely, and then to encounter it on the page, you'd immediately understand how its visual quirks beautifully justify themselves. How, in this case, oddness is rightness. And how, if one *must* trample on all the sensible, helpful rules of punctuation and capitalization and spelling, this is indeed a beautiful way.

In addition, you might realize that its opening question isn't rhetorical. The poem offers an answer to its *Who are you?* The shadowy child beside the window presents us with a lovely, unspoken reply: *A poet.*

CHAPTER NINETEEN

Song Lyrics

Back in the early forties, a young conscientious objector turned Presbyterian missionary settled among the Funesians. His name was Lyon Chapman Garner, and he stayed for three years, from 1941 to 1944. At the end of his stay, writing to his parents in Grosse Pointe, Michigan, he announced his abject failure to effect a single heartfelt conversion. He returned to the Midwest, and after the war, a newly married man, he opened a mom-and-pop concern that in time became the immensely lucrative Universal Colorfast, specializing in automotive paint.

Garner encountered no hostility or resistance among the Funesians. Perhaps he would have known more success had he done so; as it was, his hosts' mildness and unshakable affability stymied him. An accomplished debater in college (Yale), Garner was prepared to confound his hosts in theological argument, but to a man, to a woman, they resisted anything like formal disputation. And as a teetotaler (at least for the first thirty-four months of his thirty-six-month residency), Garner was a nonparticipant in the Funesians' nightly ritualized distributions of rhubarb brandy. He kept largely to himself in the evenings, listening to music on his gramophone and composing his spirited monthly column, "Local Thoughts from Far Away," for the *Grosse Pointe Point*, his hometown paper. He wrote enthusiastically of the Andes scenery, and its eccentric birdlife, but railed against the "tiny little mountain potatoes" that were the Funesians' dietary staple ("dirty, and deadly, deadly dull"). And their pickled turnips were "disgusting."

Packing up his belongings, he chose to leave behind his gramophone and his many recordings of popular music. It was through this offhand gesture that Lyon Garner worked an enduring conversion: The Funesians fell under the spell of Tin Pan Alley.

Later, postwar visitors to the Funesians reported a curious phenomenon: villagers humming and chanting under their breath, tunelessly singing about objects and encounters meaningless for them in their primitive isolation.

> They all laughed at Wilbur and his brother
> When they said that man could fly;
> They told Marconi wireless was a phony;
> It's the same old cry!

Or:

> Electric eels, I might add, do it,
> Though it shocks 'em I know.
> Why ask if shad do it?
> Waiter, bring me shad roe!

Or:

> She's gone where the goblins go below, below, below,
>   yo ho
> Let's open up and sing, and ring the bells out
> Ding-dong! the merry-o sing it high, sing it low
> Let them know the wicked witch is dead.

The Funesians were a "strikingly unmusical people," according to Garner, producing over the centuries "no instruments beyond a few primitive and indeed altogether malodorous animal-skinned drums." Yet modern American popular music had speedily permeated their culture. Though Garner had generated among them only limited enthusiasm for modern American poetry (regrettably, they showed no interest in Ezra Pound), they wholeheartedly embraced Ira Gershwin and Cole Porter and Dorothy Fields and Oscar Hammerstein.

When we today consider Lyon Chapman Garner's legacy among the Funesians, it seems obvious that the songs appealed chiefly through their quirky verbal structures. As we've seen, traditional English prosody spurned odd-syllabled lines. The poets of Tin Pan Alley, on the other hand, welcomed them, as in "It Had to Be You":

> I wandered around
> And finally found
> The somebody who
> Could make me be true . . .

Or:

> One girl for my dreams,
> One partner in Paradise,

This promise of Paradise—
This nearly was mine.

Garner's recordings introduced the Funesians to new ways
to put line and stanza together. Especially exciting was the
three-syllable cluster, a rare phenomenon in English poetry
but a favorite of the Tin Pan Alley poet, who repeatedly asked,
Am I blue?:

Ain't these tears
In these eyes
Tellin' you?
Am I blue?

The triple cluster might be somewhat disguised on the page,
as in George M. Cohan's stirring World War I battle cry:

Over there, over there,
Send the word, send the word over there,
That the Yanks are coming . . .

So prepare, say a pray'r,
Send the word, send the word to beware.

But the Funesians were absorbing the sounds not on the page,
as in sheet music, but as sounds coupled to melody, in which
case the lyric might more accurately be transcribed this way:

Over there
Over there,
Send the word,
Send the word

Over there,
That the Yanks
Are coming . . .

Something similar might be done with the Beatles' "Yesterday," which looks like this:

Yesterday
All my troubles seemed so far away
Now it looks as though they're here to stay
Oh, I believe in yesterday

but sounds like this:

Yesterday
All my troubles seemed so
Far away
Now it looks as though they're
Here to stay
Oh, I believe in
Yesterday.

A conclusion gradually clarifies: The true enjambments of a
song are not those demarcated by the lyricist on a page, but
those created by the natural groupings of the melody.

Meters were stable in traditional prosody, but some Tin
Pan Alley songs were waltzes, lending themselves to abrupt
(though oddly smooth) shiftings from anapestic to dactylic
meter and back again:

The **corn** is as **high** as an **el**ephant's **eye**,
An' it **looks** like it's **climb**in' clear **up** to the **sky**.

Oh, what a **beautiful mornin'**,
Oh, what a **beautiful day.**

Or from anapests into something less clear:

And if **you** should sur**vive**
To a **hun**dred and **five**
Look at **all** you'll **derive**
Out of **be**ing a**live.**
And **here** is the **best** part,
You have a **head** start . . .

CAROLYN LEIGH, "YOUNG AT HEART"

Innovative structures opened up inventive wordplay:

Mister Harris, plutocrat
Wants to give my cheek a pat
If the Harris pat
Means a Paris hat
Bébé
(Ooh la la!)
Mais je suis toujour fidèle, darlin', in my fashion
Oui, je suis toujour fidèle, darlin', in my way.

COLE PORTER, "ALWAYS TRUE TO YOU IN MY FASHION"

Or:

You must contain yourself, restrain yourself,
And train yourself to gain your self
Control.

DOROTHY LANGDON PREVIN, "CONTROL YOURSELF"

What did it matter if the Funesians didn't know who Wilbur and his brother were? Or what an electric eel was, or shad roe, or, indeed, what a waiter was? For that matter, what did it matter if they were not a musical people? For it turned out you hardly needed to love music in order to love collections of words born and available only through music. A new home for the imagination beckoned. Melody was the midwife to alternative dwellings, new places for language to live.

But now the scene shifts from the Andes and the 1940s to Chicago and the present day. Not long ago, during a layover in O'Hare International Airport, I ordered a bowl of soba noodles and, scuttling around the crowds, secured an empty table. Naturally, televisions encircled me. A football game was unfolding on the nearest one and I heard a sportscaster announce with a chuckle, "Well, he's not about to go gentle into that good night."

On the one hand, there was something madly improbable in hearing a line from a notoriously obscure Welsh poet, dead now for two-thirds of a century, applied to an American football game. On the other, Dylan Thomas's elegy for his father blended right in—for how could anyone or anything appear out of place in a modern airport? We plunk ourselves down in some International Food Court in America's heartland, hunching over our soba or chimichanga or kielbasa while seated beside somebody dining on shrimp vindaloo or moo goo gai pan or vegan chopped liver, and all the while, sprung from huge silver aircraft, noisy waves of disgorged arrivals wash in, dressed for some wildly distant climate and setting. It's a glimpse into a future where most people are tanned and everybody is jet-lagged—and there's no such thing as an incongruity.

I'm guessing the sportscaster was repeating a catch-phrase rather than making an allusion. He was a variation on Molière's Monsieur Jourdain, who proudly discovered he'd been speaking prose all his life; our sportscaster was primed for the happy realization that, week after week, he'd been spouting poetry. Of course it's no surprise when we hear somebody unwittingly quote or—more often—paraphrase Shakespeare. The sportscaster might well have said, "in my mind's eye," or "there's method in his madness," or "fair's foul." What was noteworthy was that the poet whose phrase had entered broadcasting argot was a creature of modern times.

We've recently come to the close of a matchless century in American verse—but have any of its poets infiltrated everyday language? Robert Frost, perhaps. You can picture our sportscaster vaguely summoning two diverging roads in the woods, or the miles still to go before we all get some sleep. But poets of more recent vintage? As wonderful as, say, Robert Lowell or John Berryman or Elizabeth Bishop or James Merrill was, they're unlikely to embellish *Monday Night Football*.

No, the modern poets who have colored the modern vernacular are a coterie of men and women who, by and large, hardly defined themselves as poets. They were lyricists. If it's impossible to imagine our sportscaster parroting Lowell or Berryman, it's easy to imagine his declaring that something's "de-lovely" or somebody has "plenty of nothin'," that "everything is coming up roses" or it's hard to "keep 'em down on the farm after they've seen Paree"—phrases either coined or popularized by, respectively, Cole Porter, Ira Gershwin, Stephen Sondheim, and Joe Young.

For that generation of Americans born in the first forty or so years of the twentieth century, the American popular song, whose golden age lasted roughly from 1925 to 1950, was something absorbed osmotically, unavoidably; it was the foreground music of their lives. To others born a little later, like me, into an age where rock had supplanted pop, a taste for the old standards was a lateral, haphazard acquisition. I was twenty-two, fresh out of college, when my first "real job" found me as research assistant to a writer who worked all day to the sounds of Tin Pan Alley standards. In the first month, I mostly disliked the music; in the second, I detected many things to admire, scattered throughout so much that was corny and regrettable; by the end of the summer, I'd renounced my citizenship in the Woodstock Nation—a change of status solemnized on the evening when, after work, I trotted off to the music store and purchased my first Sinatra album (*Only the Lonely*). But the oddest aspect to my conversion was the discovery that the music of Tin Pan Alley was—literally— coming out of the walls. Though often muted to a conspiratorial whisper, and frequently diluted into Muzak, it was spinning over supermarket PA systems, wandering through hotel lobbies, pumping through service stations, loitering in public waiting rooms. The music had been there all along, I tardily surmised, but I'd only recently learned to differentiate song from song—and, more to the purpose, only recently reached a point where the swoop of a clarinet, or a few soupy strains of a violin, evoked elaborate chains of lyrics.

Here was a different sort of poetry from what I'd studied in college, divergent not merely in its tools but also in its, so to speak, place of work. It was a poetry of the street: of the civic meeting place, the market, the transit lounge. It had flourished independent of academia—where, meanwhile,

a long-standing debate was (and is) going on about the possible "decline" of the role of poetry in American life. To my
mind, it's clear both that the decline is unquestionable and
that nobody has made the point more wittily than Randall
Jarrell, who once remarked, "Tomorrow morning some poet
may, like Byron, wake up to find himself famous—for having
written a novel, for having killed his wife; it will not be for
having written a poem." Yet if in the twentieth century serious poets were gently elbowed to the margins of American
society, the core position they once occupied was taken up by
pop lyricists—and to understand what *they* were up to, you
had to look at poetic structures afresh. Here was a new landscape, a new architecture.

One of my most valued reference books is Robert Gottlieb
and Robert Kimball's *Reading Lyrics*, which gathers the words
to more than a thousand American pop songs composed from
1900 to 1975. To thumb through its pages is to be struck by
how much passionately lived life it reflects, by how much of
our twentieth-century panorama it encompasses: Prohibition,
the Depression, two world wars, the battle for civil rights, all
manner of passions and pastimes. With these words, Americans courted one another and held one another, explained
and entertained themselves, laughed over a goofy pun and
sought solace when feeling hopelessly unloved. And in *Reading Lyrics,* one is struck, too, by how often the "word sling-
ers" more than held up their end—crafting bright phrases and
spry rhymes not only for appealing melodies, artful films, and
evergreen Broadway hits but also for lackluster tunes, shoddy
movies, and creaky, unrevivable shows.

While lyricists were claiming prerogatives once reserved
for high-minded poets, they were also compensating for a
retreat at the other, "low" end of literature—the domain of

untutored folk poetry. In the twentieth century, that perennially fertile artist, Anonymous, finally fell on hard times.
The creator of so much vibrant American work, particularly ballads ("John Henry," "Frankie and Johnny," "Casey
Jones," "Stagolee"), suffered an extended writer's block.
(The century's best anonymous lyric may be "The Burglar of
Babylon"—only it isn't anonymous; it's an Elizabeth Bishop
poem that draws on the techniques and cadences of the old,
unnamed ballad writers.)

Much of the literary piecework that Anonymous reliably provided—ditties and slogans, naughty epigrams, brief
explosions of high jinks and nonsense, day-to-day rhymed
accounts of minor frustrations and triumphs seemingly too
banal for the serious artist—was appropriated by the lyricist.
Especially in the case of lesser-known songwriters, we find
a situation akin to the old anonymous poet, whose stanzas
gained currency even as he himself remained unheralded.
Few people know who wrote the lyrics to "Happy Days Are
Here Again" or "Santa Claus Is Comin' to Town" or "Bye
Bye Blackbird"—all included in *Reading Lyrics*—but these are
words strung like power lines across our landscape; friend to
friend, stranger to stranger, we are connected by them.

Reading Lyrics is arranged chronologically, by authors' birth
dates, and its forward journey tells various evolutionary tales.
Over time, some song species went extinct, or linger only as
relicts. Meanwhile, new forms were cohering and others were
branching off. The early songs of naked patriotism associated
with George M. Cohan—"You're a Grand Old Flag," "The
Yankee Doodle Boy"—largely disappeared in later decades,
their sentiments perhaps mutating into various country-and-
western pieties. The song of social protest, too—although
never a significant strain in American pop—marched off,

toward folk and rock music, from which many anthems of the antiwar and civil rights movements were drawn. (Tame as it now looks, a pop song like that Depression-era tale of financial reversal "Brother, Can You Spare a Dime," with lyrics by E. Y. Harburg, was initially banned from the radio as incendiary. The American pop lyric was rarely hospitable to insurgency.)

One common appetite unifies the songwriters: a penchant for American slang, a taste for the native vernacular. It's there in the first decade of the century, for even while Cohan was busily waving the flag, he was proudly talking turkey ("And that ain't a josh / She's a Yankee, by gosh," "Music to please the gang / With plenty of biff and bang"). And you find it in the book's final pages, in the lyrics of Sondheim ("It's not I'm antisocial / I'm only anti-work. / Gloryosky, / That's why I'm a jerk!") and Fred Ebb ("I know a whoopee spot / Where the gin is cold / But the piano's hot").

Slang contributes much of the coruscation in Irving Berlin's "Top Hat, White Tie, and Tails," written for one of my half-dozen favorite movies, *Top Hat*. Although the song embraces an elegant formality on two levels—the clothing it celebrates and the prosody it implements—it sparkles with colloquialisms. The singer is puttin' on his top hat, dudein' up his shirt front, polishin' his nails, in an atmosphere:

That simply reeks with class;
And I trust
That you'll excuse my dust
When I step on the gas.

The gentleman the song was written for, Fred Astaire, may have epitomized suavity, but he also embodied razzmatazz,

and in *Top Hat* he breaks into these words minutes after creating a ruckus in a somnolent London gentlemen's club. Those
dozing Brits clearly needed a dose of American moxie, and
Fred gave it to them by detonating a clattering explosion with
his neat, polished feet.

By Tin Pan Alley convention, the rawness of slang was
often highlighted, as in "Top Hat, White Tie, and Tails," by
a formal setting. Rhymes were exact, grammatical niceties
respected, enunciations clean. Singers were, you might say,
talking up—employing a more elevated discourse than their
everyday speech. You hear it when Billie Holiday cries "Give
your heart and your love / To whomever you love" in Ted
Koehler's "Don't Worry 'Bout Me." Or when Sinatra asks
"Whom can I run to" in Harburg's "April in Paris," or sings
the phrase "Just within a trice" in Tom Adair's "Violets for
Your Furs." (This sort of high diction occasionally runs into
tonal inconsistencies, as when Sinatra, in the more swingin'
mode he adopted after leaving Columbia Records, began regularly dropping his *g*'s—adding a somewhat discrepant touch
to lines like "Night and Day, why is it so / That this longin'
for you follows wherever I go?")

If Tin Pan Alley talked up, rock music habitually talks
down, producing its own anomalies. Hard as it is to envision
some member of the Sinatra Rat Pack asking, in real life,
"Whom can I run to," it's harder still to picture Mick Jagger,
who studied at the London School of Economics, unironi-
cally observing, "I can't get no satisfaction." Spanning half a
century in the history of a rapidly evolving country, the songs
of *Reading Lyrics* maintain at least one constant: they rhyme.
And the same holds true today. Whether you the songwriter
are a hip-hop artist or a straight-up rocker or a rapper or a

throwback folkie, you're likely a rhymer. In this regard, the contemporary poet who has abandoned rhyme has distanced himself from song—from the music of the streets. (A precarious place for a poet to reside, it seems to me.)

Defending his decision to exclude "The Owl and the Pussycat" from his anthology, Kingsley Amis, editor of *The New Oxford Book of English Light Verse*, argued that light verse can never be beautiful. Although this strikes me as an unnecessarily restrictive view, it does seem largely valid for American pop lyrics. When they drift toward the conventionally—the poetically—beautiful, lyrics cross into the terrain of either the art song or the folk song. Certainly, the lyric poet's traditional mother of beauty—Mother Nature—has almost no place in the pop song. When she does make an appearance, she's likely to don a carnival guise. We're far closer to the natural world of Byron than of Wordsworth, as where Lorenz Hart (first employing, with *greenery/scenery,* a rhyme dear to Byron) concocts a song of pastoral bliss:

> Just two crazy people together.
> While you love your lover, let
> Blue skies be your coverlet—
> When it rains we'll laugh at the weather.

Or where Oscar Hammerstein extols the rich Oklahoma soil:

> The corn is as high as a elephant's eye,
> An' it looks like it's climbin' clear up to the sky.

Or where Hoagy Carmichael evokes a Hoosier tranquillity:

> Some old lazy river
> Sleeps beside my door,
> Whisp'ring to the sunlit shore.

Still, given the profusion of topics and themes and moods the American pop song has entertained over the decades, it's scarcely surprising if something approaching pure beauty has occasionally slipped in. The close to Cole Porter's "In the Still of the Night" has some of the elongated, chiming musicality of Edward Lear and his—yes—"The Owl and the Pussycat":

> Or will this dream of mine
> Fade out of sight
> Like the moon
> Growing dim
> On the rim
> Of the hill
> In the chill,
> Still
> Of the night?

And in its deft expansions and contractions, as well as its plea for a precisely graduated understanding, Johnny Burke's "Moonlight Becomes You" recalls the quatrains of Louise Bogan:

> If I say I love you,
> I want you to know
> It's not just because there's moonlight, although
> Moonlight becomes you so.

Reading Lyrics provides an illuminating sidelight to the Library of America's two-volume *American Poetry: The Twentieth Century*. Much of the most poignant poetry in the twin volumes is surpassingly bleak (T. S. Eliot, Robinson Jeffers, Ezra Pound, Theodore Roethke), and the prevailing atmosphere is, for long stretches, suitably harrowing. *Reading Lyrics* offers a corrective, continually reminding us of how much lighthearted joy was simultaneously being generated by poetry—the poetry of the lyricist. Page after page, there's no mistaking the sheer glee fused into the making of these songs. "*No tears in the writer, no tears in the reader,*" Frost once remarked. I'm not sure I agree, but I'm confident of a corollary truth: *No laughter in the writer, no laughter in the reader.* Cole Porter, Ira Gershwin, Lorenz Hart, Frank Loesser—surely they were smiling as they came up with "Let's Do It, Let's Fall in Love," "They All Laughed," "The Lady Is a Tramp," "Luck Be a Lady."

It's not always easy to distinguish one Tin Pan Alley lyricists from another, largely because their aims were so similar. Again and again they told the same two stories: He or she hurt me; he or she healed me. The characters inhabiting the songs are typically as insubstantial as the glints and shadows thrown by a disco ball—originally known as a glitter ball, back when it and Tin Pan Alley were emerging novelties. The characters hardly matter. What matters, what differentiates one song from another, is the freshness and dexterity with which it lays out its familiar tales of heartbreak and heartmend.

The best lyricists were quick to acknowledge that what they were doing wasn't what Shakespeare or Donne or Keats once did. They were problem solvers: fixers of broken songs, broken revues, broken plays and movies. Self-described craftsmen, they shared the craftsman's sense of a guild membership, a collective undertaking.

As a result, a monument like *Reading Lyrics* ultimately becomes much more than the sum of its parts. Few of its lyrics boast that linguistic savor that demands a second reading—and yet we return to the words, by way of the melodies, again and again, and find them ever satisfying. Together, they construct a sort of verbal metropolis whose prosody—whose architecture—is novel and disorienting and enlivening. Yes, we may often confuse the individual songwriters. But we love them collectively, and the golden age blurs into a shared golden mist. As we lose their names, we seem to hear something as disembodied as our language itself freshly coming into its own—ballyhooing with its everyday élan.

◻

CHAPTER TWENTY

Poetry and Folly

Architects have a useful term that has no clear counter-part among poets. They speak of a *folly* with affection and approval. It's defined by the *Longman Dictionary of Contemporary English* as "an unusual building that was built in the past as a decoration, not to be used or lived in." And by *Webster's* as "an often extravagant picturesque building erected to suit a fanciful taste." In this case, preferring *fanciful* to *unusual,* I'd plump for *Webster's,* since its definition makes way for the willfully whimsical, the perversely peculiar. On the internet I recently came upon an upside-down church, its steeple pointing toward Hell. Now *that's* one fanciful construction.

Over the years, buildings have been laboriously constructed to resemble dogs, cats, hens, mushrooms, hats—as if to literalize the Marvin Gaye song "Wherever I Lay My Hat (That's My Home)"—boots, beer glasses, cars, sailing ships, and God knows what else. Such structures reflect the dogged domestic lunacy at the word's French root, *folie,* which carries associations of both madness and a cherished abode. In the poetry world, too, we find complex assemblages that evince a plodding, contented, brick-by-brick madness, even if we don't typically refer to them as follies. Consider "Washington Crossing the Delaware," by David Shulman.

Shulman was a champion Scrabble player and contributor to the *OED*. His poem, a sonnet, was written in 1936. In none of its fourteen lines will you find the following letters: *b, f, j, k, m, p, q, u, v, x, y, z*. Why not? Because they fail to appear in the poem's title, of which all fourteen lines are precise anagrams (e.g., since there are four *e*'s in "Washington Crosses the Delaware," four *e*'s must appear in each line; three *a*'s means three *a*'s; and so forth). Much more remarkable: The poem, whose first line is "A hard, howling, tossing water scene" and whose last line is "He's astern—so go alight, crew, and win!," actually makes a fair amount of sense, and follows a discernible meter, and rhymes responsibly. Though it's hardly a good poem, I've read far worse by poets operating without a single restriction in the world (other than lack of talent, industry, and imagination).

But the anagrammatic sonnet, like the house contrived to resemble a teapot, enkindles more curiosity than inspiration. The most compelling follies, whether architectural or poetic, are those whose primary goal isn't the merely bizarre or even the fiendishly difficult; rather, their aims and appeals are aesthetic.

Such is the case with two recentish books that sport with our notions of follies, John Hollander's *Powers of Thirteen* (1983) and Greg Williamson's *A Most Marvelous Piece of Luck* (2008). Hollander's volume might be described as thirteen raised to the fourth. There are 169 poems (thirteen times thirteen) each consisting of thirteen lines, each containing thirteen syllables. This is fertile material, for the emotional fascinations of the number thirteen are long-standing and considerable: It is defiantly prime, it remains notoriously unlucky (dine with a dozen other people only if you're planning a Last Supper), and it suggests the deliberate superfluity of the baker's dozen. Its power is encapsulated in a single word: *triskaidekaphobia,* or fear of the number thirteen. Not surprisingly, there are some lovely things threaded through the book's 28,561 syllables (13^4):

> I went out without you yesterday for a slow hour.
> The lichens which in the right light give a choral tongue
> To the rising rock were simply plastered over it;
> The fir woods began just as its circle of shadow;
> The sun leaked down to the floor in interesting ways;
> Here was here and there was there . . .

Even so, *Powers of Thirteen* feels too long—too devoted to its predetermined goal of 169 poems. For all the book's length, it paradoxically winds up feeling claustrophobic. We're reminded that *folly* is a sonic cousin to *failure.*

Something similar might have been predicted for Greg Williamson's *A Most Marvelous Piece of Luck,* one of the most self-constricted books I know. It consists entirely of rhymed sonnets—sixty-nine of them—which sounds rigid enough, but Williamson goes the form one better by subjecting it to a range of quirky restrictions: In every sonnet, the title is identical to the last word or words of the poem; the ninth line of each opens with *Until;* and the closing six lines invariably intimate or chronicle a death.

The potential pitfall here is cavernous: the threat of sameness and depletion in anything so formally scripted. It's a danger Williamson largely circumvents through sheer

cleverness: There's a superabundance of wit and wordplay—
outrageous puns, fractured homilies, garbled quotations,
double entendres.

A Most Marvelous Piece of Luck recalls those planetarium
shows that, in their vertiginous final minutes, whirl the audience through the cosmos. The first two poems are "Time"
and "Space." We begin with a bang—the big bang—and
drift steadily homeward across the universe, until we're in the
thick of modern life: poems about trains, jets, and rock music,
marijuana and beer and tacos. After lunch, so to speak, we
journey back outward, to "The Hubble Constant" and "The
Ten Spacetime Dimensional Universe."

This is light verse in the most capacious sense, less in
the line of Ogden Nash and Phyllis McGinley than of James
Merrill and L. E. Sissman; it makes room for the lyrical and
weighty.

Here is "Easter Island," in which a spoof on UFO con-
spiracists finishes as something closer in spirit to Shelley's
"Ozymandias" than to the *National Enquirer*:

> The statues, we now know, were carved in place, then
> Transconveyed across (some thirteen tons)
> The lonely, trade-wind-whipped terrain by spacemen
> Using laser beams (see Williamson's
>
> *The Secret Places of the Lion*), but
> That's science, and you contemplate, out there
> In mid-Pacific, the obsessive glut
> Of clenched jaws and the thousand-mile stare
>
> Until, your excavations at an end,
> You see, with peerless eyes, the oblong sun

> Go down, and see in your own rocky highland,
> Its leaning headstones and the endless wind,
> Resigned, enisled, cut off from everyone,
> Your kinship with the tribe
>   of Easter Island.

That lovely pun on *headstones* encourages the reader to look deeper (is *enisled* a play on *annihilation?*), and the pun on peerless is better still: These are the unexampled eyes that see everything and nothing at once.

Charming, too, is the way those stone heads, in their bodiless improbability, recall architectural follies. Silently, they speak both of spiritual hunger and the air of physical displacement so common to the best follies, nostalgic for environs abandoned but not forgotten. Hence the profound appeal of the landlocked lighthouse in the forested valley a thousand miles from the sea; of the obelisk in the Ozarks; the leaning campanile in the Badlands. And hence the picturesque charm of all those classical ruins—*built* as ruins, centuries and centuries after the sun went down on ancient Greece and Rome—scattered across the English countryside. Like the skull once perched on the medieval scholar's desk, such ruins are memento mori. Even as, two hundred years ago, the gleaming Georgian manse was materializing, the ruins beside it foresaw its eventual razing.

Consider two short poems—ruinous poems, both favorites of mine—about Native Americans. The first is Robert Frost's "A Cliff Dwelling":

> There sandy seems the golden sky
> And golden seems the sandy plain.
> No habitation meets the eye

Unless in the horizon rim,
Some halfway up the limestone wall,
That spot of black is not a stain
Or shadow, but a cavern hole,
Where someone used to climb and crawl
To rest from his besetting fears.
I see the callus on his soul
The disappearing last of him
And of his race starvation slim,
Oh years ago—ten thousand years.

The second is John Fandel's "Indians":

Margaret mentioned Indians,
And I began to think about Indians—

Indians once living
Where now we are living—

And I thought how little I know
About Indians. Oh, I know

What I have heard. Not much,
When I think how much

I wonder about them,
When a mere mention of them,

Indians, starts me. I
Think of their wigwams. I

Think of canoes. I think
Of quick arrows. I think

Of things Indian. And still
I think of their bright, still

Summers, when these hills
And meadows on these hills

Shone in the morning
Suns before this morning.

The two poems have much in common: subject matter, brevity, simplicity of language. Both are less about Indigenous peoples (the poet in each case modestly disclaiming any expertise about them) than about distant worlds, vanished civilizations. The poems could equally be about Kushites, Carthaginians, Akkadians, Jōmons. They share a sweet, childish tone, established in their opening lines. (Indeed, I met Fandel's poem not in *The New Yorker*, where it first appeared, but in an anthology of children's verse.)

For all their resemblances, I think of "A Cliff Dwelling" as an admirably solid, typically Frostian construction. On the other hand, Fandel's poem looks like a folly.

Frost's poem is in rigidly regular iambic tetrameter. (Andrew Marvell would have felt at home.) Rhymes are all exact. (Alexander Pope, ditto.) The poem is working in a centuries-old tradition.

Fandel's poem has no meter, other than an insouciant adherence to a three-beat line. It has no conventional rhyme scheme, only a set of couplets whose paired end words are identical. One can envision Fandel in the poem's early stages, playing around, his scribbled notes drifting toward a draft. He discovers a fair amount of repetition and—the lovely moment of folly—resolves to build a poem whose surprise resides in its sameness.

I like the way he fails to explain or account for himself. Who is Margaret? His wife? His daughter? And why does the poem take the queer form that it does? The poem feels at once casual and callow—increasingly childlike by the time we hit the fifth repetition of *I think*. As is often true with Elizabeth Bishop, the poem feigns a jaunty naïveté, a stubby, unstudied declarativeness. But this sort of repetition ultimately cries out for variation, which arrives in that splendid moment where we alight upon the second *still*. For this is a new *still*, a different *still*. The first is an adverb, the second an adjective. The first adds a note of qualification, the second a splash of lyricism. It's all quite beautifully, simply done, and deftly mirrored in the final stanza, where the first *morning* looks like a noun but is in fact an adjective, and only the second *morning* is that real thing, a noun, an entity, an event, the very day you're inhabiting at this moment.

As far as I can determine, Fandel never again employed this form. In this, too, "Indians" fits with a folly: a cultivated air of idiosyncrasy, an essence rooted in rarity. Architectural or poetic, the folly's true domain is a mystical, ideal Land of the One-offs.

No modern poet in English created so many exciting one-offs as Louis MacNeice, whose dark imagination kept locating improbable spaces in which to hole up for the night. A poet's poet, he is read especially by those hoping to chance upon something odd and marvelous that might be borrowed or stolen. Recall "The Sunlight on the Garden," an amazingly intricate and lovely poem, and (in *Webster's* sense of an "extravagant picturesque building erected to suit a fanciful taste") perhaps the finest folly in the language. MacNeice wrote, prosodically, some of the queerest poems of our time. He fused a revolutionary's appetite for novelty to a conservative's reverence for established discipline. (In 1953, when asked to address the question "What do I believe?" MacNeice responded, "What I do believe is that as a human being, it is my duty to make patterns and to contribute to order—good patterns and a good order.")

Like Marianne Moore (the subject of chapter 22), he created unusual designs as a matter of reflex. But in Moore's case, once you've adjusted to her guiding procedures (her syllabic verse, her **light rhyme,** her wayward indentations), you generally know where you stand. Having read a stanza, you can safely extrapolate the form to follow. With MacNeice, though, the underpinnings may be slow to declare themselves, as in the four-part "Nature Notes." Its first section is entitled "Dandelions":

> Incorrigible, brash,
> They brightened the cinder path of my childhood,
> Unsubtle, the opposite of primroses,
> But, unlike primroses, capable
> Of growing anywhere, railway track, pierhead,
> Like our extrovert friends who never
> Make us fall in love, yet fill
> The primroseless roseless gaps.

What is the prosodic contract here—what do these lines intimate or promise about what's to come? Almost nothing. For who in the world would predict that each of the succeeding stanzas would begin with *Incorrigible*? That each second line would end with *childhood*? That each third line would incorporate *opposite* and each fourth line *unlike*? The rules here may be self-generated, but they're unbending; they stipulate with precision the definitions of both obedience and violation to the form—a form that, naturally, bears no relation to anything you'd find in any handbook of prosodic terms.

Some of MacNeice's most interesting experiments arise in a small scattering of poems that wed disparate stanzaic configurations. Here is the opening of "Hands and Eyes," which brings together (a typically unlikely MacNeice *mélange*) a farmer, an infant, and a monkey:

> In a high wind
> Gnarled hands cup to kindle an old briar,
> From a frilled cot
> Twin sea anemones grope for a hanging lamp,
> In a foul cage
> Old coal-gloves dangle from dejected arms.
>
> Of which three pairs of hands, the child's are helpless
> (Whose wheels barely engage)
> And the shepherd's from his age are almost bloodless
> While the chimpanzee's are hopeless
> Were there not even a cage.

In formal terms, the two stanzas share little: The first has six lines, the second five; the first has no rhymes, the second has one; the first (alternating dimeter and pentameter) flows, the second congests. Perhaps they're randomly conjoined? And yet MacNeice holds to their alternating pattern until the seventh and final stanza emerges as a hybrid: a seven-line form that borrows from each prototype. When its techniques are dissected in this fashion, a poem like "Hands and Eyes" may appear bloodless and academic. On the page, though, with its contrapuntal music jostling in your ears, it comes off as novel and invigorating.

"House on a Cliff" is another short poem that sets up its own rules and expectations:

Indoors the tang of a tiny oil lamp. Outdoors
The winking signal on the waste of sea.
Indoors the sound of the wind. Outdoors the wind.
Indoors the locked heart and the lost key.

Outdoors the chill, the void, the siren. Indoors
The strong man pained to find his red blood cools,
While the blind clock grows louder, faster. Outdoors
The silent moon, the garrulous tides she rules.

Indoors ancestral curse-cum-blessing. Outdoors
The empty bowl of heaven, the empty deep.
Indoors a purposeful man who talks at cross
Purposes, to himself, in a broken sleep.

The human portrait here is typically sketchy. Perhaps the subject is a lighthouse keeper, or a farmer. We know, anyway, he's reticent and indrawn; uneasy about aging; troubled in his ancestral legacy. We know he finds no peace anywhere, out or in. Formally, I suppose you could call this a traditional poem—what could be more conventional than rhymed iambic pentameter quatrains? But within its orthodox format the poem announces another pattern, one so odd and so strident as to drown out traditional harmonies. The poet does some delicate work with a sledge-hammer. We have a poem of eleven scattered sentences, each beginning, alternatingly, with *Indoors* or *Outdoors*. The poem poses a technical problem, which might be described as *How do you stop the hammer blows?* Or, *What device will bring this slam-bang construction together?*

The answer lies in that phrase *cross purposes*—or better still, *cross / Purposes* (the enjambment enhancing and summing up the dynamic balance of tensions). The poem floats away. Both the Indoors and the Outdoors dissolve—or are carried off—into the likewise conflicted domain of the man's unconsciousness. It's an adroit solution. At times, MacNeice's poems partake of the spirit not so much of the chess player, who naturally focuses on plausible lines of play, as the chess problemist, who relishes positions that wouldn't normally arise. He shares with the problemist both a love of ingenuity for its own sake and a penchant for outlandish configurations.

In no area is MacNeice's influence potentially so salutary as in his prosody—or let's call it his restless urge to create singular, weird-looking objects. In the twenty-first century, much formal verse (all those blank-verse narratives, those earnest quatrains) has a wayworn feel, and various once-recherché forms have been done to death. (Is there a reader of contemporary poetry left in America who doesn't shudder on turning a page and discovering yet one more sestina?) Contemporary poets of a prosodic bent—those in whom the creative impulse is indissolubly tied to an impulse to fabricate patterns—might look to MacNeice as a replenisher.

Now and then, what originates as folly becomes something else: a signature form, a full chapter in one's oeuvre. Consider Richard Wilbur's "Thyme Flowering Among Rocks," which opens this way:

This, if Japanese,
Would represent grey boulders
Walloped by rough seas

So that, here or there,
The balked water tossed its froth
Straight into the air.

Here, where things are what
They are, it is thyme blooming,
Rocks, and nothing but—

Having, nonetheless,
Many small leaves implicit,
A green countlessness.

The very first line is a tip-off. *Japanese* prepares us for the haikus to follow, even as the poem simultaneously, wittily insists on how un-Japanese it is. No, we will renounce that rich Eastern tradition of attaching symbols to every element in a garden. We are going to be Western, where "things are what they are" and facts are facts. . . .

Of course it's all an artful joke, for *nothing* here is what it is. A small and simple blossom, the thyme flowering among rocks, is neither small nor simple. It is really time itself, brooding among rocks: We're back in the land of ruins. (In an earlier poem, "Epistemology," Wilbur warns, "But cloudy, cloudy is the stuff of stones.")

The poem disavows things Japanese by another means, as well: its rigorous adherence to clean, clarion rhyme. (All fourteen of the poem's paired rhymes are exact.) Rhyme has no place in the classical Japanese poetry evoked with Bashō, though it has always been a complaisant beast of burden in Wilbur's stable.

Hence, for this special occasion—this blending of botany and Bashō, of Western rhyme and Eastern syllabics—Wilbur went and erected a folly. He created a sort of teahouse for himself in his home in the Berkshires of western Massachusetts. And my guess is that he saw it as such, as a one-off, and had no plans to redeploy the form.

But redeploy he did. Over the next few decades, he enlisted the form in three more poems about botanical subjects: "Signature," "Alatus," "Zea." Put all four together and you have some 124 lines of verse, in which the formal requirements of both traditions, East and West, syllable count and exact rhyme, are punctiliously respected. What begins as folly eventually, through repeated use, loses its air of idiosyncrasy and becomes a viable, potentially useful structure for a variety of occasions.

In *Anterooms*, his final volume, he returned to the form four more times. What had once looked like a one-off had become the book's dominant mode. One of the four was "A Measuring Worm," here reprinted in its entirety:

This yellow striped green
Caterpillar, climbing up
The steep window screen,

Constantly (for lack
Of a full set of legs) keeps
Humping up his back.

It's as if he sent
By a sort of semaphore
Dark omegas meant

To warn of Last Things.
Although he doesn't know it,
He will soon have wings,

And I, too, don't know
Toward what undreamt condition
Inch by inch I go.

Wilbur was eighty-six when the poem appeared, and I think this little creation is an improbable masterpiece. (What could be better than the understated elegance and enormousness of *undreamt condition?*) I'd go further: No American poet of such an advanced age ever wrote a finer poem.

"A Measuring Worm" originated with a minute observation: the way in which a caterpillar, hunching up its back, approximates an omega shape. As a man reaching the omega of his own life, Wilbur had found a metaphor of profound personal significance.

The poem bears close connections to "All but Blind," by Walter de la Mare, a poet whom Wilbur adored:

All but blind
In his chambered hole,
Gropes for worms
The four-clawed mole.

All but blind
In the evening sky,
The hooded Bat
Twirls softly by.

All but blind
In the burning day,
The barn owl
Blunders on her way.

And blind as are
These three to me,
So blind to someone
I must be.

Both poems insist that our eyes are not the final arbiter. What we cannot see must be taken on faith. Wilbur's "Measuring Worm" is a matter-of-fact poem about miracles. Or one might better say that what begins in human folly ends in divine madness.

◻

CHAPTER TWENTY-ONE

Dining with the Funesians

(Gerard Manley Hopkins)

A performer stands up, a poem is about to be recited. Perhaps we're at a funeral. We're at a wedding. A high school graduation. A honky-tonk bar, here's an open mike, it's a girls' night out.

Assuming you're the speaker, and the poem your creation, no guidance is required; you're the expert, and you'll read it just as you believe it should be read. But let's say it's someone else's poem. Shakespeare, Emily Dickinson, Edgar Guest— whatever the source, the odds are you've received no instructions on how to proceed. Generally, poems don't tell you how they wish to be recited.

Contrast this with the world of classical music, with its strict and elaborate codes for public recital. The birth of musical notation, which allows a modern composer to choreograph every aspect of a performance, is an inspiring story, lovingly set out in Thomas Forrest Kelly's *Capturing Music*. It's a tale of refinement sparking refinement down the centuries. My handy little dictionary of musical notation runs some 355 pages—all of them devoted to illuminating a composer's intentions.

With the invention of the metronome, in the early nine-teenth century, desired tempi could be established within frac-tions of a second. Modern chromatic tuners will adjust pitch to indiscernible degrees of fineness. But not all instruction is so mechanical. In the modern era, composers have often offered personal-sounding advice, as in Mahler's "cheerful in tone and cheeky in expression." The ever-unconventional Eric Satie took this impulse out to the furthest edge, propos-ing that one passage in a piano piece be conveyed "like a nightingale with toothache."

Among poets, Vachel Lindsey (1879–1931), who barn-stormed across America practicing "higher vaudeville," was a rarity in providing counsel on how to read his poems aloud. In "The Santa Fe Trail," the reader is advised that one pas-sage is to be orated "like a train caller in a railroad station" and another is "to be brawled with a snapping explosiveness ending in a languorous chant." But Lindsey was sparing in his annotations. Readers seeking the most minute advice, of a nicety analogous to what musical notation allows, must even-tually turn to Gerard Manley Hopkins.

Like so much else in his life, Hopkins's publishing history was singular. A convert from his family's High Anglican-ism to Catholicism while an undergraduate at Oxford, later a Jesuit priest, Hopkins repeatedly swore off the writing of poetry as a vanity and distraction from his duties to God. Wayward in his application to verse, he was still more so in pursuit of publication. Few of his poems appeared during his lifetime (1844–1889), and it wasn't until 1918, as modernism was everywhere burgeoning, that this mid-Victorian poet belatedly arrived in book form.

In truth, he belonged among those iconoclastic mod-ernists, for he was something altogether new, disassembling and reassembling language with the best of them. And he belonged back among the Victorians, given his sometimes quaint diction and his distrustful suspicion that irony's mode was a temptation to be resisted as ungrateful and ungodly. (Irony was the modernists' universal currency.) In addition, he belonged to a spiritual zone far removed from both of these worlds, one as detached and timeless as those high-minded constellations of clouds perpetually rolling over his poetic landscapes.

His innovations were partly a matter of vocabulary. He loved obscure, pungent, punchy monosyllables, often agricultural and dialectical in origin. If you feel fully at home with terms like *degged, flitch, fashed, pashed,* and *shive,* you must be either an ancient Lancashire farmer or a young grad student preparing a thesis on Hopkins.

But his newness was chiefly a matter of cadence and harmony. He adored compaction and his syllables fell in bizarre thick clusters. In a letter to his friend the poet Robert Bridges, he set out seven different diacritical markings for how his sonnet "Harry Ploughman" ought to be read. A caretlike symbol indicated "strong stress." A fermata asked the reader to "pause or dwell on a syllable, which need not however have the metrical stress." A subtending arch rendered the syllables above it "extrametrical; a slight pause follows as if the voice were silently making its way back to the highroad of the verse." And so forth.

From the outset of this book, *Rhyme's Rooms* has been rooted in hypotheticals, beginning with those outlandish Funesians, who "hear things the rest of us don't hear." But when you place Hopkins among them, suddenly they feel far less fanciful. Theirs is a jubilant encounter. The Funesians gladly make room for him at one of their bare wooden tables.

And oh, how they glow at the sight of those seven distinct aural indicators. Order triumphant! Progress at last! Bring out the mountain potatoes, bring out the pickled turnips, the time's come for a priestly feast.

No poet before Hopkins sounded quite like him, or looked like him on the page. Consider a line from "Spelt from Sibyl's Leaves": "Her fond yellow hornlight wound to the west, her wild hollow hoarlight hung to the height . . ."

Well, a real mouthful. Though it looks like a *pair* of lines at least, it's merely line three in what Hopkins called the "longest sonnet ever made." Note how intricately, syllable by syllable, the sound contours of "her fond yellow hornlight" and "her wild hollow hoarlight" mirror each other, *hornlight* and *hoarlight* as close to identical twins as distinct words can be.

While the line may sound purely ornamental, it captures a specific dusky moment. The sun just now setting is an ancient sun, evoking those primeval lamps in which animal horns, pared and whittled to translucency, sheltered and shed a vulnerable flame. Sunset yields to hoarlight (ice light, starlight) and to the vacancy (hollow) of the night sky. One more day . . . but what a day! Note, too, how "wound to the west" and "hung to the height" square off as alliterative pairs: The music enacts a kind of protracted cosmic balance. You won't find in Milton (Hopkins's great model) or in Shakespeare a systematically more complicated line.

And much the same might be said of line fourteen: "Where, selfwrung, selfstrung, sheathe- and shelterless, thoughts against thoughts in groans grind."

Again, alliterative pairs; symmetries; identicalities (*thoughts/ thoughts*); and variations off the identical (*groans/grind*). Again, near homonyms (*selfwrung/selfstrung*), although this time, to vary the music, Hopkins has placed them in the first half of the line. It's all the sonic equivalent of a fun house hall of mirrors. Some sounds are reflected truly, but most of the notes bend, convexly or concavely, away from themselves.

Or take the first two gargantuan lines of "The Leaden Echo and the Golden Echo," a song for the water maidens of St. Winefred's Well, where a pristine source percolated up from the earth in divine acknowledgment of a brutal martyrdom. The poem begins by asking how beauty, in a perilous and destructive world, is to be safeguarded:

> How to keep—is there any any, is there none such,
>   nowhere known some, bow or brooch or braid or
>   brace, lace, latch or catch or key to keep
> Back beauty, keep it, beauty, beauty, beauty, . . . from
>   vanishing away?

While the lines may seem confusing and intimidating (even though I've left off Hopkins's idiosyncratic accent marks in hopes of momentarily reducing confusion and intimidation), it's apparent that the music is complex and compressed, rich and strange. To read the lines slowly, aloud, is to lift aloft a birdlike flock of echoes—rising, plunging, regathering, repurposing—that Hopkins alone had the ear to hear.

A musical parade of such lines could be extended indefinitely. But even with the few I've provided, it's obvious that Hopkins, of all the poets we've examined, most exemplifies the paramount lesson the Funesians would impart: He reminds us of how narrow are the sonic sectors our poets have traditionally worked inside, how amplitudinous the range beyond. More than other poets do, he tests our hearing. Which naturally raises another question: Who *was* this man—seemingly so straitlaced, so dutiful, so fixed upon spiritual compliance and piety—who kept blasting all our civilized expectations, who kept urging us into musical spaces unsounded before?

He was a great one for taking the long view. So it's hardly unexpected that contemporaneous theories of art for art's sake held no appeal for him, given that all art, all everything, derives from God. Nor is his poetic obscurity surprising, since all mysteries are unriddled in God's eye.

Yet the more you read Hopkins, the clearer it grows how fervently he wished for comprehending readers. His links to the modernists sometimes disguises this desire. Yes, when he writes a phrase like "that side hurling a heavyheaded hundredfold / What while we, while we slumbered," he sounds closer to E. E. Cummings than to anybody in the nineteenth century. And the creatures in a line like "As kingfishers catch fire, dragonflies draw flame" feel more like denizens of one of Marianne Moore's bestiaries than William Wordsworth's. Yet Hopkins showed little tolerance for what would be, in the next century, the modernists' common acceptance of obscurantism—especially the idea that certain emotional states are necessarily, rightly ineffable. It's hard to picture Eliot or Pound or Moore doing what Hopkins regularly did when Bridges complained a passage was opaque: He would obligingly supply an abundant prose paraphrase. Even when Hopkins's words hurtle like a river in spate, he can be counted on to have in mind some fixed phenomenon that he longs to impart.

This sense of arcane but discoverable meanings lends an air of sharp decisiveness to minute matters of Hopkins criticism. The most authoritative version of his poems, published in 1990, presents learned ornithological debate over what is going on, aerodynamically, with the kestrel glimpsed in the first stanza of "The Windhover":

> I caught this morning morning's minion, king-
>   dom of daylight's dauphin, dapple-dawn-drawn
>   Falcon, in his riding
> Of the rolling level underneath him steady air, and
>   striding
> High there, how he rung upon the rein of a wimpling
>   wing
> In his ecstasy!

What exactly does it mean for a bird to have "rung upon the rein of a wimpling wing?" Such discussions have a point only if Hopkins's words are more than words—if one might behold, behind all his verbal arabesques, a real bird doing real things. Since our primary human duty is, as he once wrote, to "give God glory and to mean to give it," any strain of poetry that fares too far from the world of His creation risks triviality, if not ingratitude.

Hopkins saw the very notion of "religious poetry" as something of a pleonasm—a favorite term of his when dismissing somebody's laxity of thought. While art for art's sake was predictably unsympathetic, the degree to which Hopkins chose to make a spiritual virtue of sharp-sightedness was not necessarily to be expected. But in a private world like his, where a tiny and easily overlooked bluebell could ring out a message of divine reassurance—he knew "the beauty of our Lord by it"—the alert observations of the born naturalist became not merely a gratification but a joyfully embraced responsibility.

In one of his sermons, Hopkins spoke of the world as "word, expression, news from God." Surely, given their source, no such bulletin should ever be overlooked, and we are all tasked with constant vigilance. He was pleased to discover "nothing at random," in even the most out-of-the-way places, as another journal entry makes clear:

> Looking down into the thick ice of our pond I found the imprisoned air-bubbles nothing at random but starting from centers and in particular one most beautifully regular white brush of them, each spur of it a curving string of beaded and diminishing bubbles.

This notion of an imposed watchfulness may help to explain Hopkins's passion for ephemera. He was a great one for studying, with a scientist's calibrating eye, melting crystals, rainbows, lightning, rising steam clouds, the iridescence of a pigeon's neck. The vocabulary of his observations often bore a scientific tinge: "the laws of the oak leaves," "horizontally prolate gadroons," "very plump round clouds something like the eggs in an opened ant-hill." Indeed, in many of his journal entries he sounds nearer in spirit to his troubling contemporary Charles Darwin than to anything we'd expect from a poet-priest. Of all passing natural phenomena, drifting clouds drew him most profoundly, their never-to-be-duplicated patterns serving as unignorable jottings on the chalkboard of the sky.

Admittedly, it's sometimes difficult to tell precisely what phenomenon Hopkins is describing. Just as ornithologists may argue over the windhover's flight, meteorologists could have a field day sorting out some of his more eccentric annotations:

Standing on the glacier saw the prismatic colors in the
clouds, and worth saying what sort of clouds: it was fine
shapeless skins of fretted make, full of eyebrows or like
linings of curled leaves which one finds in shelved cor-
ners of a wood.

But if readers can't always picture the cloudscapes Hopkins
so painstakingly sets before them, his journals deliver something rarer and more inspiring yet: Their minute observations
eventually add up to a vision of the world, and a portrait of
the retiring man himself, in all his potent susceptibilities and
vulnerabilities, his rapturous ardors and self-imposed asceti-
cism. His first glimpse of the northern lights is particularly
memorable and endearing:

This busy working of nature wholly independent of
the earth and seeming to go on in a strain of time not
reckoned by our reckoning of days and years but simpler
and as if correcting the preoccupation of the world by
being preoccupied with and appealing to and dated to
the day of judgment was like a new witness to God and
filled me with delightful fear.

If Hopkins witnessed God in the skies, a reader may behold
in his journals one of the gods—one of the immortals of
English poetry—likewise revealing himself through an implicit immanence.

Readers familiar with Hopkins criticism recognize a
recurring tension, a schism, between an ultimately secular

outlook and a divine interpretation of events. It's a clash of viewpoints at the heart of—among other things—how we choose to regard Hopkins's chaste romantic life. His orientation was apparently homosexual, and one might plausibly interpret his flight to the rigors of the Church as an unconscious avoidance of unnerving attractions. But from Hopkins's angle, any homoerotic longings were a species of sinful temptation, to be overcome through prayer and perhaps physical mortification. Predictably, most modern Hopkins criticism is secular at heart, though without always acknowledging how distorted—how weirdly misguided—Hopkins himself would find all interpretations of a spiritual life that negate the spiritual. For him, a failure to see how divine promptings informed his shaping, active internal essence—his "inscape," to employ his own term—was to miss everything of his life that mattered.

Viewed from the liberal mores of our own era, Hopkins can come across as a bit of a prig. This particular literary revolutionary was, whenever he stepped away from his poet's notebook, a great espouser of orthodoxy. Although he revered Milton's poetry—perhaps the largest single influence on his own—he had trouble forgiving Milton his support for loosening the divorce laws ("he was a very bad man"), and while sensing profound affinities with Whitman ("I always knew in my heart Walt Whitman's mind to be more like my own than any other man's living"), he avoided his poetry as the work of a "very great scoundrel." In his letters, he was quick to upbraid friends and family. Where others might have found a tonic irony, he commonly saw corruption, as in this stern admonition of his dear friend Bridges: "And yet let me say, to take no higher ground, that without earnestness there is nothing sound or beautiful in character and that a cynical vein much indulged coarsens everything in us."

When Hopkins's journals first appeared, some critics were pleasantly surprised to find nuggets of humor. I can't say I find many. Although he could be amusingly mock peremptory, Hopkins was a limping humorist at best, as in his few scraps of light verse or a spoof-Irish letter to a sister ("I'm intoirely ashamed o meself"). The inchoate roots of much everyday humor—aggression, resentment toward authority, irreverence, sexual tension—were scarcely impulses he'd foster. Even so, his earnestness may have had an oddly liberating effect: It probably made possible some of his more outlandish experiments with rhyme.

Hopkins regularly concocted rhymes that seemingly belonged more to Thomas Hood or Byron or Ogden Nash than to a grave religious poet who was wrestling with questions of divine justice, spiritual estrangement, the fragility of earthly beauty. How could one possibly employ, as Hopkins did, rhymes like *pain, for the / grain for thee* or *ruin / crew, in* in poems that meditate on shipwreck and tragic drowning? Or *boon he on / Communion* in a lyric about initiation into the mystical rites of the Church? Only a sensibility radically extracted from conventional trappings of humor, from that entire milieu of snappy banter where everyone's greatest fear is to be made a fool of, could have employed such clownish tools on so grave a poetic mission. In his rhyming, as in so many of his excesses, he was blessedly spared that clarity of sight which would reveal to him how near to ludicrous he could appear.

.   .   .

If poetry isn't an end in itself, but an instrument for elaborating that praise of God which is our chief moral duty, then it must forever be testing itself against the empirical beauties of creation. Hopkins was tormented by a sensation of falling short. The skies he captured in his journals, the flowers he planted in his poems—their real-life models reproached him with their effortless excellences.

This poet who saw each day as "news from God" stalked through the natural world resolutely fixed on noting its often overlooked perfections—the glistening miniatures, the quiet accords and oppositions of hue and shape, the in-between things for which, as in some pre-Adamic state, there were no names:

> Glory be to God for dappled things—
> For skies of couple-color as a brinded cow;
> For rose-moles all in stipple upon trout that swim;
> Fresh-firecoal chestnut-falls; finches' wings . . .

He took it as his especial mission to extol whatever was "counter, original, spare, strange." In this he divagated broadly from the tradition of nature verse of his time, and those critics intent on stressing his continuities to Tennyson, Wordsworth, and Thomas Gray often lose sight of what makes Hopkins so compelling: his singularity. Neither his Nature nor his nature was theirs.

There's a long and exalted tradition of English pastoral poetry, extended into the twentieth century by poets like Auden and Roethke, in which natural objects revert to archetypes: trees, flowers, and streams become Trees, Flowers, Streams. But this approach to the universal wasn't Hopkins's; rather, he observed of his own temperament that "the effect of studying masterpieces" only made him wish to "do otherwise," and that "more reading would only *refine my singularity*." His approach—support for which he found in the medieval theologian Duns Scotus—was by way of ever-greater particularity and individuation. Recall "As kingfishers catch fire . . .":

> Each mortal thing does one thing and the same:
>   Deals out that being indoors each one dwells;
>   Selves—goes itself; *myself* it speaks and spells;
> Crying *What I do is me: for that I came.*

This brings us to the lip of one of my two favorite lines that anyone ever wrote: "I say more: the just man justices." Hopkins's determination to take as his subject nature's multiplicity, in all its lumpy quiddities, accordingly became fused with a belief that only a new language, a new justicing prosody, was up to the task. The poem in which Hopkins praises creatures "counter, original, spare, strange" is itself a strange animal: a "curtal sonnet," in which both octet and sestet have been truncated to three-quarters their normal length. Even while he embraced that creaky form, the sonnet, Hopkins seems to have been temperamentally unable to work in conventional forms conventionally. His nature poetry embodies a conviction that, in rendering the teeming biological world, accuracy demands stylistic extravagance—a notion that likewise would have clicked with Darwin, who as he was preparing to publish *On the Origin of Species* remarked in a pair of letters, "Truly the schemes & wonders of nature are illimitable" and "What a wondrous problem it is,—what a play of forces, determining the kinds & proportions of each plant in a square yard of turf."

. . .

Hopkins's prosody is a complicated business, partly because he experimented in so many different directions, partly because he wasn't always clear or even consistent in his rationales. In his letters, he can seem determinedly mystical and befuddling, as in his discussion of "outrides," which he defines as an "extrametrical effect," a phrase not counted when the line is scanned. "It is and is not part of the meter," he explains—and might be a physicist talking about inherently unplaceable subatomic particles. For him, prosodic issues that most other poets would regard as purely mechanical brimmed with religious significance. In a letter to Bridges that employed some of the eccentricities of punctuation that flourished in his poetry, he noted, "I hold you to be wrong about 'vulgar,' that is obvious or necessary, rhymes. . . . It is nothing that the reader can say / He had to say it, there *was* no other rhyme: you answer / shew me what better I could have said if there had been a million. Hereby, I may tell you, hangs a very profound question treated by Duns Scotus, who shews that freedom is compatible with necessity."

The innovation Hopkins took most pride in was what he called "sprung rhythm," a prosodic system in which all unstressed syllables (the "slack") are metrically irrelevant: One measures only the number of stresses in a line. The scansion to one of his best-known poems, "Spring and Fall," is a puzzle until one realizes that all lines, despite varying lengths, contain four stresses. Here are the final lines in conventional dress:

Now no matter, child, the name:
Sorrow's springs are the same.

Nor mouth had, no nor mind, expressed
What heart heard of, ghost guessed:
It is the blight man was born for,
It is Margaret you mourn for.

And here they are adorned with Hopkins's own accents where
he thought these might be overlooked:

Now no matter, child, the name:
Sórrow's spríngs áre the same.
Nor mouth had, no nor mind, expressed
What heart heard of, ghost guessed:
It ís the blight man was born for,
It is Margaret you mourn for.

Students of prosody may call this "pure stress verse" and map
it through Coleridge back to Anglo-Saxon and *Beowulf*. In
any event, it wasn't a system that Hopkins claimed to have
invented, but to have reinvigorated and regularized. Its
resurgence might restore English poetry to "the rhythm of
prose, that is the native and natural rhythm of speech, the
least forced, the most rhetorical and emphatic of all possible
rhythms." In a more exultant mood, he declared, "Sprung
rhythm gives back to poetry its true soul and self. As poetry
is emphatically speech, speech purged of dross like gold in the
furnace, so it must have emphatically the essential element of
speech."

  For all his eager willingness to coin terms to illuminate
his experimentation, the truth is we don't have a honed and
supple-enough vocabulary to capture all the avenues he ventured down. I've mentioned his habit of turning rhyme inside
out, reversing the roles of external sounds (falling at line's

end) and internal sounds. Since Chaucer's day, poets have customarily relied on external sounds (usually enhanced by exact rhymes) to create a poem's primary echoes, with internal sounds contributing (through assonance, consonance, the occasional chime of an internal rhyme) an enriching yet muted accompaniment. But Hopkins sometimes "raised the volume" of the internal music to the point where it became primary and the end rhymes secondary. In "The Leaden Echo and the Golden Echo," how can a reader possibly be expected to hear that *girlgrace* rhymes with *face,* some hundred-plus syllables earlier, in a line like the following (and it *is* all one line): "Winning ways, airs innocent, maiden manners, sweet looks, loose locks, long locks, love-locks, gaygear, going gallant, girlgrace . . ."

But his most significant innovation may have been his pioneering use of what might be called rhyme clusters: burly packs of corresponding syllables resoundingly bumping and ricocheting off one another. Typically, he blended exact rhymes with sonic siblings, as in "wears man's smudge" and "shares man's smell."

So, "Warm-laid grave" yields to "some-life gray," "darksome burn" to "horseback brown," "forward falling" to "forehead frowning." With the exception of light verse, most English rhyming has restricted itself to one or two syllables. You might say of Gerard Manley Hopkins that he chose to ring bigger bells.

Bells abound in his poems and journals. The bells in "As kingfishers catch fire . . ." are especially lovely. When swung, each one "finds tongue to fling out broad its name." Not all the bells are auditory: One thinks of those beloved bluebells, voicing themselves visibly—announcing their identity, pealing their inscape, though the color-call of their hue.

Ring/wring was perhaps Hopkins's favorite pun. No surprise there: Between them, the two words all but encapsulate his fate. The earth's clouds, its clean stars and muddled thickets, its streams and flowers and birds—daily, inexhaustibly, in their several ways, they ring out a hymn to the glory of the Lord. Meanwhile, a lone and lonely man, the sole culpable creature in sight, must unceasingly wring his spirit (purifying it of sin) and wring his language (purifying it of sloth). And must do so in abject gratefulness, if only to bring justice to the wonders allotted him.

CHAPTER TWENTY-TWO

Drinking with the Funesians

(Marianne Moore)

Imagine a passionate and well-read lover of poetry—a gentleman of congenial if conventional tastes—coming upon Marianne Moore's "The Fish" in 1918, the year it first appeared. From his point of view, it's quite remarkable just how many missteps and outright errors are committed in the first seven lines. Here's the opening stanza and a portion of the next:

THE FISH

wade
through black jade.
    Of the crow-blue mussel-shells, one keeps
    adjusting the ash heaps;
        opening and shutting itself like

an
injured fan.

    First—foremost—it's unacceptable to bleed title directly into text this way. The poem carelessly breaches a handsome wall that has stood intact for centuries.

And our poetess has forgotten to capitalize the poem's first word—and the first words of succeeding lines.

And lines of one syllable are deficient. Likewise deficient, or at least inadvisable, are three-syllable lines. Nor, for that matter, is it correct to open with a couplet whose rackety rhymes stand a mere three syllables apart. Such a thing might be suitable in a nursery rhyme ("Lucy Locket lost her pocket . . ."), or as a display of jocose levity. But whatever its intentions, the poem clearly is neither children's ditty nor light verse.

The second couplet, so much lengthier than the first, imbalances the stanza. And if you're going to adopt rhyming cinquains—an untidy form—don't conclude the stanza with a raggedly unrhymed line. What we have is cumbersome—inharmonious. Indeed, in a mere thirty-four syllables it's striking just how many reasonable expectations she thwarts.

And these are merely the structural problems! Imagery and diction are negligent and confused. As a word painter, the woman lacks an accurate palette. Jade is properly green, not black. Black is what we expect from a crow—not the blue we encounter here. As a punctuator, too, she is delinquent, as that semicolon attests. And as a coiner of metaphor and simile, she is fanciful to the point of illogicality; ashes belong to a desiccated landscape rather than to this marine environment. And an *injured* fan? Obviously, the word she was seeking is *damaged*. And fish don't *wade*—people do. Hasn't she forced an unfortunate rhyme?

As it happens, "The Fish" was the first Moore poem to make an impression on me, back in high school days. Although many years ago, vividly I recall the submerged impact of its opening lines. In the mostly undisturbed murk of my brain

they generated a glimmer, finned and darting, and I, naturally, swam off in spirited pursuit.

It didn't take me too long to discern that Marianne Moore
wasn't getting all that many things wrong. She was getting
things right. But more than that, far more exciting than that:
She was getting things right while looking wrong, as inevitably transpires when somebody lights upon novel ingenuities
of construction.

Viewed as an architect, Moore seems to me to be, along
with Whitman, the most innovative and liberating of all
American poets. She's the closest thing we have to a Gerard
Manley Hopkins. Originality seemed to come to her, or come
upon her, effortlessly. Even in her earliest lyrics, assembled
with the conventional tools of iambics and exact rhymes, she
nurtured eccentricities. She was drawn to three-syllable lines,
as in "Ennui," a poem written when she was twenty-one (and
left uncollected):

> He often expressed
> A curious wish,
> To be interchangeably
> Man and fish;
> To nibble the bait
> Off the hook,
> Said he,
> And then slip away
> Like a ghost
> In the sea.

Like the swan in "Critics and Connoisseurs," venturing
out to appraise "such bits / of food as the stream / bore coun-

ter to it," Moore relished a swim against the current. And in her use of rhyme she swam against centuries of tradition. This was true not merely in her celebrated use of quirky and little-used rhymes: light rhyme, **apocopated rhyme,** sight rhyme, and all the rest. Having new destinations in mind, she swam against the simple, ancient *flow* of rhyme.

As we've seen, rhyme tends to condense as a poem courses toward conclusion. Even in unrhymed verse, poets often look toward rhyme for a terminating resonance. And with rhymed poems, there's likely an amassing musicality. Masculine rhymes may yield to longer, more plangent feminine rhymes. Or couplets become triplets. Or internal rhyming converges and clarifies in the final stanza(s).

Against this trend, consider a youthful little poem of Moore's called "To a Steam-Roller," a lyric of three quatrains. Here's the first of them:

> The illustration
> is nothing to you without the application.
>   You lack half wit. You crush all the particles down
>   into close conformity, and then walk back and
>   forth on them.

Like many of her early poems, this is an exercise in veiled vituperation. We don't know who the *you* is, but he (I assume it's a he) is blind to subtlety and gradation. (Indeed, he resembles the conjectured fellow in the first paragraph of this chapter.) Each stanza follows an A-A-x-x pattern. Our target is dismissed quite nimbly in the opening couplet. But the dismissal in the final two lines is anything but nimble. These unrhymed lines go in for mimicry, and they're as clunky, as

plodding, as *you* himself. The four lines demonstrate, in miniature, a distinguishing motion in Moore's verses: a contrar-
ian's movement from the mellow to the rough or raucous. We
shift from the conventionally poetic to the prosy, *away from*
rather than *toward* rhyme.

Like Hopkins, Moore regularly overloaded a stanza's
internal music, so that any external structure—like a rhyme
scheme—is outshouted by the din within. Consider "Progress" (later known as "I May, I Might, I Must"), a four-liner
that to my ear is her first wholly successful verse:

> If you will tell me why the fen
> Appears impassable, I then
> Will tell you why I think that I
> Can get across it, if I try.

The poem originates in a swamp, and its voice is that of a
will-o'-the-wisp, floating above the muck and fetor. Picture
the twenty-one-year old poet, Marianne Moore from Kirk-
wood, Missouri, submitting it to a modern workshop. She'd
likely be advised that those insistent, cheek-to-jowl *i* sounds
are excessive and discordant. Half an hour later, a happy compromise might be arrived at:

> If you will tell me why the fen
> Appears impassable, I'll then
> Explain to you the way that I
> May get across if I but try.

Problem solved. The ailment's cured—though not without
death to the patient. For it turns out that the poem's upbeat
message was of less moment, was less interesting and beguil-

ing and vitalizing, than the stout, plucky rolling of long *i*'s (five of them!) in the last two lines. (Readers who object to my practice of disassembling and rewriting poems might consider an observation from Derek Walcott's Nobel Lecture: "Break a vase, and the love that reassembles the fragments is stronger than that love which took its symmetry for granted when it was whole.")

Something similar—another exhibition of the internal drowning out the external—arises in one of her later and loveliest poems, "Bird-Witted." Here are the first six lines of the penultimate stanza, in which a deadly stalking cat approaches three fledglings on a branch:

> A piebald cat observing them,
>   is slowly creeping toward the trim
> trio on the tree-stem.
>   Unused to him
> the three make room—uneasy
> new problem.

Previous stanzas have established that the rhyme scheme here is A-B-A-B-x-A. (You mightn't otherwise guess this, since the A's and B's of this particular stanza are a murmurous mesh of *m*'s.) Meanwhile, and much louder, we have an explosion of t's: *toward the trim trio on the tree-stem.* It's a phrase that for decades has accompanied me on nature walks (*toward the trim trio on the tree-stem*), down long airport corridors (*toward the trim trio on the tree-stem*), in footsore lines at the post office. Musically, if it were a little less, it would be too much. Surfeit alone is sufficient here.

A joy in itself, "Bird-Witted" is additionally treasurable as a crown jewel in *What Are Years* (1941), Moore's last indispensable volume. Though she lived for three more decades, steadily creating and revising, her best work lay behind her. Yet there was an earlier period of roughly a decade and a half, from the late twenties into the early forties, when all her structural and tonal innovations fused into something peerless.

The light rhymes; the tallied syllables; the surprise enjambments; the scurrying speed of her lowercased lines; the occasional anagrams (*sown/snow*) and spelling games; the abrupt shiftings between burly and attenuated rhymes; the likewise abrupt dictional vacillations between the "poetic" and the "prosaic"; the marrying of a workaday to a recherché vocabulary; the queerly corrugated patterns of indentation—these were the conjoined elements of a number of masterpieces like "The Steeple-Jack," "No Swan So Fine," "The Plumet Basilisk," "The Pangolin," "The Mind Is an Enchanting Thing." No English-language poet predecessor had quite prepared a reader for experiences like these. It's no surprise that Auden, one of her most appreciative and perceptive readers, confessed that he "didn't know what to make of her at first."

As an undergraduate at Bryn Mawr, Moore fell under Darwin's spell, and her poetic development might be seen as an instance of speciation: a trait evolving here, another there, and another, until eventually you arrive at something new under the sun: a creature autonomous and nameless, demanding a new nomenclature.

The title poem in *What Are Years* is one of my all-time favorites. (I chose it as epigraph to my first book.) The opening stanza and the middle stanza are merely brilliant, but the third and last strikes me as perfection:

So he who strongly feels
behaves. The very bird,

> grown taller as he sings, steels
> his form straight up. Though he is captive,
> his mighty singing
> says, satisfaction is a lowly
> thing, how pure a thing is joy.
>   This is mortality,
>   this is eternity.

Moore was fond of attaching quotations to her poems, as supplementary notes, and she might here have drawn upon Montaigne: "The most express sign of wisdom is unruffled joy."

Moore in this stanza is deploying an old authorial trick, delivering a new object as if it were a previous acquaintance. We encounter "the very bird," and a reader pauses, takes a moment to ask, *What* bird? Mysteriously and magnificently, out of nowhere, an alien avian has materialized, and we must wait a couple of lines to discover he is encaged.

There's a becoming modesty to the enterprise, signaled by the lack of capital letters, the muted rhyming, the casually run-on sentences, the sparsity of adjectives, the ordinariness of the vocabulary. Yet there's nothing modest about the closing pair of lines, which, though the poem is composed in syllabics, resonate with the trim clarity of an iambic trimeter couplet. They say in effect, *Here is death, and here is life, and I the poet have placed the two in balance.*

Ethical rhetoric came naturally to this granddaughter of a pastor and sister to a minister, and perhaps her religious background contrived to make her, more than any other poet I know, reliant upon *is* and *are*—those natural building blocks of the writer speaking of eternal verities. Any modern writers' handbook would routinely caution against such weak and bloodless verbs—sound advice, generally. But Moore's career,

as Jarrell pointed out, was "one long triumph" over her limitations, and she achieved some of her choicest effects with just
such bland and blunt tools. In "What Are Years" all but one
of the last six verbs is *is,* and yet the lines conclude with the
colossal airborne grandeur of church bells tumble-tolling on
a frosty autumn morning.

Of the couple of dozen poets I've most frequently turned
to over the years, Moore is the one who inspires in me the
sharpest feelings of inadequacy—an ever-compounding sense
of the difficulty of doing justice to her work. She can be hard
going. This is partly a matter of her wild inconsistencies. Her
punctuation was more than erratic—often flat-out wrong,
assuming ordinary rules of logic obtain.

But they don't. Moore relished the trappings of hard
logic—she loved, in effect, the syllogism's *ergo.* But she played
fast and loose with them. She composed analogical chains
that collapsed on inspection ("Diligence Is to Magic as Progress Is to Flight") and she trafficked in what might be called
"false parallelisms," as in "the enslaver is / enslaved; the hater,
harmed." (One expects the hater to be *hated*, and yet how telling is that softer substitute.) She habitually conjoined unlike
classes of objects ("oratories and wardrobes," "its rock crystal
and its imperturbability"), as if in alliance with the Lewis
Carroll who wrote, in *The Hunting of the Snark,* "You may
seek it with thimbles—and seek it with care; / You may hunt
it with forks and hope." The difference between them is that
Carroll really *was* a logician—by profession—whose Wonder-
lands were typically erected upon rule-bound substructures,
like the concealed chess game driving the plot of *Through
the Looking-Glass.* Moore, on the other hand, was comically

unmathematical. As a college student, filling out a scholarship application, she couldn't remember the year of her birth, so she calculated it—and wound up off by two years!

Yet the prime obstacle for a reader intending to do her justice always has been those eccentricities of construction. Anybody who has seriously read Moore knows the experience of suddenly ascertaining that two lines you didn't believe were meant to rhyme were meant to rhyme. The rhyme may be so "off" as to be all but inaudible (*the* and *be*), but due respect for her craftsmanship compels you to discover the patterns in all their intricacy and to evaluate them carefully.

Some of these are singular enough to leave even a Funesian wondering whether he has imbibed a little too much rhubarb brandy. Consider "To Victor Hugo of My Crow Pluto," which consists of fifty-three lines, fifty-two of which terminate in the sounds of *oh* or *oo*. The mind reels as if with drink. You have to stop and ask, *Who on earth would write this way?*

Moore behaved oddly—unpredictably—even in dealing with her own structural oddities. It became something of a routine. First, she would settle upon a peculiar and elaborate configuration of lines and rhymes; then she would laboriously fulfill its many demands; and then, finding some portion of her work displeasing, she would ruthlessly excise lines or stanzas, shattering the forms she had so painstakingly created. "The Steeple-Jack" provides a prime example. It was published in 1932, with thirteen matching stanzas of six lines. She later dropped a stanza. In 1951, far more drastically, she dropped five stanzas and portions of two others. The poem's patterning wasn't merely rumpled; it was ripped apart.

And she made little effort to conceal the violence done. She was like somebody who chooses to forgo cosmetic surgery after an accident. (Sometimes it *is* best to leave things alone.

It's been said of the young and handsome Marlon Brando that he became still handsomer after breaking his nose.) In its truncated 1951 form, "The Steeple-Jack" highlights its own imperfections, parades its own self-dissatisfaction.

Aesthetically, the poem sets us down in one of those quirky neighborhoods whose governing principle of design is sometimes described as "deliberate imperfection"—a willful cultivation of the marred or flawed, linked to the Japanese notion of *wabi-sabi*, to Navajo weaving and Punjabi ceramics, even to jazz, whose extemporaneity insists that error isn't error so much as a call for exploration. (The mistake lies not in the dropped note but in the failure to follow the pathways it reveals.) This is an artistic arena where you pointedly display missteps, irresolutions, uncertainties—a lack of finish in the double sense of polish and termination.

We're miles away here from the sensibility of a Robert Frost or a William Butler Yeats, who prided themselves on not breaking a sweat, on making the difficult look easy. As Yeats put it in "Adam's Curse":

> "A line will take us hours maybe.
> Yet if it does not seem a moment's thought,
> Our stitching and unstitching has been naught."

The numerous published revisions of "The Steeple-Jack" effectively say something quite different: *I've worked on this for years and, as you can see, it won't come right.*

There's a handsome humility at play throughout Moore's poetry, not in her ambitious shapes but in the soul of the worker working within them. The shapes themselves do not share or accommodate our shortcomings. They are uncompromising, and their demands may well be superhuman. When Moore establishes line counts approaching twenty syllables, she's working with patterns only a Funesian might hear.

In her attitudes toward poetic form, she resembled Cummings, whose work she revered ("a concentrate of titanic significance"). In his *Six Nonlectures,* he recalled his exhilaration as a young man on coming to view poetic structures as independent vessels: "each of these forms can and does exist in and of itself, apart from the use to which you or I may not or may put it."

I don't know whether Moore knew *A Mathematician's Apology* (1940), the little classic by G. W. Hardy, but it's her kind of book. She would have felt at home with two of its cardinal notions. The first is a belief in an abstract reality beyond us: "317 is a prime, not because we think so, or because our minds are shaped in one way rather than another, but *because it is,* because mathematical reality is built that way." And the second is the primacy, in all mental disciplines, of pattern creation: "A mathematician, like a painter or a poet, is a maker of patterns." Hardy continues: "I believe that mathematical reality lies outside us, that our function is to discover or observe it, and that the theorems which we prove, and which we describe grandiloquently as our 'creations,' are simply our notes of our observations."

Observations, as it happens, was the title of Moore's second collection, in which an idiosyncratic "maker of patterns" fitted her constructions to a world outside her. Her patterns were often most felicitous when portraying animals, especially creatures unfamiliar to her readers: jerboas, frigate pelicans, pangolins, the paper nautilus (a form of octopus).

Although to many readers such exotic creatures might appear almost mythological—like the unicorns and dragons she also entertained in her verses—they were, in fact, as real as real. Moore took great pride in the accuracy of her delineations. Like us, these creatures of hers were genuine inhabitants of planet Earth, making their way in the world. And the patterns Moore designed for them were likewise genuine, making their way, too, in the world—the world of poetic creation, that enchanting realm of "imaginary gardens with real toads in them."

With similar care and gusto (a favorite word of hers) Moore trafficked in rarefied abstraction. She had a born ser-monizer's appreciation for the poetic pilgrimage from the material to the incorporeal. The exhilaration is patent when, moving obliquely but ineluctably, she lands upon some prize homily: "the power of relinquishing / what one would keep; that is freedom" or "Mysteries expound mysteries." Or "What is more precise than precision? Illusion."

Other poets have favored abstract language, but I know of none except Hopkins who so felicitously combines this with a truly fresh-eyed surveillance of the natural world. The pre-cisely noted attributes of her small, remote creatures had a way of crystallizing abruptly into expansive moral apothegms. The veering speed of these transitions created some of the most startlingly beautiful effects in American poetry. After observ-ing at some length the ant-eating pangolin, she arrives at a personal artistic credo, "To explain grace requires / a curious hand," and springs from there—a characteristic marriage of the physical and temporal—to the notion that "Humor saves a few steps, it saves years." Like the desert rat, revered for its ability to launch itself "as if on wings, from its match-thin hind legs," Marianne Moore moved by leaping back and forth, back and forth between the physical and the abstract, as in the conclusion to "Nevertheless":

The weak overcomes its
menace, the strong over-
comes itself. What is there

like fortitude! What sap
went through the little thread
to make the cherry red!

If she ultimately espoused spirit over body, heaven over earth, this allegiance is all the more remarkable given how brilliantly she paid tribute to the planet's flora and fauna, its oceans and glaciers and bogs and shifting skies. Moore's poems are famously unforthcoming—you can study them for years and derive little sense of her family, friendships, jobs, and littler sense still of the nature of any balked hopes and private losses. Even so, in a modest poem like "Nevertheless" we glimpse an essential, perhaps *the* essential, intimate truth about her: how extraordinary was this woman whose poems could love the world so eagerly, embracingly, intoxicatedly, and yet love another world still more.

CHAPTER TWENTY-THREE

The Essential Conservatism
of Poetry

Over the years, critics and poets of various stripes have marveled at the essential conservatism of poetry. It remains recognizably itself across the decades—across centuries, millennia. Shakespeare would have had little trouble processing Robert Frost (even if *processing* bamboozled him). They are two peerless sonneteers, separated by a sizable three hundred years, but place them within the same rolling railway car of an anthology and they chat companionably. Time drops away. Outside, pretty pastoral landscapes unfold. Inside, the two masters compare notes. As they contemplate each other's work, they might occasionally wonder who wrote what. Here are ten lines drawn from their sonnets. It's a rare student of mine who scores 100 percent in identifying which belongs to whom.

> Midsummer is to spring as one to ten
> Or ten times happier, be it ten for one.

And:

> Be that as may be, she was in their song
> Who all in one, one pleasing note do sing.

And:

For the wood wakes, and you are here for proof
Upon that blessed wood, whose motion sounds . . .

And:

My breathing shakes the bluet like a breeze
For never-resting time leads summer on.

And:

Back up a stream of radiance to the sky
Cheered and checked even by the selfsame sky . . .

(The first line of each pair belongs to Frost.)

Am I stacking the deck a bit in selecting Frost as a touch-stone? Sure. Shakespeare would have a harder time assimilating Marianne Moore or E. E. Cummings or William Carlos Williams or John Ashbery. Still, he'd catch not just the gist but the aims and mechanics of most of the poems in *The Oxford Book of Modern Verse*—or, for that matter, in *The Ecopoetry Anthology* or in *Nepantla: An Anthology Dedicated to Queer Poets of Color* or in *The Best of Best New Zealand Poems*. Whether or not such verses charmed him, he would quickly plumb their working principles, their underlying prosody. Would grasp how the poems were made and what their aspirations were.

Wandering the palace of a thousand years of English-language verse, paying special attention to the crowded and eclectic rooms devoted to the twenty-first century, Shakespeare would undergo far less disorientation than his contemporary Peter Paul Rubens would experience in the Museum of Modern Art, or than another contemporary, Claudio Monteverdi, would meet at the Venice Festival of Contemporary Music.

Why is this? Why would poetry venture less far afield than other arts? Any definitive answer—uniting political and social history, literary trends, the crossbreeding of languages and the biochemistry of language acquisition—is beyond our reach here. But it seems plausible that poetry's conservatism is tied to how early in life language is acquired and how difficult it is to undo what is seeded in infancy. With other art forms, the roots may lie less deep. Like many fans of classical music, I was touched by the South African soprano Pretty Yende's explanation of how she came to opera. At the age of sixteen, watching TV with her family, she saw a British Airlines commercial with background music from the "Flower Duet" of Delibes's *Lakmé*. At school the next day, she inquired of her teacher what those heavenly sounds had been. Told they were opera, she vowed to become an opera singer.

The poet lays the groundwork much earlier. The plump infant lying supine in a bassinet, cheerily babbling nonsense, is hard at it. There are complicated configurations of lip and teeth and tongue and larynx needing to be marshaled. Experiments must be conducted daily, data assembled and tested and retested, before an initial *Mama* or *Papa* can be voiced.

You may reach opera stardom in your twenties without having heard an aria before the age of sixteen. But you cannot become a poet, or a writer at all, without first enrolling in the superadvanced course in language acquisition known as Infancy. Poetry comes to most of us quite early. It spills in through nonsense chants during bedtimes and bath times, health advice ("An apple a day keeps the doctor away"), overheard traffic advisories ("Take Five—Stay Alive"), toilet counsel ("If it's yellow, let it mellow; if it's brown, flush it down"—a phrase coined during a California drought), singing commercials, and the lovely, bouncy mini-genre known as skipping-rope rhymes—as well as, one hopes, through Mother Goose and Robert Louis Stevenson and Lewis Carroll and A. A. Milne. As future readers of poetry, we are conditioned long before we know the word *conditioned*.

Linguistic researchers have confirmed that various skills will be acquired in life's earliest years or not at all. Those founders of Rome reared by a wolf, Romulus and Remus, doubtless were superb warriors, with a fine-nosed, vulpine instinct for bringing down a formidable foe, but lousy communicators.

Consider John Locke and his conception of the human brain as a tabula rasa. In the centuries since, how cluttered his once-empty blackboard has become! And how obvious, nowadays, that language was *never* acquirable by the mind's scratching letters on a blank slate. The essential work had to be wrought over millions of years, by Mother Nature, laying down the hardware and software, the neural programs allowing the newborn to begin assembling meaningful sounds. There's a far shorter distance between T. S. Eliot's *The Waste Land* and the blathering infant in the bassinet than between the infant and some prehistoric, prelingual ancestor whose hungry hunter's eyes, picking over their own desolate wasteland, had no oral outlet. The infant all but has the poem written.

That our earliest dealings with poetry precede most everything, including active memory, helps explain why prosodic systems are so resistant to change. Their configurations are in our blood. A hundred years ago, the future poet may have been brought up on Mother Goose. And perhaps today it's Dr. Seuss. (From Goose to Seuss—let the rhyming begin.) But the underlying prosodic systems are compatible. We're in a Land of Short Lines and Obvious Symmetries, of Proximate Rhymes, of Pure Stress configurations that repeat and echo one another. As little listeners, still preliterate, we start assembling a house of language, which turns out to be both our childhood home and, decades on, our assisted-living facility; we adopt its architecture for the duration.

I spoke earlier of my happy discovery that at a very young age my daughters intuitively understood what a prosodic contract is. They could sense when an adult did "funny things" to a line of verse. And they knew the slight, enlivening shock provided by those funny things, and hence were beginning to prepare—only let a few decades elapse—for the artful wrenching rhymes and enjambments to be found in a poem by John Donne or Robert Browning or Robert Lowell or Amy Clampitt.

Poets have sometimes attempted, in a deliberative fashion, to import into English a new prosodic system, as when Campion experimented with quantitative verse or Longfellow erected the towering trochaics of *Hiawatha*. But such efforts inevitably wind up struggling against less intellect-driven templates. The sophisticated poet means to forge a new prosody—which is to say, new patterns of expectation—but finds herself thwarted by the primordial systems of childhood, hardened into instinct. Successes are few. It's a rare day when a Marianne Moore or a Gerard Manley Hopkins emerges to suggest patterns both novel and viable: a new musical concourse.

The triumph of free verse in our time—much the dominant mode—illustrates the notion that it's often easier to eliminate pattern than to replace it. As a would-be replacement, Marianne Moore's syllabics are exquisitely lovely and yet fragile; at the slightest challenge, they default into iambics, subsumed by the more dominant form. All such efforts at prosodic replacement point to a pretty paradox: The patterns of expectation formed in earliest childhood, which fostered our initial love of poetry, become a bulwark discouraging later innovation. At day's end, it's hard to compete with "Hey, diddle, diddle, / The cat and the fiddle, / The cow jumped over the moon . . ."

The wholesale replacing of one strict prosodic system by another, equally strict or stricter, isn't merely a rare phenomenon; call it a once-in-a-millennium occurrence. It has occurred only once in English, anyway. Sometime in the fourteenth century, the pure stress verse (aka accentual verse) of *Beowulf* and the *Pearl* poet gave way to **accentual-syllabic meter,** which tabulates both accents and syllables. What's amazing is how thoroughgoing the substitution turned out to be. It was like the Olympians replacing the Titans: The ground heaved once and new gods reigned and the old ones all but vanished.

Recall the literal infinity of possible meters. To create a metrical system, all that's required is some reliable yardstick, however whimsically or weirdly chosen. You might logically expect, then, that we'd have dozens of viable, well-trafficked meters—instead of the paltry handful that see any real use. And how much more paltry still are the number of flourishing, identifiable forms within those meters—structures with an established name and tradition and rules of construction. The nineteenth century generated one prosodic experiment after another, yet few innovative forms took hold. (The limerick remains a spunky but minor exception.) In the twentieth, we had a resurgence of some outré older forms (the sestina, the villanelle, the ghazal) as well as the altogether new double dactyl. But again, the contents of the poet's toolbox were left largely unchanged.

Consider a hypothetical poem written in a novel form: Each line must contain five and only five appearances of the letter *o*. The poem begins with an epigraph ("To be or not to be—that is the question") as a model specimen. You read along and every line respectfully follows format. Then arrives, without warning, a line without a single *o*. ("Oh," you say.) Theoretically, this constitutes a sizable surprise. Yet it's hard to imagine any reader responding strongly and freshly, as a child will when "something funny" rumples a line. As adults, we may be quite good at enumerating the rules, but we lack the conditioning to register such infractions viscerally.

This is where I've found the Funesians—to whom we're bidding a farewell—so helpful. They clarify the limitations under which poets traditionally labor. And they are, implicitly, a force for innovation. They remind us that *there are other poetries out there*. They urge us to go on exploring new methods of walking (or swimming or tunneling) to the undiscovered. They ask us to ponder how our bodily confines, in conjunction with our training, tether us to a narrow ambit. Gently, all but omnisciently, they propel us ahead of ourselves.

Admittedly, to speak of our limitations may seem a little perverse. Yes, our poetry is narrow—and yet how inestimably rich, how capacious beyond all measure: What a treasure trove we've been given! Let the painters boast that painting is supreme. Let the composers elevate music above the other arts. But the poet sees in *The Oxford Book of English Verse* or *The Norton Anthology of Poetry* an unrivaled apex. Indeed, the poets can be rich even when being pointedly humble, as when Pope brilliantly characterizes humankind as the "Sole judge of truth, in endless error hurled: / The glory, jest, and riddle of the world!"

And so we veer, with our Funesians as docents, between awe at the magnitude of past accomplishment and a tantalizing sense of something greater. As Cummings put it: "listen: there's a hell / of a good universe next door; let's go." Just one valley over from us, the Funesians are chanting of finer poetry than any we know, and occasionally, nights, their voices waft in on the breeze. In what is for me the greatest of all plays, Caliban declares, "Sometimes a thousand twangling instruments / Will hum about mine ears." Even this lowly creature—Caliban the "poisonous slave," the servant prone to "gabble like a thing most brutish"—is obsessed with musics he's untrained to hear.

Viewed in this light, poetry's conservatism, its hostility to innovation, is something to be resisted—even resented. Isn't it an obstacle? Obstructing us from the appreciation of harmonies beyond our daily range? Those twangling instruments—might they not be the legendary music of the spheres?

But try another perspective. Look the other way round, and the conservatism of poetry appears admirable—indeed, something to be encouraged at every step. If conservatism means a reluctance to change—well, where poetry is concerned, change inevitably signifies loss. And who could argue against minimizing losses? What we love best must be conserved. Our task is a search for "the secret of durable pigments" (Nabokov's phrase), where objects of art stand outside the hazardous, everyday whims of mutability, the thoughtlessly cruel corrosions of age.

The irony here is that poetry is by essence a thing of

flux. Language knows no permanence. And as any language alters, all the utterances of yesteryear, however picturesque or poignant, gradually drift away, willy-nilly. The enchanted island of *The Tempest* is incrementally more distant in 2020 than it was in 2019. Which is why a resentment springs up toward the very thing that makes poems possible: the growth and warpage of language over time.

Language is so intricate a delta of fine and far-reaching streams that an alteration in one area may disturb the flow in some uncharted, unlikely spot. A tiny example: the slangy *bod*. The word is winsome in its way, and irresistible for caption writers of magazine covers, forever promising a brand-new bod (just two weeks!), a leaner bod (easy exercises!), a hotter bod (they'll be drooling!). In the interval since *body* was first stripped down to *bod* (dated to 1933), the trim colloquialism has come to incarnate our intimate fantasies of sexual prowess and self-glorification. Meanwhile, all those enviable bods on the beach—women with sleek, gleaming glutes, men with six-pack abs—may look both inveigling and harmless. But in truth they're undermining Shakespeare's *Hamlet*. In act 3, coming seriously unstrung, the prince contemplates suicide by way of a ferocious stiletto, a *bare bodkin*.

No matter how sober/scholarly the modern reader aspires to be, the antiquated phrase fosters images not only of cold steel but of sun-warmed flesh. We can't help hearing echoes of *People* magazine, where dependably week after week some aging supermodel stuns with her new bikini bod. (Hard to say whether Shakespeare would have found *supermodel* or *stuns* the more amusing here.)

In an earlier chapter I introduced one of my favorite poem openings, that of Amy Clampitt's "The Sun Underfoot Among the Sundews":

An ingenuity too astonishing
to be quite fortuitous is
this bog full of sundews . . .

But in the four decades since I came upon the poem, for-tuitously, these lines have become tarnished or threatened. More and more, people appear to be using *fortuitous* as a fancy way of saying *fortunate*, rather than—aptly—to signify what is random. Such people will inevitably misread the poem, and the stakes could hardly be greater: for Clampitt is talking, after all, about the nature of life's operations on Earth.

Another tiny example: *every man Jack*. Though hardly a common phrase in my childhood, I knew it as a classy way of saying *everybody* (or—for you southerners—*y'all*). But when teaching T. S. Eliot to undergrads a few years ago, I met utter puzzlement when we encountered *every dog Jack*. "He's play-ing off the phrase *every man Jack*," I explained.

Extended puzzlement. None of my students recognized the original phrase. Eliot's little joke was lost, the dog kaput. In that glorious, elongated string of lights that is *Old Possum's Book of Practical Cats*, one little bulb had gone out.

Humor—light verse generally—suffers unduly from teeny shifts of language. Comedy is a more sensitive plant than trag-edy, which has a cactile way of weathering those droughts where meaning is temporarily mislaid. The tragedian can survive a good many trips to the glossary; humor, however, might be defined as the delicate sprig that perishes in the journey between text and footnote. An explicated joke is no joke at all.

My trifling examples underscore a grander principle: Lan-guage often behaves as a zero-sum game. Add something to it here, perhaps a fine and witty neologism, and a subtraction results elsewhere. A person's—a people's—working vocabulary is only so extensive. As new terms enter, old ones slip away. It's a little like a small island's fauna—introduce a new species of bird today and a native species goes extinct tomorrow. Occasional visitors to the island might declare that little has changed, since birds on each visit can be seen fluttering and singing in the trees. But this is hardly consoling to the long-term inhabitants, if what went extinct was the more beautiful, the more musical species.

Poetry lovers will naturally form attachments to words unjustly fallen out of favor. The dictionary marks their obsolescence curtly, with an unsentimental *obs.* I'm fond of *foison,* so sadly *obs.,* whose synonyms (plenty, abundance, satiety) lack the old term's trappings of harvested opulence. In recent years, some of *foison*'s work has been taken up by *loaded*—as in *loaded nachos* or a *loaded baked potato.* But there are contexts where *loaded,* however loaded up, makes an unsuitabler substitute, as in *Measure for Measure*:

> As those that feed grow full, as blossoming time
> That from the seedness the bare fallow brings
> To teeming foison, even so her plenteous womb
> Expresseth his full tilth and husbandry.

Even now, *foison* sings of plenty—a plenty lost.

Linguists have estimated that the average English speaker has an active vocabulary of twenty thousand words and a passive vocabulary of about forty thousand. In most cases, the number flattens in middle age; evidently, we become word-sated. Wherever the number of words stays fixed—whether in an individual or in a society—the ushering in of a new word may mean the forgetful chucking out of an old one. And any shifts to the poetic lexicon—losses of connotation within a word, losses of whole words—inevitably means that earlier passages of poetry are dwindled or denatured. There is a potent, if implicit, threat inside Pound's *Make it new.*

One of my favorite novels is *A Tale of Two Cities*, which I've regularly taught over the last three decades. Increasingly, my students wrangle with its verbosity, its backhandedness, its outworn vocabulary. They have trouble seeing that a Dickens novel limited to a mere four hundred pages is a streamlined affair. And they have trouble identifying its genre. They struggle to understand that the book is the Victorian equivalent of a modern-day thriller, complete with a car chase (carriage chase). The novel's diction impedes them as it wouldn't have fifty years ago, and still less a century ago. The book's language gets in the way; and potential readers are lost; and a marvelous story suffers a partial death.

If only the language would do the impossible thing and stay still! Who wants to see *A Tale of Two Cities*—or *The Prelude* or *The Rape of the Lock* or *Twelfth Night* or "The Wife of Bath's Tale"—eddy away from us? And if this feels like an illogical conservatism, it's nonetheless based in gratitude and love.

And yet—how enticing is that *Make it new!* How irresistible the opportunities open to the poet embracing a fresh-coined word, a fresh sentence construction. One shares his mischievous joy when Auden in his last book (*Thank You, Fog*, 1974) opens a stanza like this:

Out there still the Innocence
that we somehow freaked out of
where *can* and *ought* are the same . . .

Auden couldn't have written the stanza a decade before. He had to wait for the startling slang term—*freak out*—to arise and gain currency.

The sensitive poet, the sensitive reader—both wind up on a seesaw, torn between wanting nothing to change and everything to change. Language must freeze, as a means of preserving its finest fruits. Language must flow, ripening new sounds, new meanings.

Of course one might argue that these are idle or moot impulses. What do they matter? Don't the great rivers of language go their way indifferently, independent of us, their makers? And yet, our power to direct the flow mustn't be underestimated. This is where the scholar materializes, offering an indispensable service.

One of the scholar's chosen tasks is to make water flow uphill—to restore to us lost currents, words and cadences that have already drifted by. Recall how Dryden revered Chaucer but misread his meters, unaware that various *e*'s had fallen into silence in passing out of Middle English. Today, through scholarship, we have a far better understanding of Chaucer's prosody—we *hear* Chaucer better—than Dryden could.

Even so, one can only speculate about how much we still get wrong. If a resurrected Chaucer could attend a modern seminar in his poetry, surely he'd wonder what odd dialect everyone was spouting. (Or as Pandarus has it in *Troilus and Criseyde*: "O mercy, god, what unhap may this meene?") Who can doubt that implications and inflections have been mislaid or mangled since the fourteenth century? Nonetheless, we've come closer to Chaucer over the ages. Time's waters have been partially reversed.

On a global stage, Hebrew represents the great feat of

linguistic conservation. It all sounds crazily impracticable: the notion, rooted in the nineteenth century, of transforming a "dead language" (one no longer the native language of any community) into a live one. In seeking to seize the reins of language, the notion hums with the ancient hubris of the builders of the Tower of Babel.

But in this case, no tower collapsed. The result wasn't many languages springing from one. Rather, it was one deriving from many. Israel's adoption of Hebrew as its official language, in 1948, serves as a sweeping lighthouse over the streaming oceans of the Earth's languages. It signals a miraculous harbor.

Most such attempts to engineer language are doomed to failure, but there are successes here and there. In 1986 I interviewed Baldur Jónsson, the head of the Icelandic Language Committee. Though it had no formal authority to dictate vocabulary or usage, his committee served in a coordinating role, with other more specialized committees, seeking to create an Icelandic suitable for modern objects and concepts. Jónsson described himself as a "philologist, though you might say my field is language planning."

Their charged task was all the more noble given that Icelandic is Europe's oldest living language, the one least changed over the last thousand years. Modern Icelandic remains remarkably close to Old Norse, providing today's Icelanders with easy entry into the twelfth-century sagas and poems that are their country's masterworks. (Imagine if we could read *Beowulf* with little assistance.) Iceland's greatest heroes, the very myths and chronicles of the country's creation, endorsed the impulse.

Jónsson offered a small example. "Let's take the word *skjar*, which is now used to designate a computer screen. The word originally referred to a window—a certain type of obsolete window in a turf house. So somebody got the idea of using the word for this new type of window. . . . The danger is that the new word will swamp the old. Some people think we shouldn't have taken this *skjar* and used it in this modern sense. We terminologize—as it is called—words from the common language. But in certain cases we have to make sure we don't go too far, throwing unwanted associations into our old poetry, for example. . . . One must be careful with living words."

Thirty-plus years later, young people in Reykjavík do not speak of a *screen,* but a *skjar.* The adoption was a success. Still, technology ensures that new words keep coming, and the efforts to assimilate them must be unceasing. I've read that Iceland has the world's highest percentage of people online. Information—most of it in English—streams into the island nation at incalculable rates. And among its literary people, especially those of an older generation, there's a growing unease about the future of their language—that is, their literature, that is, their culture.

Iceland in its smallness (about the size of Kentucky, with less than half a million speakers of its language worldwide) provides a heightened example of the vulnerability that all languages, all cultures confront. Whatever the future holds, we can be sure it will come on an obliterating flood of subverted and subverting terms.

Language must freeze, language must flow. Paradoxes abound, and meanwhile one must also allow for how the new sometimes unexpectedly revives the old, as in the denouement of Eliot's *Four Quartets:*

We shall not cease from exploration
And the end of all our exploring
Will be to arrive where we started
And know the place for the first time.

In the late 1910s, Picasso entered his "classical period," for me the most beautiful stretch in his long and ever-startling career. His reexamination of ancient statuary led to monumental paintings of pale blocky figures of an ethereal sentience and beauty. They looked like nothing under the sun, while also resembling some of the oldest statuary in the dustiest museums we've ever assembled. The paintings compel us to revisit galleries we thought we knew, there to discover that the ancient figures have awakened. No, that isn't quite right. The statues haven't changed—which is all to the good, since we wish to conserve them. But in being compelled to see them afresh, *we've* changed, which, too, is all to the good.

◻

CHAPTER TWENTY-FOUR

The Essential Radicalism
of Poetry

I spoke earlier of a TV sportscaster's praise for a football star who wasn't about to go gentle into that good night. Here was that miraculous thing: a line of twentieth-century poetry abloom in the gritty soil of the American vernacular.

Of course Dylan Thomas wrote in English. Rarer still—perhaps rare as unicorns or sasquatches are rare—is the snippet of *foreign* poetry that nudges its way into our parlance. In all of German literature, the line perhaps best known in America—familiar to many MFA poetry students, anyway—is "*Du mußt dein Leben ändern*," or, "You must change your life."

The line concludes a much-translated sonnet by Rainer Maria Rilke, "Archaic Torso of Apollo." I've read more than a dozen versions, and feel confident, while not knowing German, that "Archaic Torso" is great literature—though I haven't yet met the translation that seems a great poem. But there are numerous good ones. Stephen Mitchell's quietly off-rhymed rendition concludes this way:

> Otherwise this stone would seem defaced
> beneath the translucent cascade of the shoulders
> and would not glisten like a wild beast's fur:

would not, from all the borders of itself,
burst like a star: for here there is no place
that does not see you. You must change your life.

Transfixed, Rilke stands meditating before a chunky fragment of classical statuary. Or you might say he's meditating
on poetry—even on this particular poem. And in his meditation he taps into a familiar, tonic vein of poetic reproach—the
perennial summons to a better self than the one we muster on
a daily basis.

One way or another, poems frequently urge a change of
life. And virtually *every* poem offers another prompt: *You must
change your clock.* (Perhaps the one is a rephrasing of the other.)
I began this book with the assertion that "All poems begin
by saying the same thing": *Slow down.* Even an unambitious,
trifling poem demands it: *Rethink your thinking about time.*

Modern life feeds us a steady diet of accelerants. Sometimes literally so. (A Red Bull anyone?) But most are figura-
tive, arriving as imperative whispers from our friends or our
jobs or our providers of entertainment, from the radio, the
TV, the computer. And the more our lives speed up, the more
clamorous the exigency grows. I'm old enough to recall when
a sixty-second commercial was a TV norm. But such leisure-
liness will hardly suit a world where, as one recent study has
it, "between 34%–49% of TV viewers are constantly using
another screen—phone, tablet or computer—during commercial breaks." The study also noted: "79% of Millennials
are distracted by other devices during TV commercial breaks
either 'most of the time' or 'all of the time.'" Recently, we've
seen the debut of the lightning-strike commercial of six
seconds. . . . Peddle ten products in the time once allotted
for one!

Yet the quiet discipline of poetry, our obstinate and indrawn and plodding and precious beast of burden, refuses to quicken its gait. It clip-clops down the ages, balky and oblivious. A contemporary of George Herbert, coming upon his fine double sonnet addressed to his mother, would have required roughly the same amount of time to peruse it as a modern reader would need for Elizabeth Bishop's brooding double sonnet "The Prodigal" (my favorite of her poems). In the intervening centuries, hordes of time-saving inventions have unfolded, but we've yet to contrive a better, more efficacious way to read poetry than how we've always best read it— aloud, and slowly. In their carefully sequenced substances, the two double sonnets show more resemblance than difference, a kinship clarified when you contemplate a medium like the movies—whose earliest fans were mesmerized by black-and-white figures, gesticulating jumpily and soundlessly, captured by equipment so heavy and cumbersome that it was seldom shifted during the process of creation. We call it *film,* referring both to those early images and to the latest creation by the great Almodóvar, but the word encompasses different art forms.

In its travels down the centuries, poetry has been a far more stable pilgrim than the other arts, and even than other literary genres. Consider the essay. Pick up the nineteenth century's Matthew Arnold or John Ruskin or Thomas Macaulay, or pick up the eighteenth century's Samuel Johnson or Edmund Burke or Edward Gibbon, and the first thing to strike any contemporary reader is the prose's unhurriedness, its confident copiousness. Johnson wasn't being merely whimsical—he was being prescient—in entitling his essays *The Rambler,* for his excursions ramble more nowadays than in the eighteenth century, when hours were more spacious and indirection more welcome. Much the same is true with novels. . . . Pick up *Great Expectations* or *A Tale of Two Cities*. Those massive volumes represent the *taciturn* Dickens—trimmer by hundreds of pages than *Martin Chuzzlewit* or *Bleak House* or *David Copperfield*.

Yet to speak of poetry's unhurriedness is to illuminate but half the picture. There's another way to look at poetry. Rotate the view, and it behaves differently. Under the right circumstances, poetry can be a giddily rapid means of transport.

I adore Anthony Trollope's portly novels (I've read more books by him, I suppose, than by any other author), but I enter them with some effort. After two of three chapters, I'm typically not wholly engaged, and I proceed partly out of a justified confidence that an enchanter's spell is indeed being woven, albeit gradually. By contrast, after devoting fifteen minutes to reading Tennyson closely, I've undergone a speedy immersion into nineteenth-century cadences, a nineteenth-century sensibility. Recall Marilyn Monroe: Poetry saves time. Or put it another way: Poetry asks us to slow down, so we may speed up. Of all literary genres, poetry is the most successful time traveler.

"[Y]ou cannot get away from the present moment," remarks the skeptical Medical Man in the first chapter of *The Time Machine*. Of the dozen most beloved novels in my life, H. G. Wells's "scientific romance" may be the oftenest revisited, partly because it's much the shortest. Bless its brevity. Voluminousness might have been predicted from Wells, who had at his disposal—in a literal sense the phrase seldom wields—all the time in the world. By temperament, he was a tireless polemicist, and given the book's premise (a machine that whisks a person through the eons with the ease of a TV remote navigating hundreds of channels), you might have expected frequent stops, accompanied by bulging historical analyses. But Wells stops only twice: first at an imminent dystopian human future (a mere 800,000 years away), then at a distant prospect stripped of humanity, some thirty million years off, where a dying Earth lifelessly cools, icy and abandoned as any churchyard gravestone at year's end.

Until our scientists provide us with Wells's time-traveling device, poetry remains the most dependable instrument for uprooting us from one time zone and bundling us into another. It's a gift that poetry, especially brief poems, shares with painting: sensations of dissolved time, of unclockable moments. Such feelings are far less common in theater or music or fiction—all dependent on substantial duration, time's metronomic tick-tock. To this lover of Dutch painting, wandering through *The Oxford Book of Short Poems* (each entry briefer than a sonnet) is to suggest, over here, the humming self-sufficiency of a Vermeer interior; over there, the almost unnoticed horizontal grandeur of a Ruisdael landscape; and there, the call to empathy in one of Rembrandt's elderly subjects. You take the work in whole, at once. You're one with the author, whether he wrote last week or last century.

I'm not often asked by a student what our primary goal as readers ought to be. But should the question arise, I have an answer prepared. Our task is to connect meaningfully with lives as remote as possible from our own. This distance may be defined geographically. (I'd recommend to my students the novel set in Buenos Aires or the Japanese Alps or the Australian Outback over one set in their hometown.) Or this distance may mean transgressing boundaries of gender or race or religion. Or—for me the most significant—it may mean crossing temporal thresholds, venturing back into earlier centuries.

I find it easier to read eighteenth-century poetry than

eighteenth-century prose, seventeenth-century poetry than seventeenth-century prose. Long-standing structural continuities lend assistance to the reader of poetry. Perhaps the poem you're examining is three hundred years old. Still, its form may be familiar (a sonnet, a villanelle). And its underlying prosodic architecture may be familiar (accentual-syllabic meter, most likely). You've meandered away, into a foreign century, yet a poem's stanzas—those conveniently stable shapes—are arranged like stepping-stones, beckoning you onward. A dense paragraph of prose, on the other hand, may stand before you like a wall.

Given all this, why do so many literature-loving folks engage with poetry so rarely? Why is it reserved for special occasions? Sometimes, admittedly, there's something profoundly moving in this very rareness. As a teenager, I regularly shoveled snow for a neighbor (a retired insurance man), who, knowing of my interest in poetry, proudly informed me that he'd written in his life one, and only one, poem: a tribute to his deceased wife, a victim of cancer in her forties. His elegy—memorialized by a fanciful calligrapher, and opulently framed—embellished his living room mantel. And for me he remains, all these years later, both lovable and inspirational. Without quite aiming to, he was pleading allegiance not merely to a beloved spouse but to a holy flame of art.

But the question stubbornly reiterates: Why do our friends turn to poetry so seldom? As they readily declare, they loved that poetry course they took twenty years ago (thirty? forty?) on Chaucer (Milton? the Romantic poets?). But somehow down the years the pleasures of verse dropped away. (Down in their basements, where they keep a mildewy box of college textbooks, Trollope is overheard whispering, "By the common consent of all mankind who have read, poetry takes the highest place in literature.") I've spoken perhaps too glibly of the ease by which poetry transports us out of time and place, for it's an ease maintained only through practice. Poetry is an efficient time machine for the reader accustomed to reading poems. For others, the little machine may malfunction. The unpracticed may come upon a poem by Wordsworth and discover that it fails to transport them to the Lake Country in the early nineteenth century. No, it shuttles them a much shorter distance, to adolescence and an austere high school English classroom whose teacher has just now announced a pop quiz.

Some readers carry a lifelong sense of having betrayed the high schooler they were, the one who (pop quiz or no) came to poetry eagerly, indiscriminately—who welcomed it not merely for its beauty but also perhaps for its ability to speak to the fundamental loneliness and emptiness and phoniness of the human experience. (My own experience with poetry in my early teens was probably typical: I much preferred bad adult poetry to good children's poetry, which I mostly came to appreciate only when childhood, alas, lay far behind me.) Something went amiss in their relationship with poetry— which is to say, with language at its best. This is a realization to confess both ruefully and puzzledly: *I'm not sure why that is.*

In truth, such self-recrimination may be uncalled for, since the failing may be less personal than societal. An accelerating society is one unconsciously hostile to poetry's old-fashioned, snail-mail tempi. Elizabeth Bishop used to lament the modern rise of a tightly scheduled, tightly scripted childhood. Poetry, she suggested, gestates not merely from heartbreak and passion and revelation but also from sheer boredom—the child who, for lack of anything better to do, steadily watches the clouds pass. For this is fertile boredom, guiding the young soul in upon itself. Societies where we're rarely alone even when we're alone—where solitude comes accoutered with a phone and earbuds and a screen—discourage verse. Poetry is forgiving of almost any shortcoming we show it, except the disloyalty of inattention.

Poetry has always been the most democratic of art forms, hospitable to every willing participant. Other forms are more restrictive. Classical music has largely belonged—performers and composers both—to those with access to instruments and training and performances, those with the funded leisure for long and unremunerated practice. Drama, too, has thrived beside privilege. The oeuvre of a Molière, who was an official supplier of court entertainments, is unimaginable outside aristocratic patronage. The poet, on the other hand, will often flower without external support. The writing of poetry exacts few resources, demands little or no outside recognition. As such, it's a natural haven for the socially ill at ease and the maladroit, the oddball and the ne'er-do-well.

Poetry has sometimes meant salvation for souls too fragile or hypersensitive or damaged to participate in collaborative ventures. It's impossible to imagine a John Berryman or an Emily Dickinson or a John Clare weathering the demands (of scheduling, of compromise with others, of accommodation to controlling financial interests) required for a career on the theatrical or concert stage, in the movie studio, or even in a newspaper or magazine office. (When Elizabeth Bishop became poetry critic of *The New Yorker*—a job she'd solicited—she reassured herself that it would mean writing "just 4 or 6 times a year." But she never managed to submit a single piece.)

Poetry has provided refuge for the exiled diplomat, for the freed slave, for the on-again, off-again schizophrenic, for the formerly burly and now shell-shocked soldier. Poetry has provided a home for kings (like Henry VIII, who ought to have specialized in headless lines) as well as his court's toadies, for an elevated president (Abraham Lincoln) and for any soul of equally humble origins. (Could *any* birthplace sound more inauspicious—more poetic—than the Lincoln family's Sinking Spring Farm?) Poetry isn't merely democratic but radically democratic, erecting a domain where you're only as worthy as your phrases are incisive. It's a province of solitaries, of souls hopelessly lonely except when bedded with a muse.

Poetry's openness to eccentrics and cranks and misfits fosters a landscape remarkable for its extreme features. It revels in queer contours, harsh outcroppings, pointed unlovelinesses. Not surprisingly, its inhabitants are frequently opinionated and uncentered and off-putting. I've spoken often here of Cummings—a favorite of mine—but one mustn't forget how irksome he can be on the page, how smug and overweening in his attestations of humility. It's all there in that proudly modest "i" of his. As a poet—working alone, accountable to no one, not needing to balance any budget or accommodate any coworker—Cummings pursued his virtues and vices with unchecked gusto. He felt free to be himself (a good thing), and to boast about it (a bad one). And how deeply Cummingsesque Cummings's best poems are. No one—*nobody, ever*—has written that cherishable thing, a Cummings poem, as well as Cummings has.

In its radical freedom, poetry has provided a hostel for the one-hit wonder, the one-poem poet. Most big anthologies of English verse find a place for Chidiock Tichborne (d. 1586), and almost none include more than one. (Apparently, he left behind only three.) A devout Catholic, Tichborne was convicted of treason in a plot to replace the religiously intolerant

Queen Elizabeth with Mary Stuart. Writing from prison on the day before his execution, he included a verse in a letter to his wife. A mere three stanzas, eighteen lines. Here's the middle stanza:

> The spring is past, and yet it hath not sprung,
> The fruit is dead, and yet the leaves are green,
> My youth is gone, and yet I am but young,
> I saw the world, and yet I was not seen,
> My thread is cut, and yet it was not spun,
> And now I live, and now my life is done.

The next day, he was hanged and, while still alive, disemboweled.

Tichborne's story dead-ends there, at the gallows—were it not for a single verse in which, with blazing simplicity (the poem consists solely of monosyllables: 180 of them!), a prisoner sang with luminous grief of life's promises unfulfilled, its joys forcibly forgone. Chidiock Tichborne was a young man who died an unspeakable death; yet the poem written at death's door continues to speak. At one stroke, he joined the canon.

A special burnish, a kind of quivery haloing effect, attends the one-hit wonder. Theirs is a fleeting grace and charm bestowed more often upon the poet than upon the fiction writer, playwright, essayist. A poem's brevity is of great advantage here. You the reader chance upon somebody you'll never meet again, and yet the interchange—perhaps lasting less than a minute—is indelible. A fundamental communication is established, a regrouping of the world. But for this sole encounter, for this brief lyric, the poet you're entertaining would have joined those untold billions of Earth's inhabitants, alive or dead, with whom you never forged any significant connection.

I've read much of what Conrad Aiken (1889–1973) published, both poetry and fiction, but for me he is, like John McCrae ("In Flanders Fields"), a poet who wrote one poem. Aiken's "Morning Song," from *Senlin*, enthralled me in high school, and all these years later the spell is unlifted. It seemed back then to integrate, in a way I'd never experienced, the lushest romanticism with a cool, even astronomical detachment:

> Stars in the purple dusk above the rooftops
> Pale in a saffron mist and seem to die
> And I myself on a swiftly tilting planet
> Stand before a glass and tie my tie.

The verse presents you the reader with a mirror, into which Conrad Aiken peers and sees himself. And you likewise gaze there and you glimpse—almost as close as your own face—an unprepossessing but noble personage, whose name is Conrad Aiken.

More deeply than any other art form, poetry is invested in the mysteries and rites and consolations and frustrations of memory. European literature originates with a prodigy of memorization, those hundreds of years of oral transmission between the composing of the *Iliad* and the *Odyssey* and their alighting upon papyrus. And ever since, in ways large and small, poetry has worked into memory's recesses, sometimes unbeknownst to the recipient. There's a lovely anecdote about Randall Jarrell floating with companions in a midwestern swimming hole on a sweltering summer day. He begins to recite Frost's "Provide, Provide." Stanza follows stanza as

Jarrell dawningly ascertains that he has succeeded, without conscious effort, in lodging by heart its twenty-one lines. He exalts, and we with him. The refreshed body bobs and floats; the words bob and float above it.

Poetry is the art form nearest to the insomniac, for whom it may provide as much curse as blessing. In the ever-expanding middle of the night, when phones and textbooks and computers must be sensibly avoided, when you're really alone with that off-putting presence, yourself, how deeply unsettling verse can be. You fail at recalling a line from a poem you know as well as—as what? The names of your parents? The date you were born? Elizabeth Bishop conveys this particular desperation with piercing simplicity in her lengthy meditation on loneliness (or insomnia), "Crusoe in England." Marooned on his desolate island, Robinson Crusoe fragmentarily recalls some lines from Wordsworth: "They flash upon that inward eye, / which is the bliss . . ." And the missing phrase? The crucial missing word? It is—painfully—what is omnipresent for Crusoe, or for any sleepless soul: solitude.

Of the ancient Greek goddesses, Mnemosyne may be the one fallen on hardest times. Nowadays, memorization has dropped away as a schoolroom practice. During those years when poetic recitation held a sizable and official slot in the American curriculum (roughly from 1875 to 1950), the rationales behind it were many and sometimes mutually contradictory: to foster a lifelong love of literature; to preserve the finest accomplishments in the language down the generations; to boost self-confidence through a mastery of elocution; to help purge the idioms and accents of lower-class speech; to strengthen the brain through exercise. These days, I'm deeply touched when recalling how a former colleague, the Russian poet and Nobel laureate Joseph Brodsky, required his undergrads at Mount Holyoke to memorize more than a thousand lines of poetry over the semester. Today, it looks like such a quaint gesture.

Yet Brodsky's life story remains instructive. Before emigrating from the Soviet Union to the States, in 1972, he was persecuted by the Soviets for "social parasitism." He was deposited in prison, and in mental asylums. (The term doubtless deserves quotation marks.) At one point, he was banished to frigid Archangelsk, by the White Sea. Throughout his long and compulsory journeying, he carried few possessions, but he hoarded a great many poems within.

Joseph could be a difficult colleague—prone to estrangements with those fondest of him—but always inspiring. I remember once—my dearest memory of him—meeting up in the parking lot of a convenience store early one bitingly cold New England morning. He was on a cigarette run. Snow in the air, wind picking up. Our encounter would surely have been brief, except in passing I made the happy mistake of mentioning that I'd been reading Swinburne's poetry. Swinburne? Joseph was launched, and for the next ten minutes—as we stamped our feet for warmth and hugged our chests—he rattled on about Victorian verse. A former exile to the Arctic, Joseph Brodsky wasn't about to let any discussion of poetry be derailed by mere weather.

He entertained a haunted sense of everything pared away, down to the soul, to the irreducible you. Fate might so arrange it that you're stripped not merely of your phone, your computer. It might also steal any means you have of listening to music. Deprive you of all access to art museums, or art books. Or books at all. And what will be left? Which form is yours inalienably? Poetry.

It wasn't as though he thought any of his students might

eventually find themselves exiled or imprisoned. But each might face intervals of isolation when a particular poem was called for, as solace or confirmation. And if it wasn't there, a precious opportunity was lost.

In the quarter century since his death, I'm struck by how even this rationale for memorization begins to look obsolete. Brodsky saw memorized poems as a sort of larder, laid up against the hungers of extended solitude. But we're far less solitary today than even a few decades ago. Let's say you're out and about on a gorgeous afternoon in October. You're ambling through a picturesque park, and you wish to recall—but can't quite summon—the opening lines of Keats's "To Autumn." With a quick tap-tap-tap, you have it on your screen:

> Season of mists and mellow fruitfulness,
> Close bosom-friend of the maturing sun . . .

You're back in the nineteenth century, but you're also residing in the twenty-first, where machine memory superannuates brain memory.

Even so, in their divergent ways, those two exiles, Brodsky and Crusoe, point to the peculiar energies released when we possess poetry—or it, us. To speak in terms of ownership makes sense. For a memorized poem becomes your own. You *have* it in a way you don't typically have a beloved novel, a favorite essay—or a string quartet, or a favorite painting on a favorite wall in a museum. Poetry is more intimate than all that. It belongs not so much to the museum or the concert hall as it belongs to *you*. And belongs with a kinlike closeness. The best argument I know in support of that outmoded practice, the memorization of verse, is that it provides us with knowl-edge of a qualitatively and physiologically different variety:

You take the poem inside you, into your brain chemistry, and you know it at a deeper, bodily level than if you simply read it off a page or a screen. I like how the critic Catherine Robson put it in *Heart Beats: Everyday Life and the Memorized Poem*: "If we do not learn by heart, the heart does not feel the rhythms of poetry as echoes or variations of its own insistent beat."

I suppose what I'm doing here, in my concluding chapter, might be termed a defense of poetry. That's a loaded phrase, actually, venerable and distinguished. There's a lithe, lovely line of argument to be traced from Sir Philip Sidney's "The Defence of Poesy," written around 1580, through Thomas Campion's "Observations in the Art of English Poesie" (1602) and Samuel Daniel's "A Defence of Rhyme" (1603), and finally to Percy Shelley's "Defence of Poetry," composed in 1821. At times the poets contend with one another, especially Daniel with Campion. (Daniel rightfully points out that, when adopting a prosody, one's language shouldn't be slotted into a preexisting system; any fertile system must evolve out of the language's own peculiarities.) But among the four poet-writers, similarities outweigh differences. Each of their essays frets about contemporary poetry's ability to uphold the gold standard of the classical past, speculates on future directions, and ultimately reinforces the role of poetry as an ethical agent. Poetry is, for all four, a moral directive.

These days, any argument linking art to moral betterment will likely leave a tinny ring. It all sounds so overly earnest and out-of-date. One can imagine all four essays being swept aside by a single line from W. H. Auden's elegy for Yeats: "For poetry makes nothing happen."

It's an unforgettable line. Auden's delivery was impeccable. His pronouncement could so easily have soured. It might have come across as glib, or hostile, or self-pitying, or self-congratulatorily nihilistic, or fashionably languid. But the line doesn't stir any such response. Auden has enfolded it in a three-part poem of exquisite gratitude and loveliness. The reader trusts him. There's an implicit nobility in taking such artistic care over something that—confessedly—will alter nothing. It's admirable: how artistry undermines his own assertion.

In its note of wise resignation, the line makes Shelley's most high-flying dictum, his blazoning attestation that "poets are the unacknowledged legislators of the world," sound callow and self-aggrandizing. If we accept Shelley literally, and further accept—as we must—that the poet's role today is much dwindled, then a descent into a collective anarchy seems a foregone conclusion. With no functioning legislators, we're bound for Thomas Hobbes's vision of an existence "nasty, brutish, and short."

Sidney speaks of poetry as the "first light-giver to ignorance" in the "noblest nations and languages that are known." Campion calls it "the chief beginner, and maintainer of eloquence, not only helping the ear with the acquaintance of sweet numbers, but also raising the mind to a more high and lofty conceit." Daniel speaks of the "sacred monuments" of English verse, "wherein so many honourable spirits have sacrificed to memory their dearest passions, showing by what divine influence they have been moved, and under what stars they lived." Shelley observes that poetry "awakens and enlarges the mind itself by rendering it the receptacle of a thousand unapprehended combinations of thought" and further observes that poets are "the inventors of the arts of life and the teachers, who draw into a certain propinquity with the beautiful and the true that partial apprehension of the agencies of the invisible world which is called religion," and still further observes that poetry is "the source of whatever beautiful, or generous, or true can have place in an evil time," and goes on to declare that "Poetry is a sword of lightning ever unsheathed." (I confess to a deep fondness for Shelley's soaring grandiosities.)

These are voices from a vanished kingdom. They sound so out-of-date—and all the more distant in a world where time relentlessly accelerates.

And yet they're Sidney, Campion, Daniel, Shelley. They are speaking to whatever is best in us, and they are to be ignored only if the best is something no longer valued and coveted.

Poetry makes nothing happen?

Poetry in our time is a generative impulse challenging the calendars by which we live, the values by which we register our prosperity. Our calendar is out of whack, it declares; our values must realign with what is precisely and mindfully and lovingly wrought.

Poetry is a routine that shatters routine. Poetry is the force that induces you, on a night of savage weather, to throw on a greatcoat and venture out to check how the moon's faring against the onslaught of wind and rain.

Poetry asks to be revisited—as true friends will ask. If its requests are urgent, they are also patient, spanning the millennia, for time is on its side. Poetry insists that we read and reread and reeducate ourselves, outfitting ourselves for a changed life. It is our purest call to what is purest within us.

Poetry improves people.

□

Accentual-syllabic meter: the dominant meter in English formal verse. It is a system that counts both accents and syllables, and is typically assembled through the use of one of four metrical feet: the **iamb,** the **trochee,** the **anapest,** the **dactyl.** It allows us to predict both how many accents and how many syllables a line will have. For instance, a poem written in iambic trimeter (da-DUM da-DUM da-DUM) and one written in dactylic dimeter (DUM-da-da DUM-da-da) will each typically have six syllables, despite having a different number of accents.

Anapest: the metrical foot that goes da-da-DUM. It's a frequent substitute for the iamb in poems written in loose (as opposed to strict) iambics.

Apocopated rhyme: Typically, a rhyme that pairs a one-syllable word with the first, stressed syllable of a two-syllable word, as in *strange/ranger* or *field/wielding.* A rare variant, beloved by Marianne Moore, W. H. Auden, James Merrill.

Caesura: a natural break or pausing place within a line, often marked by a comma, semicolon, period, et cetera. Naturally, longer lines tend to have more caesuras than shorter. Victorian poets had a special fondness for the fourteener, a fourteen-syllable line that almost invariably had a strong caesura near the middle, typically after the eighth syllable, resulting in that 4:3 ratio so beloved by English poets. The caesura can serve, then, to create patterns not immediately visible on the page.

Dactyl: the metrical foot that goes DUM-da-da. Something of a rarity in poems written in iambics.

Enjambment: the phenomenon where one line runs over into the next, without terminal punctuation. Often used more generally for the art or strategy of breaking lines.

Exact rhyme: a rhyme in which, typically, initial consonant sounds differ, followed by identical vowel sound and consonant sound: for example, *pound* and *sound*. Sometimes there is no final consonant sound (*pow* and *sow*), but an exact rhyme presupposes the existence of a shared vowel.

Feminine ending: a line ending with an unstressed syllable. In metrical poems this additional syllable is often considered extra-metrical: It leaves the overall structure largely unaltered.

Feminine rhyme: a two-syllable rhyme (as opposed to the one-syllable **masculine rhyme**) in which the first of the two syllables is accented. While *man* and *van* are masculine rhymes, *mannish* and *vanish* are feminine rhymes. Note that the second syllables in a pair of feminine rhymes are typically identical.

Formal poem, formal poetry: poetry written in some poetic form, as opposed to free verse. The term has nothing to do with that other sense of formal—decorous, prim, dressy, et cetera. An obscene limerick is a formal poem.

Heroic couplet: a rhymed pair of lines (usually exactly rhymed) in iambic pentameter.

Iamb: a metrical foot consisting of an unaccented syllable followed by an accented syllable. The foot that goes da-DUM. It's the most common, the basic foot in English.

Iambic pentameter: a line, consisting of five iambs, that goes da-DUM da-DUM da-DUM da-DUM da-DUM. Historically, it has always allowed for metrical substitution(s), typically a **trochee** for an iamb.

Internal rhyme: Most rhymes occur at the ends of lines. Internal rhyme arises when rhymes arise from other places within the lines.

Light rhyme: A sort of mirror image of **apocopated rhyme.** Again, we usually have a one-syllable word paired with a two-syllable word, though in this case rhyming on the latter's second, unstressed syllable: *sea/mighty* or *old/cuckold.* A Marianne Moore specialty.

Masculine rhyme: a one-syllable rhyme. Note that the rhyming words may each have more than one syllable, as in *mezzanine/ gasoline.*

Metrical systems: There are only three important metrical systems in English: **pure stress meter, accentual-syllabic meter,** and **syllabic meter.** These three, in combination with the non-metrical system of free verse, will account for 99 percent of the poems you ever come across.

Off rhyme: a catchall term for pretty much any sonic connection that isn't an **exact rhyme.**

Prosodic contract: one of my favorite poetic terms. The implicit deal that a poem establishes, the promises it appears to make in its opening lines. Much of what is most distinctive about a poet can be discerned in the way she subsequently conceals, adheres to, modifies, or breaks the initial terms of the contract.

Pure stress meter: a meter in which only the stressed syllables are counted and the number of unstressed syllables may vary widely. Gerard Manley Hopkins refers to this meter as sprung, and the unstressed syllables as the slack.

Relative stress: evidently a more confusing notion than it ought to be. See the opening to chapter 6. In essence, the idea that stress within a foot ought to be measured autonomously, independent of feet around it. If one syllable in a foot carries slightly more stress than any other or others, it should be seen as the defining accent. We will know that this notion has not been fully understood and embraced so long as we hear critics speak of pyrrhic feet.

Rhyme decay: typically, the process where, over time, shifts in pronunciation result in an exact rhyme devolving into an off rhyme.

Rhythm: in our context, probably should be spoken of only as speech rhythm. The way a line of poetry actually sounds when delivered aloud. In formal poems, the pattern of stresses a speaker gives it. It works in counterpoint to the meter, sometimes in conformity with it and sometimes in opposition. Note that speech rhythm may vary greatly from speaker to speaker, so that rhythm is far less determinate than meter.

Rim rhyme: a term of great beauty that both pinpoints and embodies its own definition. In its purest form, it consists of two words that front and back share consonant sounds but that differ in their internal vowel sound: for example, *light/late, feel/fail, rim/ rhyme.*

Syllabic verse: poetry written in a form that counts syllables but not accents, which vary from line to line. Stanzas will consist of a repeated pattern of syllable counts. It is commonly associated with Japanese verse forms like the haiku, though its earliest proponents in English (Marianne Moore, Elizabeth Daryush) seem to have drawn their inspiration from elsewhere.

Trochee: a metrical foot consisting of an accented syllable followed by an unaccented syllable. It goes DUM-da. As such, it's the mirror image of the iamb, for which it is often substituted.

PERMISSIONS CREDITS

ACKNOWLEDGMENTS

In my early twenties I promised myself I'd write a book about English-language poetry, and in my early sixties a tardy realization dawned that my book better get started if it meant to get done. Though the goal remained constant over the decades, my thinking naturally evolved. Some of the material in *Rhyme's Rooms* appeared in earlier forms, though everything has been modified, more often substantially than slightly.

I'm grateful to various editors who helped pilot those earlier pieces into print, in particular Sara Lippincott at *The New Yorker,* Sasha Weiss at *The New Yorker*'s online *Page-Turner,* and, especially, the late Barbara Epstein at *The New York Review of Books.* A list of relevant publications follows, many of them offering discussions lengthier than *Rhyme's Rooms* allows.

Chapter Seven: For the marvelous and painfully neglected Peter Kane Dufault, see my "Barely Sighted Lives," *The New York Review of Books,* October 20, 1994. Also see "Postscript: Peter Kane Dufault (1923–2013)," *The New Yorker, Page-Turner,* June 7, 2013.

Chapter Fifteen: For a longer discussion of Daniel Hall, see "Getting Things Right," *The New York Review of Books,* September 19, 1996. For Charlotte Mew, see "Small Wonder," *The New*

York Review of Books, January 15, 1987. For Theodore Roethke, see "Glassed In," *The New York Review of Books,* April 17, 2008.

Chapter Nineteen: For a survey of E. E. Cummings, see "Mr. Lower Case," a review of *Complete Poems, 1904–1962,* in *The New Yorker,* January 26, 1992. For more about Swenson, see "Reading Through Someone Else's Eyes," *The New Yorker, Page-Turner,* July 17, 2014.

Chapter Twenty-One: For a review of *The Poetical Words of Gerard Manley Hopkins,* see *The New Yorker,* October 20, 1991. For a discussion of his "terrible sonnets," see "Comforting Talk," *The New Yorker, Page-Turner,* May 20, 2014. See also "A Passionate Clamor," *The New York Review of Books,* April 29, 2004. Father Hopkins, that sad and beautiful and unpushy soul, somehow nudges his way into most of my discussions of poetry. See also my preface to *Mortal Beauty, God's Grace: Major Poems and Spiritual Writings of Gerard Manley Hopkins* (Vintage, 2003) and "Name-Calling," *The New Yorker, Page-Turner,* February 28, 2014.

Chapter Twenty-Two: See "Digesting Hard Iron," a review of *The Poems of Marianne Moore,* in *The New York Times,* January 4, 2004.

Chapter Twenty-Four: See "Why We Should Memorize," *The New Yorker, Page-Turner,* January 25, 2013.

Various friends have kindly offered suggestions along the way. Thanks are due to David Sofield, William Pritchard, Richard Kenney, Eric Sawyer, Rebecca Sinos, Greg Williamson, Willard Spiegelman, John Chapman, Richard Lyon, and Jamie Bernstein. Special thanks to Hilary Leithauser for her nettlesome precision.

A NOTE ABOUT THE AUTHOR

Brad Leithauser is the author of seventeen previous books, the most recent of which is the novel *The Promise of Elsewhere*. He is a former theater critic for *Time,* and the recipient of numerous awards and honors, including a MacArthur fellowship and a Guggenheim fellowship. In 2005, he was inducted into the Order of the Falcon by the president of Iceland for his writings about Nordic literature. A professor in the Writing Seminars at Johns Hopkins University, he divides his time between Baltimore, Maryland, and Amherst, Massachusetts.

A NOTE ON THE TYPE

This book was set in a version of the well-known Monotype face Bembo. This letter was cut for the celebrated Venetian printer Aldus Manutius by Francesco Griffo, and first used in Pietro Cardinal Bembo's *De Aetna* of 1495. The companion italic is an adaptation of the chancery script type designed by the calligrapher and printer Lodovico degli Arrighi.

Typeset by Digital Composition, Berryville, Virginia
Printed and bound by Berryville Graphics, Berryville, Virginia
Designed by Maria Carella